EASY BLOOD

Mike Layton

DRAGONRED PUBLISHING

Library of Congress Catalog number 96-96996

ISBN 0-9654533-0-8

Layton, Mike
Easy Blood, Ronald Reagan's Proxy Wars in Central America

320 pages, index
1. Introduction—2. travels in Central America—
3. history of U.S. intervention—4. Nicaragua—5. El Salvador—6. Honduras, Guatemala, Costa Rica, Panama—
7. Cuba—8. Armies, Church, adventurers, death squads, land
reform, press distortions, political cowardice, U.S. economic
policy

First edition 1997

DragonRed Publishing
P O Box 11612
Olympia, WA 98508

Printed by Gorham Printing, Rochester, Washington

CONTENTS

CENTRAL AMERICA

MEXICO

BELIZE

GUATEMALA

Guatemala ★

HONDURAS

Tegucigalpa ★

EL SALVADOR ★

San Salvador

NICARAGUA

★ Managua

COSTA RICA ★
San Jose

PANAMA ★ Panama

COLUMBIA

Introduction

DURING THE DECADE OF THE 1980S WHEN THE PEOPLE OF the United States were looking the other way their government was waging two bloody wars against neighbors who had never done them any harm. Occasionally a newspaper article or a television special revealed fragments of semi-secret efforts in Central America to prevent some vaguely defined disaster. But most United States citizens were little aware of those wars or if they were, who was on our side and who were the bad guys.

I was one of them when I first visited the region on my way home at the end of a six-week tour of Latin America. I had no reason to reflect on the purity of my country's actions. The idea that we of *el Norte* were to blame for the poverty and misery I found wherever I went was absurd. The El Salvador colonel's reply to the man whose wife had been raped by his troops that "these things happen in war and it is not important," was terrible, but it was not my affair. A bystander, I failed to find words for the Nicaraguan war widow who lost a foot and an eye in an ambush. Her seven-year-old son was killed and another son, a toddler, was maimed for life. But that was a problem for Nicaraguans, not for me.

Reality came slowly. As I returned again and again to Central America seeking answers a disturbing awareness grew that my government, with my tax money, was complicit in making many of these things happen. I am a patriot; I served in the United States Army in two wars as a paratrooper and as a Green Beret officer and I choke up when the flag goes by, when the Star Spangled Banner is played. As a political reporter and believer in our democratic system of self governance I tried to be skeptical of both government and of its critics.

On that first visit in 1978 I was thinking of writing some see-no-evil travel magazine articles about the region and maybe a book for travelers. I was skeptical of stories of United States interference in Central American affairs although I had prepped myself on the history of our interventions which I was convinced were just that—history. Mostly I rejected tales from natives and American citizens alike of United States bullying and disregard for the sovereignty of small nations. I knew, and still know, America-haters, people whose bile is so bitter they will acknowledge nothing good about their own country. I am not one of them. For a long time I could find a rationale for what Uncle Sam was doing to the throw-away countries in his "back yard."

United States companies cutting timber, mining gold, raising cattle and introducing new farm crops into Central America were providing jobs and paychecks to people who needed them. So the pay was low? So was the cost of living, for the time being. A rising tide lifts all boats. I saw the shiny new Texaco stations in El Salvador, the supermarket in Honduras, the posh hotels in Guatemala. These folks were joining the modern world.

My own experience, training guerrillas in Korea to help block Soviet Union domination of the Far East, stifled any early doubts. So too, later, would being kicked out of Cuba for daring to visit without an invitation or escort strengthen my distaste for monolithic and authoritarian communism. I accepted United States Department of State charges of communist subversion in Central America and the need for quick and strong counter measures. I had seen for myself what the communists did to Korea and East Germany. I had known some people in the Central Intelligence Agency and found them to be bright and dedicated; for many years I never doubted their assessments of the world's dangers.

Only slowly did I become aware of the real reason the Reagan Administration was waging murder against a helpless people. My Epiphany began in 1983 in the war zone of northern Nicaragua when a peasant woman proudly showed me her new ability to read and write.

Ronald Reagan made his wars in Central America a litmus test of patriotism; Nicaragua's Sandinistas, in his shallow view, took some of their ideas from Marx (ignored were their borrowings from the gospels of the bible) and ergo, they were communists. And ergo they were liars, not to be trusted, and worse, they were almost at our gates. Just a two-day drive from Harlingen, Texas. Once Harlingen went, the whole United States would be threatened by these conniving skulkers. Doubters shared the guilt. What congressman wanted it said of him in a subsequent election campaign that he "lost Nicaragua?"

Reagan had help from a strange source—Fidel Castro, whose megalomania and crusades against "imperialism" made him the perfect communist. Castro has much to answer for, including obscuring, behind the fog of his exaggerated rhetoric, his country's genuine achievements. But even he, in his wildest manipulations to liberate the poor in the name of communism, never caused as many deaths as Reagan's crusades against the people of Nicaragua and El Salvador and our toleration of near genocide in Guatemala.

I have tried to keep my focus in this book on Central America but the Latin American world can't be compartmented so easily, any more than the countries of Central America can be examined singly, in isolation from their neighbors. I glance at Mexico and the nations of South America for another reason also; I have come to believe that the actions of the United States, through all our historic involvement with Latin America, dating from the Monroe Doctrine of 1823, have been almost always, in every way, detrimental, even when we have been most sincerely trying to help.

7

Among experiences from my fifteen-year journal of growing outrage and disillusionment are the brutal arrogance of the military, theirs and ours; drug running; death squad encounters; a Catholic Church torn by schisms and losing souls and revenues to fundamentalists; enormous debts; disastrous economics and appalling poverty and their causes. I report here insights gained from talks with farmers, business people, the newly literate, recently liberated women, victims and persecutors, priests and lay religious workers, soldiers and guerrillas, academics and diplomats, teachers and children.

Personal adventures include being caught up in a rally the late dictator Anastasio Somoza of Nicaragua staged for himself to revile President Jimmy Carter for his human rights crusade. I relive hitchhiking through Nicaragua on Russian dump trucks and cattle trailers during the Reagan Contra war; of Honduran soldiers openly stealing my books because they were "military secrets"; of chasing Salvadoran guerrillas by taxi; of posing as a minister to visit political prisoners in El Salvador's notorious Mariona prison; of a bloody beating in broad daylight on the sea wall along the beautiful Bay of Panama in the days when Manuel Noriega was the pet toad of former CIA Chief George Bush. They added up to a good way to learn Spanish.

As an unofficial "official" observer of the 1984 El Salvador election, I listened to foreign service officers at a United States embassy party present a crazy parody of a briefing so far from reality that rather than laughing I found myself sharing the embarrassment they must have felt.

They weren't alone in being abused by higher authority; for two years the editors of my own newspaper would not let me write about Central America because my stories from there differed from Ronald Reagan's version of the United States role in El Salvador and Nicaragua. I was being censored at the same time my newspaper was denouncing Nicaragua's censorship of La Prensa, a newspaper of almost comic irresponsibility. In sorrow, but in anger too, I tell of the cowardice of American editors and the failure of most newspapers, in the face of Reagan and Bush Administration manipulation, to tell the public what really was happening in Nicaragua, El Salvador, Guatemala, Panama and Honduras.

I was forced to accept some truths I at first refused to believe, to admit to myself that accounts of two wars and the miseries of five nations were being slanted on a vast scale and at the highest levels to promote a myopic political agenda. The American media were being fed lies, by their government, and those lies were being repeated to the public as the truth with almost no challenge by intimidated or fearful editors and publishers and by columnists currying favors. This book tells who was shading the truth, and why.

I still walk a line between the new American imperialists on one side who believe our power gives us the right to bully our weaker neighbors, and the leftists who link every child's death in El Salvador, Guatemala, Honduras or Nicaragua to deliberate policies plotted in Washington, D.C. Actually, in one sense the situation is worse even than the paranoiacs believe. If there were a grand plan to oppress our neighbors it might be possible to focus public debate. Instead of a conspiracy, however, United States policy toward Central America is a basketful of half-baked and ever-changing little schemes concocted by various interest groups for their own benefit. Usually there is no connection between them, and often they are in conflict. That's what makes it all so insidious; how do you roll back a policy that isn't a policy, how get a handle on diverse and poorly formulated actions that never make a whole and almost never trace back to any accountable body?

Years after the United States called off its proxy army, the Contra, Nicaragua's misery index was measured in sixty five percent unemployment and the destruction of its forests. El Salvadoran Army officers, confident that the United States would continue to protect and finance them, cheered on the death squads and gave them cover. American officers looked the other way and tolerated murder. Terrorized Guatemala was a country under occupation by its own army while North American tourists looked but did not see. Honduras, for a brief time on a roll financed by United States bribes, attempted to bring the military to heel but sank back into the poverty that always provides an alibi for the generals to take over. Panama, where Latin American corruption blossoms as lushly as it did before George Bush's "I'm-no-wimp" invasion and the jailing of Manuel Noriega, is once again drug money launderer to the world.

Even if peace were not an illusion, a greater threat from Central America lurks in history's road ahead for the United States. It's one we deplore but can't forestall, a massive migration, largely illegal, unstoppable. This human tidal wave driven from the south by mindless economic, political and military schemes concocted primarily in Washington was, and to a degree still is, rooted in hysteria over a communism that never existed, and beckoned northward by glittering consumer goodies and the wages with which to buy them. The hysteria these gentle invaders bring with them is far more dangerous to our liberties than the phantom invasion armies dreamed of by the right wing that for forty years called our political tunes.

I am not an expert on Central America, even after fifteen years of travel there; but I am a trained and, I think, an honest observer. The book that follows tells what I saw and heard between 1979, when the people of Nicaragua, tired of tyranny at home and bullying and exploitation from the north, said *basta*, enough, and what the end of that experiment in early 1990 meant to Nicaragua and to its neighbors. I dedicate this book to the tens of thousands of Americans whose personal, on-the-ground witness I believe prevented Ronald Reagan from invading Nicaragua or sending American troops into El Salvador.

1

Somoza Stages A Rally For Himself

A LINE OF TRUCKS, THEIR UNTUNED MOTORS RUMBLING AND belching engine exhaust, stretched out of sight in both directions in the dim light of Managua street lamps. Each ratttle trap vehicle was packed with silent men clinging to the sideboards or to one another. The sounds had awakened me and for a time I stood back from my window in the pre-dawn chill and watched that ghostly parade. Then, still puzzled, I went back to bed.

After breakfast the next morning the trucks with their mute cargoes were still groaning along the street when I faced the sun on the front veranda of the Nicaraguan *hospedade*. Joining me was the landlady, who had an English surname and spoke of her vacations in Canada. Why all the trucks and men on this early Sunday morning?

"The dictator is holding a meeting, a demonstration for himself," she said, her dark eyes looking at me in what I thought was a rather uncivil way. This was March of 1978 and Anastasio (Tachito) Somoza had learned his public relations, her message said. "It is to show you, you North Americans, that he is well loved in this country.

"These men," she said, "have come from all over the country. Their bosses must send them, at the dictator's orders. It is for your President Carter."

She touched my elbow. "Come," she said, steering me into the street between two trucks whose human freight stared down at us without expression. On the other side of the street we looked out onto a field of weeds sweeping toward the profiles of shattered buildings against the morning sunlight. Beyond them sparkled the deceptively blue waters of polluted Lake Managua.

"This was the center of Managua," the landlady said, waving her hand in a half circle in front of us. "Six years ago the earthquake destroyed it. Only a few buildings remain. You sent millions of dollars for relief. Other countries gave money and food and medicine.

"The dictator stole it all," she said. "The people got nothing. He sold the blood, North American blood, Nicaraguan blood, he and his Cuban friends. Nothing has been done. The people, ten thousand are dead, many are injured, many are sick, homes are gone, businesses are destroyed. Your government knew all this but you sent more dollars and Somoza stole them. Now there is nothing."

She spoke in a low but intense voice, looking at me all the while. "Why did you do this? Why did you send money to a thief? You knew. Jack Anderson had reports, in your newspapers, of what was happening here, but you sent more money to the dictator.

"Now your President Carter says Somoza is a bad man. But what will you do?" She spat in the dust. "Somoza is calling for this demonstration to show you that the people support him."

The demonstration, she said, was to be held in the meadow, or wasteland, in front of the Hotel Intercontinental, Managua's finest. That hotel's structure, terraced like a Mayan temple with each higher floor slightly smaller than the one below it, and its location at the edge of the quake zone, had saved it from the destruction that leveled most of the city between it and the lake. I had been at the hotel the night before, drinking beer in the bar with a mildly cynical Mississippi cotton buyer; a New Orleans tour guide free for a peaceful couple of hours from his nattering flock, and a gringo from Boston who taught English to officers of Somoza's National Guard by day and cadged drinks at night to keep himself sane.

I decided to see this demonstration although my knowledge of Somoza, and indeed of Nicaragua at this stage of my first visit at the end of a journey through all of Latin America, was scanty. I knew it was about the size of Illinois but with roughly the population of Oregon and that it had a turbulent history. I got a notebook from my room and joined the throng moving slowly toward the hotel, somewhat apprehensive among these sullen men. No one seemed to pay any attention to me, a phenomena that creates an eerie feeling at first but which I learned in later years and other visits was a Central American illusion. Tall, blue-eyed and ruddy Gringos are always watched obliquely in Central America; only little children stare. But during that walk among the crowd of demonstrators-on-demand I felt invisible.

I joined the cotton buyer and we walked through the mob, attempting to avoid the drunks, already staggering around trying to start arguments. We estimated the crowd at about ten thousand, maybe a little more. The next day the Somoza newspaper *Novedades* said it was two hundred thousand, all "*liberales*," members of Somoza's political party. The sun grew hot quickly and by nine o'clock everyone was sweating heavily. But time ran on and still there was no activity, just the men, and a few women, talking in low tones and, some of them, drinking beer. Most could not afford even that, the cotton buyer said.

At last television crews from Miami appeared and, not coincidentally, there was a wail of sirens. The crowd standing in the street leading down the hill that dominates Managua from behind the hotel parted suddenly. Jeeps with .50 caliber machine guns on pedestal mounts, World War II weapons, roared down the hill and swept into the dusty field. Soldiers, Somoza's National Guard, although they looked like North Americans in their green fatigue uniforms, helmet liners, webbing and boots, swung the muzzles of the guns across the crowd menacingly. Some men cringed but most stared back stonily. Soldiers with submachine guns and wearing blue berets had taken up positions on the hotel's top terraces far above the crowd.

Behind the jeeps came a long black Mercedes, its windows tinted, its headlights flashing. It braked to a dusty halt at a reviewing stand temporarily set up at the edge of a clump of scraggly trees near the center of the field. Flags, banners and carefully lettered signs, most in the same type face, appeared amid a small forest of waving straw hats in the immediate area of the reviewing stand. A chant went up: "So-mo-za, So-mo-za, So-mo-za." The messages of the signs and banners were the same, either hailing Somoza's good works or pledging their undying loyalty to him and denouncing the communists, Fidel Castro and, in some instances, United States President Carter. Then Somoza mounted the reviewing stand, where he stood shaded from the sun, wearing a white Guyabara shirt, open at the neck, sleeves buttoned to the wrists, waving and smiling. With his bald head, paunch and meaty face he looked like a small town banker from the midwestern United States, hardly the trim West Pointer of earlier pictures of him with his father.

Only a month earlier, Pedro Joaquin Chamorro, publisher of the newspaper La Prensa and Somoza's most prominent critic, had been murdered in a street attack a few blocks from here by what nearly everyone agrees were Somoza hirelings. Since that time the unrest that had been seething under the surface in Nicaragua for generations boiled ever hotter.

Somoza talked that day like a genuine liberal, promising state loans to small farmers and guarantees for loans from private banks to small urban businesses. He said he would extend social security to the campesinos, farm workers, and to domestic workers, and guarantee other worker rights. He talked of health care for children. Each promise was greeted by shouts from the several hundred party faithful surrounding the reviewing stand. Most of the crowd, however, stood silently, patiently, their arms folded. Nicaragua, Somoza told them, had no need of lessons in human rights "from those who whip Negroes and maintain Indians as second class citizens." It was a bald reference to the Yanquis and, specifically, to President Carter, whose talk at that time of human rights was infuriating, or frightening, Latin American dictators from Guatemala to Paraguay.

Others spoke too, among them a woman, the education minister, as well as lesser officials. There was much talk, new to me, of fealty not only to the "*unico lider*," Somoza, but also to the valiant, incomparable, illustrious National Guard. Indeed, newspapers the next day emphasized that even more than the government, the Army was the institution holding the country together. It was my introduction to the idea that the Central American military was an entity apart from the rest of the country, an institution to be respected above all others, even the presidency.

Somoza finished his speech and descended to his Mercedes and roared away behind the jeeps with the mounted 50s, sirens wailing. Men and women in civilian clothing passed out a sandwich and a bottle of Coca Cola to each man in the crowd. Then the men were herded to their trucks for the long rides back to their farms and ranches all over the country.

Later that afternoon a National Guard patrol fought a battle with "terrorists" at a roadblock near Diriamba, so the next day's *Novedades* said, and killed seven of them. The terrorists, the paper reported, had tried to block access to the demonstration, and a front page photograph showed as proof a jumble of wires, drill bits, "subversive" pamphlets, boots and boxes of cartridges and a hand lettered sign warning that vehicles passing the roadblock would be burned. Filling the back page of the tabloid newspaper were head and shoulder photographs of six of the seven terrorists, their eyes half closed in death. One had part of his face shot away. A heroic Guard sergeant had been killed, the paper said.

All of page two of the paper was filled with stories of other battles around the country that Sunday, attacks on a church, a dance hall, fights in cantinas, with guns and Molotov cocktails. The revolution was on although none of these events were being reported in United States newspapers. Not until July of 1979 would it become a full scale war, with street battles in the cities and bombings by Somoza's

15

planes of the poor barrios which supplied most of the fighters.

The war became news in the United States only after a guardsman executed a North American television newsman, on camera, for the titillation of viewers back home. Fought mostly by teenagers, that series of battles, unlike the prolonged war that ravaged neighboring El Salvador for so many years, lasted only a few weeks. It ended with Somoza fleeing to Miami with most of the money from the national treasury. Surviving Guardia fled, those who could, to Miami also, the rest to Honduras where soon the CIA began recruiting them into a counter revolutionary army, the Contra.

A year later Somoza, his grossness too much even for South Florida, went to live with his dictator buddy, Alfredo Stroessner, in Paraguay. Somoza's partiality for thirteen-year-old virgins scandalized the Paraguayans. Someone, probably a Nicaraguan named Hugo Alfredo Yrurzun, put a rocket through the windshield of his car, bringing an end to the Somoza dynasty. Somoza's bodyguards filled Yrurzun full of bullet holes and so no one knows exactly how the assassination was conceived although a Nicaraguan defector later said it was planned in Managua with the help of Cubans.[1] Every bad thing in Latin America, every back lash against oppression, was being blamed on Cubans in those years.

Truly, as President Franklin Roosevelt said in the 1940s, Somoza's father "may be a son of a bitch, but he's our son of a bitch." His family not only got its start under the guidance of the United States military, but Somoza also borrowed the bedrock maxim of his politics from American mentors: when all else fails to bring down an opponent, label him a communist. Others continue the theme all over Latin America, and it's still working, long after Communism's dismal failure in the former Soviet Union. In 1993 in neighboring Honduras, a candidate backed lavishly by the Reverend Sun Myung Moon, millionaire owner of the Unification Church, almost won the presidency. His campaign theme: opponent Carlos Reina is a communist. To prove it he showed doctored films

---

[1] Don Oberdorfer and Joanne Omang, The Washington Post, June 19, 1983.

in television commercials of Reina supposedly buddying up to Fidel Castro, hobnobbing with Nicaragua's Ortega brothers and, incredibly, visiting Panama's capitalist United States stooge, Manuel Noriega.

◆ ◆ ◆

Outside the little town of Ocotal in northern Nicaragua on the road from Jalapa, there was in the middle 1980s a "Welcome Brothers" billboard erected by the local Sandinista Party at an intersection above a sandbagged bunker. Its message for the traveler:

"Ocotal, the first city in Latin America to be bombed from the air by Yanqui Imperialism, 17 July, 1927. Where the tough guy invaders ate the dust of our rustic mountains."

It was reminder of a United States Marine Corps attack by air on the town in the long attempt to capture the "bandit" Augusto Sandino, one of the first Nicaraguans to sound the cry of "imperialism" against the Yanquis. When I first saw the sign, in 1983, Nicaraguans considered themselves once again under siege by Yanqui imperialists. The sign disappeared after Violeta Chamorro won election as president. Her government didn't want to aggravate her northern benefactors.

In 1933, shortly after the Marines turned their new National Guard over to Somoza's father, "the first Somoza," he invited Sandino down from the hills under truce for a peace conference and after a cordial dinner had him murdered. The young men who overthrew Somoza in 1979 took Sandino's name for their movement and their political party. The silhouette of the little man with the big hat became the party's symbol, plastered on doors and walls all over the country until Sandinismo was defeated by an American-sponsored war, an American economic embargo and American election campaign money in the 1990 vote that brought Chamorro to office.

The 1978 Managua demonstration on the dusty field in front of the Intercontinental Hotel remains, for me, the symbol of old style Central American dictator politics. In contrast were the "face the people" meetings inaugurated by the

Sandinistas after they led those bands of teenagers to triumph in ousting Somoza the next year at a cost of fifty thousand dead. Each week for years after the triumph, one or more of the Sandinista commandantes would hold an open meeting, sometimes in the evening, at others on a Sunday, where people in the neighborhood could air their opinions or complaints about the government.

I attended two of those meetings, both held at schools and both presided over by Daniel Ortega. One was in a poor barrio of Managua in 1983 when Ortega was still one of "the nine commandantes," and the other in 1986, in Somoto, a little town ten miles from the Honduras border, after Ortega became president. Both were plainly "press-the-flesh" politics, far more open than anything else ever seen in Central America.

The full significance of Ortega's meetings with the Nicaraguan public has never registered with United States officialdom. Nor with many United States news people who sneered at them as typical Communist manipulation of the public. Unlike Somoza's diatribe to his subjects, Ortega's were two-way encounters, a give and take with constituents that belied constant United States accusations of repression. At the Managua meeting women complained, as early as 1983, of shortages of food and other household staples in the stores. They told Ortega of inadequate school supplies. Several people denounced the police for allowing a disreputable night club to continue to operate in the face of local opposition. Nothing much was accomplished, and Ortega could only promise that food production and distribution were being improved. He brought forward the Managua chief of police to answer the complaint about the night club and I noticed a few days afterward that it had been closed.

At the Somoto school three years later, in an area to which the United States-sponsored Contra rebels were frequent visitors, Ortega arrived in an enormous Russian helicopter, frightening horses and enthralling little boys. The criticisms were sharper. When was the government going to fix the pot holes in the roads, several men demanded. When

18

was this school going to get some books for its students, another wanted to know. What was the government doing to protect farmers from the Contras, another asked.

The most impassioned criticism came from a portly woman in her Sunday best who stood up in that crowd of farmers and cowboys to protest the government's recent gift of a plot of agrarian reform land to a former Contra. Her son, who was loyal to the government and had not taken up arms against it, had been promised that land, she said. Who was being punished and who rewarded? Ortega explained that the young man who had surrendered and turned in his rifle had priority under an amnesty program passed by the National Assembly to undercut the appeal of the Contra. It did seem unfair, he said, but amnesty was a weapon in Nicaragua's defense against "Mr. Reagan's war." Her son, he assured the woman, would get his land too, at the next allocation.

Soldiers were guarding Ortega in each of these encounters but their presence paled in comparison with the elaborate security measures that routinely surround an American president. Covering an appearance by Reagan or Bush in safe Seattle during the same era was an ordeal for news reporters. Credentials had to be applied for before hand and identity cards had to be worn on strings around our necks. Getting close enough to ask questions was impossible. In Nicaragua I and others, Nicaraguans and foreigners, approached Ortega at the end of the meetings, shook hands and asked him questions face to face. Sure it was politics, good politics, democratic politics.

In neither of these encounters did Ortega distinguish himself with Solomon-like judgments or solutions. Many people seemed to go away unsatisfied. He's not an inspired speaker and definitely not the usual charismatic Latin politico, a type that all too often emerges full of bombast from the back rooms of regional political brokering. Ortega's attempts to explain government efforts to improve roads and schools and farm production and to get their crops to market, to ease the harsh conditions in which most Nicaraguans

19

live, were accepted with cynicism by some, I am sure. Except for his shyness, Ortega sounded not so different from politicians I've covered in the United States and other parts of the world. To the mother of the disappointed young farmer he laid the blame at least partly on the National Assembly. Its local delegate was also on the podium and he too didn't do much to defend the amnesty program although both he and Ortega were at least partially responsible for it. Explaining complex long-range policies is tough with any crowd and I was never certain of the response in Somoto. Neither was I certain of that crowd's reaction to Ortega's repeated references to "Mr. Reagan's war" as the cause of most of Nicaragua's troubles although there were locals, apparently party hacks, who cheered each time. Four years later that region voted for UNO, Violeta Chamorro's odd coalition of fourteen parties ranging from avowed communists to the super right in the national election, ending Ortega's presidency.

While to some the face-the-people encounters may have seemed phony, they represented at least an attempt by the Sandinistas to involve the people of Nicaragua in their government. Many of the younger people seemed to accept that as normal. Older ones had never imagined their president discussing anything with them, let alone asking for their comments. In no other country in Central America have the rulers ever attempted to take the ruled into their confidence, as Ortega and his fellow commandantes tried to do. In spite of the criticisms, the Somoto meeting, attended by three hundred rural, unsophisticated people, seemed to be a success. Maybe it was the only game in town that Sunday, but those people sat in the school yard or stood along its fringes for more than five hours listening to the over-long speeches and the give and take between Ortega, and his staff and cabinet members, and their fellow townsfolk. People came and went constantly and so far as I could see there was no attempt at coercion. The bodyguards seemed bored by it all, their faces as blank as the Secret Servicemen's who guard American presidents. Local people paid them little attention, a marked contrast to the fear displayed by many of those bored peasants dragooned eight years earlier to pack Somoza's demonstration.

The Sandinistas failed in many of their endeavors, but they tried hard to bring about a better life for their countrymen. Long after most of the world's adherents of the teachings of Marx had gone deep into cynicism and clung to power for its own sake, the Sandinistas were preaching that a pluralistic government could make a difference in the lives of Nicaragua's people. One of their first acts after the triumph in 1979 was to mobilize most of the country's college and senior high school students into literacy brigades and send them into the *campo*, the rugged back country of farms, cattle ranches, coffee plantations and small villages in a brief but intense effort to bring literacy to people who had never held a book in their hands. The effort was not as successful as the Sandinistas claimed. It did make an impact, however, primarily in imparting to the poor the radical notion that their government cared about them, that its purpose was not to oppress them, or steal their land or preside over the deaths of their children. The results of that literacy campaign were still noticeable ten years later although the war by then had ended it in most areas.

In the first five years after the revolution small, crude schools were built in nearly every community in the country. Health clinics went up also, although the medics who operated them had little more knowledge of medicine than one could obtain in a Red Cross first aid course at a United States YMCA.

By 1984 the war had put an end not only to school building, but to many of the schools themselves. The Contra specialized in attacks on schools, clinics and other public facilities, always avoiding direct battle with the Sandinista Army. Teachers, doctors, nurses, engineers, Nicaraguan or foreign, as well as public officials or any local leaders were targets of Contra assassinations.

No one will ever know, now, whether the Sandinistas would have created a benign socialist or Marxist state, with a mixed economy and a pluralistic government, the goals they proclaimed, had they been given a chance. I think most of them were sincere in their efforts, and I think Nicaragua could have evolved into a democratic socialist state. Nicaraguans are too independent to endure suppression long, especially after their ten-year taste of equality under the Sandinistas. But Reagan's war rendered the question moot. That reds-under-the-bed element in American society that until 1989 saw every effort anywhere in the world to throw off tyranny as evidence of communist subversion will always insist that without the Contra war the Sandinistas would never have permitted Central American peace. Only war would make the Sandinistas cry "uncle," they insisted.

I believe that view is nonsense, but no one can prove or disprove that either. The official line was that Daniel Ortega would "steal" the 1990 election or, if he lost he would refuse to give up the government on some pretense. Ortega proved that wrong in the eyes of all the world. He lost and turned the government over peacefully to Violeta Chamorro.

I believe Nicaragua could have become a model for all of Latin America had it been left alone. That, of course, was what worried the men who whispered in Reagan's ear. They wanted no successful social democracy in America's "backyard." I do not dismiss the Sandinistas' failings, of which there were many. Their economic policies were erratic and in many cases not well thought out.

Most visible was their waste of the crude oil they received from the Soviet Union, which was processed, incidentally, in two North American-owned refineries in Managua. I watched one evening in Esteli as teenagers cruised the streets in the American fashion, burning up gasoline that cost about 35 cents a gallon. Since it came from Russia it was, in a sense free. In the view of the Sandinistas the people, threatened by war, deserved what little relaxation and enjoyment was available to them. Perhaps it was no more irresponsible than the aimless driving in the United States that burns so much fuel to no purpose, but Nicaragua was at war and new cars and spare parts were hard to come by.

The Sandinistas also failed to mobilize the country's distribution system, a criticism made often by their free market critics who never recognized that government inefficiency was more than matched by Contra targeting of corn fields, coffee farms, granaries, warehouses, bridges and trucks. But it is true that produce did rot in fields or warehouses while market shelves were bare. Nicaragua's national currency, the cordoba, was deteriorating fast—50 percent a month inflation in 1991—and the Sandinistas' only remedy was to print new rows of zeroes on old hundred-cordoba bills.

Worse than everything else, perhaps, was the Sandinista failure to curb the Nicaraguan bureaucracy. One of the worst in Latin America under Somoza, it didn't get better under the Sandinistas except that bureaucrats became more polite and smiled more often. Bloated public payrolls weren't unique to Nicaragua; stifling bureaucracies are the norm in most poor Third World countries where the meanest government job is prized as security. But bureaucracy seems ingrained in socialism and the Sandinistas never made any serious attempts to deal with the problem. Instead they allowed the bureaucracy to grow wildly or actually nurtured it as a means of gaining political support.

"We ask people to denounce publicly their problems with the bureaucracy," Rafael Solis, secretary of the Council of State, told me. "The public has to be constantly on top of public officials. We know, for example, that some times people have to go to ten officials to get something done. We're overcoming it." But the Nicaraguan bureaucracy was almost impossible to tame.

The graft endemic to Somoza's time, which still exists throughout most of Central America, was sharply curbed, however. Under the Sandinistas Nicaragua was probably the only place south of the United States-Mexican border where a motorist could be in real trouble for trying to bribe a traffic cop. Corruption, as debilitating to public confidence in government as inflation is to faith in economic policy, had begun to re-emerge in Nicaragua as the Reagan-Bush war and embargo crippled the economy. The change to Violeta Chamorro's free enterprise UNO government and economic desperation accelerated the loosening of public ethics. By 1994 little in the way of public or private business could be accomplished without a kickback of some kind for those who appeared able to pay.

Corruption exists outside government, in private enterprises, as well, according to Myrna Cunningham, a member of the National Assembly from Nicaragua's impoverished east coast. "People have no alternatives (to accepting bribes)," Cunningham told me. "It is impossible for Managua (the government) to control it" when people are desperate. Others agreed.

Lush supermarkets offered the bounty of North America to Nicaraguans in Managua after Chamorro's election, if they had money. But by almost any other criteria Nicaragua was in worse shape in 1995 than it was before the 1979 revolution. People were hungry, most had no money or any means of earning any, and health services brought by the Sandinistas had collapsed. Education has been privatized and literacy gains reversed.

Drugs, never a problem in Nicaragua under the Sandinistas, are spreading widely, from the isolated ports on the swampy East Coast to the west. "Marijuana and cocaine abuse and glue sniffing are all serious problems as young people seek escape from their misery," said Leonel Navarro, of a church organization called CEPAD, in Leon, Nicaragua's second largest city. "Youth crime is increasing, as well as prostitution." CEPAD has a food program for pre-school children of poor families "but we can do little in the face of problems of this scale," Navarro said. "Peace is better than war but we also seek justice so people can live with dignity, and the poor are respected."

Nicaragua has been on a rocky road for more than half a century and the future looks just as bad, or worse. The Sandinista Party is still the largest in Nicaragua but it is riven with factionalism at the top and is outnumbered in the National Assembly by an even more fractious coalition. Violeta

Chamorro was in some ways only a figurehead as president, but she carried great moral authority to a majority of Nicaraguans, especially as she spoke frequently against violence. With her departure Nicaragua is likely to experience more of the savagery that has afflicted it, with United States help, for a hundred and fifty years.

2

El Salvadore and the Endless War

"CALL ME CLEMENTE," THE BOY SAYS WHEN I ASK HIS NAME. He was seventeen and described himself as a "popular teacher." He was going back to his home village in the hills of Chalatenango Department where the guerrillas ruled except on the occasional day when the El Salvadoran Army roared through to show that it could. Clemente is a handsome imp, almost pretty, thin but bright faced. When I asked if he was a guerrilla his eyes widened in innocence, he wrapped his slender arms around his body and trembled with exaggerated shakes.

"I would be afraid," he said.

When Clemente was ten the Army ordered his family to leave its farm. After a year of wandering destitute through the blighted countryside, they came to Honduras where "internationalists" escorted them over the border in defiance of hostile Honduran soldiers. Clemente's older brother stayed in El Salvador and was killed, presumably by the Army, "because he was a student" at the National University. It's a familiar story in El Salvador. When I met him after seven years as a ward of international relief organizations, west European and Scandinavian, in the Mesa Grande refugee camp, the family had decided with many others that they would rather die at home than waste away in misery. The Army grudgingly tolerated their return, perhaps because there were too many of them to kill openly in front of foreign observers.

I met Clemente and a number of other popular teachers at a leafy school yard in San Salvador. They were in the capitol for a national conference and to join students at the National University in a march through the streets to the presidential palace, demanding more money for schools. I walked with them. Many wore masks, and on our way we passed the brown, terraced and moated fortress that is the United States embassy. Ask any Salvadoran for the hierarchical order of governance in the country—who's in charge?—and the answer is, first, the United States ambassador in this cartoonish bunker. Second is the Salvadoran Army and, as sort of an after-thought third, whoever the Army allows to sit in the president's office. El Salvador was a special client of the United States, paid for if not entirely safely bought. Through the 1980s and into the early '90s, the United States poured up to $6 billion into the country in the name of financing a democracy or, from the standpoint of the Reagan and later the Bush administrations, a proxy war to hold back communist hordes gathering in our own backyard.

Who were these threats to the hemisphere's peace? One was Clemente, dangerous because he was a teacher.

There were many others. I met a little man who was a guitar maker before the war but whose instruments, made from laurel wood, were considered sinister because the guerillas entertained themselves with them in their jungle camps. He was living in Morazan Department when soldiers came to his house and workshop while he was away and smashed all his tools and unfinished guitars. Then, when his wife couldn't tell them where he was, they repeatedly raped her in front of their four children.

"I wrote to Colonel Monterrosa of the 3rd Brigade, asking him for an answer," the little guitar maker told me. "He replied that these things happen in war and it is not important. Then he told me to leave, and I went to Honduras." He returned to El Salvador five years later and when I met him the soldiers had come again and told him there were to be no shops or factories from which the guerrillas could obtain supplies. Presumably guitars were still tools of revolutionaries.

Those American taxpayer dollars at work created a hollow army of some 60,000 men good at skinning people alive and carving out tongues but of little stomach for face to face combat. The money also financed an opulent lifestyle for the Army's officers and members of El Salvador's oligarchy who enjoyed some of the finest homes in the world as well as expensive European cars, classy restaurants and the loudest all-night discos north of Rio de Janiero. More pertinent, for those Americans who aren't squeamish about letting someone else do their killing, ala "low intensity conflict," our tax dollars were creating a vast flood of refugees, people without hope seeking something, almost anything, better in the United States, most illegally. Along the way, as the main impetus of that refugee flow, our tax dollars financed the killing of some 80,000 people, most of them civilians, men, women and children, who barely understood what their murders were all about.

Clemente understood. While at the refugee camp he had obviously learned something. He had been taught, by Belgians, the rudiments of pedagogy and he was going back to his home village to teach other, younger children. That too was a familiar pattern. Six years later, at a place called Arcatao in Chalatenango, I attended a dance, a fiesta, put on by the teachers at the two-building community school. They were all teenagers, except the principal, who was twenty three.

Clemente had written his own textbooks, he told me, not entirely because no others were available. His, he explained, reflected "revolutionary thought." One could legitimately call it Marxist. The few textbooks at the Arcatao school were more bland, Dick and Jane type stuff, which may be why they survived in the midst of a war zone. If Clemente was a communist, and he shrugged off the question as "unimportant," the fault lay more in Washington, D. C. than it did in Moscow. The Soviet Union was always eager to tweak Uncle Sam by helping insurgent movements, in countries allied to the United States, whose people resented American help to the tyrants ruling over them. It must have been especially satisfying to Soviet mischief makers to find such easy pickings in our own backyard. But there was never any need for the Soviets to export revolutionary ideas. Clemente had lived his indoctrination into radicalism; it had been his life. He didn't need anyone from outside to tell him that he and his family were oppressed, that his brother was murdered because he sought an education.

Looking at this frail kid getting ready to go back into the war zone and risk his life teaching others, I was once again in awe of the courage of Salvadorans. If Nicaraguans are most impressive through their poetry and artistic temper, Salvadorans must be respected for their determination. Sure, they fled the country by the thousands, but usually only after repeated threats. Many stayed and endured. On my 1986 visit the country seemed to be not so volatile, the danger not quite as palpable as earlier. Still, one's primary emotion after a few days in El Salvador was unease. The oppression pervaded everything, even the most ordinary pursuit. You felt it when you saw the men with blank stares and automatic rifles in front of every fast food joint, the beefy men idling beside the Jeep Cherokees with the opaque windows, the nervous, fast walk as people hurry to get behind their garden walls. I was having what I thought was a leisurely chat over a beer with a labor leader late one afternoon when he abruptly got to his feet and left, explaining that it was near dark and thus dangerous for him to be away from home.

I was always amazed at the coolness of Maria Hernandez, the chief human rights investigator for Tutela Legal, at the Catholic Archbishopric of El Salvador. To my shame I was sometimes nervous just being in her office, talking to her. I could picture myself being gunned down with her by a death squad bursting in to avenge her documentation of their atrocities. She was hated by the oligarchs who own El Salvador, by the military which did its bidding, and scorned by the Americans at the Embassy who accused her of meddling and exaggeration. She was a meticulous investigator and record keeper but even if she were stretching things by

29

half, or if only a fourth of what she documented were true, that would be enough to sicken anyone. About five feet, two inches tall, slightly pudgy with a smooth face often broken by a weary smile, Hernandez's very notoriety apparently kept her alive all the years she defied Army officers, policemen and, beyond them, the men with dark glasses. "They don't dare kill her for fear of international repercussions," a North American admirer told me.

But few other Salvadorans enjoyed the immunity earned by Maria Hernandez. I learned some of what they endured when I visited an American priest, Father Jim Barnett, as he ministered to what must be the most miserable people in a world full of misery. About one million of El Salvador's six million people fled the country during the war, many to the United States and Canada, some to other Central American countries and Mexico. Another half million lived in 1986 in refugee camps within the country, nearly all of them in a periphery around San Salvador. Those were official camps. Inside the city, in vacant areas, were other, unofficial, camps, their conditions far worse. Father Barnett's parish was one of these, a squalid area of maybe two hundred acres where he estimated fifteen thousand people existed as squatters, crowded into one-room huts made of sticks and cardboard.

We walked along three-foot-wide paths, really ditches that carried the area's sewage, so narrow in places that our shoulders brushed the walls of huts on each side of us. Some of the huts, the more substantial ones, were damaged in the 1986 earthquake, nature's perverse discrimination, piling misery on people already subject to an intolerable unfairness. One woman who had been there with her five children for eight months had just finished building her hut when the earthquake knocked it down. When we visited she was wrapping the repositioned stakes with milky white six-mil plastic, a donation from a United states church.

A few privies were set up over ditches but most people *vay a montana*, go to the mountain. Food, a few hundred-pound bags of rice and beans, was distributed every few weeks. I felt a catch in my throat as a flock of giggling, chattering little girls in starched blue uniform dresses passed us on their way, Father Barnett told me, to communion in the only clothing they owned.

People whose homes were destroyed in the quake received little of the international help supposedly poured into the country. They told me, and an embassy spokesman later confirmed it, reluctantly, that a jurisdictional dispute delayed delivery of relief items. Several business factions competed for the commissions that came with distribution. Some planeloads of Mexican clothing, medicines and other material were turned back still loaded because of wrangles over who was to dispose of the stuff. Within days after the arrival of some supplies sent by church and charity groups in the United States and Europe they were showing up, for sale, in Salvadoran shops.

Villagers nodded to Father Barnett as we walked along and some stopped him to ask for help, if he knew where they could find a job, an item for the home. They were polite but I detected a resentment I hadn't seen before toward American missionaries. Barnett confirmed it. They know who helps their oppressors, he said. They blamed the United States for supporting a government that treats them, or allows them to be treated, this way. The only smile greeting us on our tour was on the face of nineteen-year-old Carlos William Ponce, who sat all day, every day, on a four-foot high mound of dirt above a slimy green sewer trench, pulling a string attached to a handmade wooden toy automobile. When he raised his arm the car came up its little track on the dirt hillside, when he lowered his arm it rolled back down the hill until he stopped it, usually, just before it ran into the sewage. Each of these countless maneuvers fascinated Carlos and he tried to tell us what he was doing, his eyes rolling around inside his head, but we couldn't understand his gibberish. His sister, fifteen, said Carlos was contented with his seven-day-a-week job. And, she added, it kept him out of the way as she and her mother attempted to feed and keep clean their brothers and sisters. Father Barnett shook his head.

There is no place for the retarded, he said, and so they are kept usually in a back room, out of sight. Some are just abandoned and wind up in state homes whose condition he can only imagine. Carlos was one of the lucky ones. We are stopped by one of the few able-bodied men in the camp—most of them are in the hills with "the boys," the guerrillas—who has a church request of Father Barnett. His youngest son, the fourteen-month-old with the bad cough, died the night before and some neighbors have chipped in enough money to buy a wooden box to bury the baby. Will the *padre* say some words? We stopped by the man's home, a one-room shanty with a dirt floor and torn cardboard walls under a sort of thatching of twisted poles and twigs. The baby's coffin, which would probably only temporarily contain his body, was on the floor. Several neighbors stopped by, and as a gaggle of wide-eyed children crowded around, Father Barnett said a prayer service. "One of every five kids here will die before the age of one," he told me.

Maria Hernandez wasn't the only woman of courage in El Salvador. Indeed, the women of the country, and women of the other countries of Latin America, could be role models for their macho men, if the men deigned to pay attention. Working with Hernandez was a group of women who dealt with death nearly every day, without her prominence to protect them, in the routine filing necessary to keep a record of the killings. These women, the Mothers of the Disappeared, defied death, defied the mean men with guns, giving a lie to their macho, asking, by their witness, what is so courageous about killing women and children?

I believe the inverse of that thought accounts for much of the ferocity with which Salvadorans, many Latins, indeed killers in every country in the world do their dirty work. It is not enough just to shoot a union worker. His tongue must be cut out, his genitals hacked off, his eyes gouged out. Hernandez told me of the mother whose eighteen-year-old daughter failed to return from a date with a boyfriend. The woman called Hernandez who called the police and then the morgue. Yes, her daughter's body was there, a morgue attendant said. When the woman went there she was led to a slab covered by a white sheet with a bulge thrusting up in the center. That could not be her daughter, the woman said; she was not pregnant. But the attendant drew back the sheet and there was her daughter, her abdominal cavity slashed open. The bulge was the head of her boyfriend. These kids were killed not because they were revolutionaries, but because the Christian Knights found them to be delinquent. They may have been fornicating or they may have been thinking about it. The usual explanation for this barbarism beyond even murder is that it intimidates others. Certainly it must do that, but it is usually so irrational, so without purpose that it fails even there; it fuels the fires of vengeance.

I think shame has something to do with it. If you are to kill someone who has never wronged you, whom you've never even seen before, you must rev up your emotional motor, get yourself into a mood for doing what normally might, or should, repel you. Cowardice, or its denial, must also be a factor. Many Latin men prate of their honor and it must be a psychological downer to visualize yourself as a fierce warrior and be ordered to kill the innocent and defenseless. Without that sudden, manufactured hate you wouldn't be able to do the job at all. So you dehumanize your victims, strip them of that last bit of dignity, their vulnerable bodies, and render them contemptible in their abject whimpering before you kill them. Murder became so routine in El Salvador that it was difficult at times to distinguish political killings from those perpetrated by religious fanatics or others originating in fender bender accidents or over neighborhood dog disputes.

It was always a good idea to visit Maria Hernandez long before or long after lunch. Her files contained thousands of accounts of disappearances, some concluded in known deaths after investigations, some never solved. For many, there were pictures of the missing people, usually family or school graduation portraits. And then, in the same file, the final pictures, taken in morgues or in the body dumping grounds. Few of the latter were recognizable; faces had been shot away, eyes gouged out, tongues cut out, ears cut off. Every conceivable way to torture and devalue a human to the ultimate nothing was there in that gallery of atrocities. I never saw all of Tutela Legal's files and pictures. Usually just the most recent month's collection was as much as I could take. On a 1986 visit I asked Hernandez if anything had changed since she and I had met two years before. "The death squads don't kill as often now," she replied. Maybe five people a month were found headless or their bodies disfigured in a roadside ditch in the countryside or a city gutter, she said. Two years earlier, at the time of an election, the daily toll was about eighty.

"The Army is more sophisticated now," Hernandez said. "But they're still torturing people and bombing them in the conflictive zones."

I told her of meeting Clemente and the other teachers and wondered if it was safe for them to go back to the homes from which they were expelled years ago. No, it was not safe, she said, although the village massacres that erupted periodically in the early 1980s were no longer happening. But, she said, the refugees had no real choice. "Life is better in the conflictive zones than it is here or in the refugee camps. Here there are no jobs. People live on charity. At least at home maybe they can grow their own beans, have some chickens."

But even that was difficult, as I saw one day when I hired a taxi for $100 a day to seek out guerrillas in one of the areas they controlled. My driver was a young man whom I will identify as Roger, because that is not his name, who drove a Mercedes taxi a year older than he. He was a garrulous companion, something of a clown and jokester, eager to give me my money's worth on our trip north out of San Salvador through a blasted landscape. For some twenty miles we drove through a silent land of no people, startling in itself in one of the world's most heavily populated countries. We saw not a single human being along that stretch of road. The only signs of life were starving dogs skulking in the ruins of houses and farm outbuildings and, wheeling above them, vultures waiting for them to die. In some cases houses had been bulldozed flat. Others had been dynamited. Appliances and plumbing fixtures were smashed. Plants in gardens had been uprooted, banana trees had been slashed at the ground. A few small villages were destroyed, the shop fronts pocked with bullet holes. A sign in front of what had once been a Texaco service station was shot almost in pieces. This was scorched earth with a vengeance and I couldn't determine who was responsible, the Army or the guerrillas.

At a bend in the road where ditches four feet deep had been dug in a staggered pattern half way across each lane, I found out, or at least got one side's explanation. A squad of about ten heavily armed men rose up out of the roadside brush as we twisted around the ditches. Several raised their rifles and we halted and they asked what we were doing in the area. Roger had blocked out crude TVs with masking tape on the windows of his old taxi, a standard sign in Central America that we were of the media and thus Kings-X in their war. I am not a fan of television or of most of its practioners, but by this stage in my life I recognized that television rated more respect than my newspaper press card, issued by the foreign press corps as a surrogate to the government. The guerrillas scorned it.

After a few questions and a very cursory look inside the car they waved us to go on. But before we left them I asked who had destroyed the homes and villages. The Army, their leader replied, surprised by my question. The campesinos who once lived here had sold food to the guerrillas, this guerrilla commander said, and they and even their neutral neighbors had been driven from their homes. Those who survived were now living in camps, some around San Salvador, some in other countries, he said.

They seemed almost indifferent to our presence once they had determined who we were and what our mission was and they didn't attempt to proselytize or propagandize us. But on the road back to San Salvador later that day, via a different route, we saw some papers fluttering beside the road and stopped. They were half-sheet size "communications from the FMLN (the Faribundo Marti Liberation Front, the umbrella guerrilla organization) to the people of Salvador," propaganda denouncing the candidates in the coming election.

"Salvadorans," the papers said, "none of the candidates and none of the political parties participating in these presidential elections...represent the interests of the people." Following that were the names of the candidates and their parties. Roberto d'Aubuisson of the ARENA Party "is the fascist assassin of Monsenor (Oscar) Romero and chief of the death squads." They described Jose Napoleon Duarte of the Christian Democratic Party as a "traitor to the people, responsible for the repression of workers in 1982 and self-delivered into the hands of the United States." Duarte defeated d'Aubuisson in the election a few days later, a triumph of American pressure and money. The sheets went on to say that the election would only prolong the war and "legalize the intervention of the North American military."

Those papers did not threaten the people for voting and I never saw any that did, in spite of accusations by the United states Embassy and the government that people were told they would be killed if they voted. One broadside to the public from the FMLN, according to the embassy, said "vote today, die tomorrow." But I never saw it and no one at the embassy produced a copy when I asked about it. Some guerrilla leaders may have made such threats. But only a few killings actually occurred in the days before, during and after election day, less, actually, than on normal days.

Roger drove me along a portion of the 20-mile-long reservoir behind Cerron Grande dam, its turbines the source of a good percentage of El Salvador's electricity. The power station at the dam and the pylons holding up wires carrying electricity away from it were frequent guerrilla targets.

Beyond it was Suchitoto, a fortress cattle town for whose possession the Army and the guerrillas fought for years. At the time of my visit the Army owned it and National Guardsmen, with their polished leather leggings and menacing AR-16 assault rifles stood at the entrance to every street. I raised my camera to take a picture of one guardsman in front of a bullet-pocked church. He unslung his rifle and pointed it at me. He won that contest; I took no pictures in the town. A few ragged civilians stood in the shade of shop overhangs along the town's rough streets and no one seemed to be working. They had no beer for sale so I bought warm cola drinks for Roger and myself and we drank them while dozens of women and children watched us. There were no young men around.

Nine years later I went back, in another rented taxi. Suchitoto was peaceful; I bought a beer and walked around, ignored by busy people going about their work. Life had improved in El Salvador, I acknowledged. Many of the blasted homes and villages were being rebuilt and new banana trees had been planted. d'Aubuisson and Duarte were dead, both of cancer. But the killings continued, perhaps more selective now, and almost certainly by the same people. The new president, Alfredo Christiani, an American educated coffee grower who speaks perfect English, accused the former guerrillas, many of them now out-in-the-open politicians, of the killings. Newspapers reporting on these murders never mentioned the death squads.

Although Roger had no dispute with what we read in the guerrilla leaflets he grew increasingly nervous as we neared San Salvador on our return. At last, about five miles from the city, he pulled the car to the side of the road and turned to me, his face solemn. The leaflets, he explained with some embarrassment, were dangerous. If the Army should stop us as we drove into the city we, and especially he, could be in serious trouble for having them in our possession. He was quiet for a moment as I waited for him to go on. I knew what I had to do, but I hoped for more explanation from him, something more revealing than I had obtained from him yet as to his feelings about this war. Instead, he sat silently, ashamed of his fear and refusing to look at me. Okay, I said, we'll throw them away, but would he mind if I kept a couple, in my shirt pocket, for souvenirs? He was smiling again and said that should be safe enough.

Roger began pestering me for another day's work at $100; weren't there other guerrillas I would like to see? He could show me some nice scenery. Salvador was famous for its volcanos. He prattled on as I tried to bring the notes in my journal up to date. I pondered if I wanted to spend another $100 for Roger's company and I stalled for time, by telling him that he still owed me an hour that day. Would he take me now to the site of a pre-election rally the next morning? Sure, Roger said, and we drove to the church where workers were putting up a sound system for the next day's event. Roger was still chattering as we left the church and I interrupted to ask him if he could take me in the morning to El Playon, the death squad dumping ground that I had heard about but never seen. Roger didn't answer and when I glanced at him his face, normally animated in grins and grimaces, was a pale mask. He looked straight ahead.

There, leaning against the front fender of his taxi was a beefy man with sun glasses, his gut hanging over his belt. As we neared the car, now silent, the man was paring his fingernails with a long switch-blade knife. He didn't look at us as we stopped by the taxi but kept on digging at his nails. Roger's normally deep brown face was a pallid yellow and he was trembling. I opened the passenger side door and got in and the man looked up, at me and then longer at Roger, heaved himself off the fender, crossed the sidewalk and resumed his manicure as he leaned against the wrought iron churchyard fence. Roger got into the car, his hand shaking so badly he could barely get the key into the ignition switch. After a moment he started the engine and we drove off. My hotel was only a few blocks away and Roger drove me directly there.

I paid him and tried to ask him about the man, whether he knew him and what his being there signified. Roger, usually so voluble, was almost mute. He took my money without counting it and waited impatiently while I got my camera and day pack from the rear seat and got out. I told him goodbye but he only grunted and drove off immediately as soon as I closed the door. There was no more salesman talk about another day's hire. I never saw Roger again and didn't want to endanger him further by questioning other drivers at the taxi stand across the street from the Camino Real and having talk get back that a nosy gringo was asking about him. But I did see other men like the one who had so frightened Roger. They were everywhere and Salvadorans told me what I had already deduced; these were death squad members.

I felt badly that I had endangered the boy with my careless questions in public, and from then on in El Salvador I tried to be more circumspect. But that was not so easy. The very next day I committed another gaffe. A Baptist church worker picked me up to take me to the El Presidente Hotel which was to be the national election headquarters and while I was there I found in the vast marble lobby on a coffee table a discarded newspaper I had never seen before. I didn't have time to more than glance at the paper before the driver beckoned me. When I had seated myself and closed the door he immediately objected to the newspaper and said I could not have it in his car. It was published by a right wing organization, he said, which made me all the more interested in reading it. But he was adamant. If he was to take me to visit the orphanage which was the object of our trip, I would have to throw away the paper. If guerrillas stopped our car we, or he, would be in real danger, he said. We were already late and didn't have time to return to my hotel to drop it off so I reluctantly stuffed it into a trash can. I didn't have time even to write down the name of the paper and I never saw another copy of it. Salvadorans walked through a miasma of fear that rarely touched visitors.

3

To Read and Write

SNOWY EGRETS STALK SOLEMN AS SENTINELS ON PARADE IN their search for worms in the furrows turned over by the oxens' wood-bladed plow. Some, seeking ticks, hitch rides on the backs of cattle grazing in the rolling green pastures stretching northward to the misty hills of Honduras just over the border. The gentle valley below La Estancia looks English in its pastoral beauty, unlike the usual tangled decadence of the tropics. A jarring note is the trail of dust raised by a convoy of trucks towing cannon eastward toward Jalapa and the war.

It is Nicaragua in the summer of 1983 and Teresa Zelaya Flores is showing me her new home, an ugly two-room concrete structure that might suffice as a granary on a modest farm in North America. But it has a floor, Teresa points out, apparently expecting me to show surprise, and there is a water pipe and spigot just outside the door. The roof is corrugated zinc. Electrical wiring is in place and the electricity will be hooked up within weeks, she says. She has never had a house with a floor before and she has always carried water from the stream several hundred yards from her old home. The old roof of palm thatch leaked. She has seen electric lights in Jalapa but she has never had a chance to flip a switch.

"Our government is concerned for us," Teresa told me as we admired the stout walls of the house and the smooth floor. It was surprisingly cool inside, in spite of the metal roof. She had moved two makeshift beds into the first room and in the second blankets were stretched out on the floor. Her oldest son, seventeen, was kidnapped by the Contra and Teresa didn't know if he was still alive. Her husband's mother and his four brothers had also been kidnapped by the Contra and no one knew their fates. The four of her eight children still at home would share this new house with Teresa and her husband, Ruben, who worked nearby on a tobacco cooperative farm, the same land he worked for Cuban absentee plantation owners before the revolution four years earlier. Before that Ruben's father owned some of that land. The dictator, Anastasio Somoza, and his Cuban exile friends took it through a legal trick Ruben still doesn't understand. Ruben told me he worked harder than he had for the Cubans, but the land was partly his and so were the receipts from selling tobacco to the state purchasing agency.

Teresa looked around the house and couldn't suppress a smile, her lips pulled back over toothless gums. She was thirty six, but looked nearer sixty, gaunt and sun dried. She had never seen a hair dresser or a women's clothing store. Before the revolution of 1979 she could not read or write; she had never gone to school. Now, as we stood in the shadowed porch fronting the house, she gently pulled my notebook from my hand and then my ballpoint pen. Carefully, almost painfully, with much tongue chewing, she wrote her name in the notebook and handed it back to me, her eyes shining with pride.

"I learned in the *alfabetization*," the literacy program the Sandinista government launched immediately after their triumph in the revolution. Her look told me she had learned more than just to read and write.

I wondered whether she could write any more than her name, and she reached down a tattered adult textbook from the exposed end of a rafter and slowly read aloud an account of a farmer taking his cow to market. It was heavily weighted with socialist or Marxist context. Such textbooks can get their owners killed by the Contra raiding across the border from their sanctuary in Honduras. Possessing such material, or even just learning to read, was itself "subver-

41

sive" in Contra eyes. Teresa knew that, she told me and an American nun who was giving me a ride, but that does not deter her. She had tasted learning and she would not be stopped. She and her husband were going on with their educations, both studying at night in the fourth grade of a continuing education program. Because they could read and write and because there was no priest at La Estancia, Teresa and Ruben had both become Delegates of the Word, authorized to conduct Catholic Church services and to lead the congregation in reading the liturgy although not to say mass or hear confessions.

Teresa scorned the Contra as ex-National Guardsmen, killers "seeking to return to power." She had an answer to the latest broadcast by the Contra's clandestine radio, operating safely from Honduras, as it attacked the government's recent food rationing plan. "They promise that if they take power there will be no more rationing," Teresa says. "Everyone will get enough to eat. Maybe they would take away rationing, but before (the revolution) there was no rationing either, but only those who had money could eat." Rationing assured her family of getting ten pounds of sugar a week, she said. It seemed a lot of sugar and I learned only later that excessive sugar in diets is the curse of Nicaraguans, and other Central Americans as well.

As we left Teresa's house we were ambushed by a swarm of about forty children from ages three to twelve years who got a lunch each day at a communal kitchen. Caressing the head of a little girl clinging to her tightly, Teresa said the girl's mother had been killed in a Contra raid. Teresa hoped to establish a cooperative to raise chickens and also to teach the people how to cultivate better gardens with a wider variety of vegetables.

Knowledge is indeed power, I thought as I left La Estancia that day, taking a salute from the resident militiaman, Amadea Martinez Ruiz, who patrolled the community with his AK-47 rifle and enough hair to clothe a horse. He was a fearsome sight and I wondered what kind of opposition he could put up against the Contra. Then I realized that his function was primarily to give the alarm when the raid came and to delay as long as possible the enemy's advance. Many militia like him were killed in raids on similar communities over the next four years as the Contra slowly strangled civil life in northern Nicaragua through murder and terror.

I never went back to La Estancia so I don't know if Teresa continued on with her school and co-op, or if she survived the war. But in later travels as the war grew in intensity and nastiness, I saw the dreams of other Nicaraguans shattered as the Contra killed teachers and destroyed their schools. Also targeted were Delegates of the Word, doubly subversive in that they accepted the teachings of Liberation Theology and thus defied the leadership of the traditional church heirarchy with its message of humility and subservience to the word of the bishops and their priests.

Reagan may have actually believed that he was fighting off an invasion by Nicaragua of its neighbors, but his handlers and advisers knew it was nonsense. What they were really afraid of was the power of an idea that had been imparted by the revolution to this toothless thirty-six year old and her husband: you have a right to be here. They had been given a sense of dignity, of their value as human beings. If they and their neighbors and friends and thousands of others in Nicaragua were allowed to chart their own destinies, people like them in other countries might begin to wonder if they too couldn't take charge of their lives. In that sense they were, indeed, subversives. And they were a threat to the corporate interests in the United States who intended to preserve Central America as a resource base and its people as a docile and cheap labor pool.

The puppets the United States purchased to pose as Contra leaders had joined in the cheering (although not the fighting) for the triumph of the revolution in 1979 after Somoza's brutalities, especially his selfish greed, became too much even for them. But they had a rude shock when the people who led the revolution and did the fighting made it clear they actually believed all that rhetoric about a *Libre Nicaragua*, its government dedicated to equality of opportunity.

The Sandinistas were socialists, or tried to be, and they certainly claimed to take lessons from the teachings of Karl Marx, but they were also nationalists, and moralistic to the point of prudishness. Most of them were never communists, except in the judgment of the American right wing, a fact relayed repeatedly back to Washington, D. C. by United States diplomats in the early 1980s. Those messages were ignored and the messengers eventually sent off to exile when they wouldn't sing the correct tune. Yet every mention of either the government or the Sandinista Party in United States newspapers or magazines was prefaced by a reference to their "leftist" bent. "Marxist-Leninist" had become a standard appellation for Nicaragua in mainstream United States newspapers. News stories of El Salvador, on the other hand, never carried the warning that its government was "right wing" or "oligarchic."

My newspaper reports from Nicaragua and the other Central American countries often prompted accusations in letters to the editor that I was a dupe of the Sandinistas or worse, one of their henchmen. One letter writer scorned me for being "led around Nicaragua by expert communist indoctrinators" for my story of Teresa Zelaya even though I went there on my own, as I always did, in this case hitching a ride with a sister of the Maryknollers. The letter writer, who identified himself as an international trader who traveled often in Latin America, said I failed to consider that "the concrete house given for free to the woman interviewed, was paid for by the United States, or some other capitalist country, directly or indirectly. Even if the house were paid for by Soviet aid, the original source of funds was the American worker, who deposited his savings in his local bank, who loaned it to the Chase Manhattan Bank, who loaned it to the Russians (or Poland or Bulgaria) who loaned it to Cuba who gave it to the Nicaraguan government for propaganda purposes. If the U.S. capitalists would not have loaned the communist block all those hundreds of billions of dollars they could not have built their arsenal and instigated (sic) the world against America," he said. Not a thought there that if his delusions were true the United States could have given or loaned that money directly to the people of Central America and thus made them our friends rather than creating enemies who saw our government as some perverse, alien evil. And there was no acknowledgement that the weapons used to kill Teresa's neighbors and probably her son were purchased with American taxpayer funds. It was such thinking, or non thinking, that made public debates over the United States course in Central America so difficult.

"There is no way the people of Nicaragua want to cease being a colony of the United States just to become a colony of the Soviet Union," said an American who lived in Managua, in answer to such nonsense. "They (the Sandinistas) will accept help from whoever will give it to them," said another.

The war was beginning to take its toll on the people by 1984 but Nicaraguans generally stood by the Sandinistas. In Esteli I talked with a businessman who owned a radio and television repair shop. A small government loan, which no bank would give him before the revolution, put him in business. He attributed the Contra war to fears that "the United States does not want to allow us to set an example for other people."

In 1993 when I visited Nicaragua that man and people like him were denied credit or loans of any kind by private banks. No government lending agency was available to help such micro entrepreneurs. Even well-off cattlemen complained that loans were denied them; only the wealthy, who were not desperate for capital, found credit available. Nicaragua had been privatized.

Among the areas that suffered most during the Contra war was the Ocotal region in northwestern Nicaragua, bombed by the United States Marines in 1927. It is, or was, a forested area heavily logged during the forty five years of Somoza family rule. It was also a source of manpower for the National Guard as young men sought work. They are very poor people, an American nun who had long worked in the region told me in 1983. Some sided with the Contra since many of the Guardia were from there. Others supported the government, the Sandinistas. But they learned that staying neutral was usually impossible. "The feeling of fear is getting closer and closer and the tensions are rising," said the nun. The Contra were coming over the border on quick raids from their safe Honduran camps, killing doctors, nurses, teachers, .

Since the revolution many schools had been built. And, the nun said, "nearly all the kids are now going to school. Before, it was too expensive and there were no teachers for public schools. Somoza solved the problem by having no classrooms. Most of the teachers are Nicaraguan although some are Cuban."

My friend the nun and others in Ocotal conceded that there were shortages of food and other basics. They insisted that with rationing there was no hoarding of food and other household staples. That changed, however, as the war and the combined effects of the United States economic blockade and the Contra attacks reduced supplies even further and some foods were not available even in the community (government) stores.

The people of Ocotal had an explanation for the shortages that was new to me. "The Sandinistas have created higher expectations and people are demanding more now," another nun said. "Coca Cola is scarce, but the people never drank Coke at all before the revolution," said a community leader and delegate of the word. "Now they can't get all they want and they complain." I wondered what Adolfo Calero, owner of Nicaragua's Coca Cola franchise in the Somoza days and in 1983 the CIA's paid Contra front man in Miami, would have thought of that. Before the revolution, people everywhere told me, the Nicaraguan bourgeois had never suffered any of the shortages endured by the majority poor. Now that they too were inconvenienced, stories of their hardships reached receptive ears in the United States Embassy and the administration in Washington.

The early years of the revolution brought many improvements in the lives of Ocotal residents. "Popular kitchens" not only fed people whose diets were deficient, but girls, future housewives, were taught to cook there. The introduction of electricity and tiny capital loans allowed small woodworking businesses to enhance their production as well as offering instruction to young apprentices. Until Contra murders drove out the survivors, six Cuban doctors treated the sick of Ocotal.

Most Nicaraguans could not afford clothing made of the cotton they grew and shipped to Japan and Europe. Instead, they bought cheaper nylon shirts and dresses, harder to wash and hotter to wear. Such anomalies were targets of the change the Sandinista Party intended to bring to Nicaragua. Change didn't always work. Tradition triumphed when the Sandinistas attempted to modernize the public market system in Managua by closing three large, dirty and disorderly markets and replacing them with a number of smaller and more easily maintained markets dispersed throughout the city, nearer to people's homes. The people did not approve. Market operators and customers protested and the Sandinistas backed down. They were never able to close the noisome Oriental Market, notorious as a gathering place for the city's petty thieves.

Reagan and the Contra were not the only enemies the Sandinistas faced; they were forever confronted by backward thinking and a superstitious cling to the past whenever they tried to apply new approaches to Nicaragua's problems. Throughout the Sandinista years and continuing now, witch doctors plied their alleged skills among a large part of the populace. As Contra depredations grew, those practioners of the old ways often were the only comfort ailing Nicaraguans had.

Daniel Ortega and the other Sandinistas, in spite of their public relations skills, seemed to have a perverse genius for making difficulties for themselves. They seemed to dare Reagan and the United States to make some new attack on Nicaragua. When Ortega went to Moscow within hours of one of Congress' rare bouts of courage—cutting off weapons shipments to the Contra—he gave many nervous congressmen all the excuse they needed not do that again.

Why did he seem to deliberately undercut sympathizers in Washington, I asked one high-ranking Sandinista. "He doesn't have to ask you for permission where and when he wants to go," snapped Ligia Elizondo, vice minister for economic planning. Ortega was on a desperate mission to Moscow, she said; Nicaragua's oil reserves were at zero. "Our president doesn't have to answer to any Yanquis."

So he didn't. But couldn't she understand how this looked to those who had sucked in their guts and voted against a popular president, how it looked to their enemies? Didn't she, or Ortega, see how recognition of the facts of political life might have made his condition, and that of his people, a bit easier? Daniel's trip was no one else's business, she said. She could never be convinced, and neither could other Nicaraguans. Actually, Ortega's trip had been planned long before the congressional showdown, but that sequence of events was never reported in the American press. The journey to Moscow was seen by editorial writers as either sheer stupidity or arrogance.

It was that very independence, that insouciant refusal to be cowed by the colossus of the north that made, and still makes, the Sandinistas attractive, at least to me. And in refusing to be "our son of a bitch," it made Ortega more appealing to his countrymen than the subservient collaborators who serve as figurehead presidents of neighboring nations.

One of the most hateful aspects of the Reagan-Bush political warfare against Nicaragua was the refusal to acknowledge that the country's record in education, in social welfare and especially in human rights, spotty as it may have been at times, was light years ahead of those other countries which those two administrations liked to refer to as "fledgling democracies" in spite of their viciousness and indifference to the well-being of their people. The official line from Washington was that Nicaragua was a "totalitarian dungeon," that it was oppressing its people and persecuting the church. All those charges far better fit Guatemala, Honduras and El Salvador than they did Nicaragua, and top officials in Washington knew it. But acknowledging those truths did not fit the larger design, and officials of those two administrations continued to repeat the distortions.

The Sandinistas were long accused of corruption, on the personal, household level. But those charges, seized on with glee by the rightwingers in the United States, always had an unsubstantial tone to them. Nicaraguans I talked to never believed them and I noticed that even the most virulent opposition seldom made much of them. The top commandantes were accused of seizing the mansions of exiled rich Nicaraguans and of taking their cars and even their women.

One of the basics of propaganda, which has long since carried over into political warfare in United States politics, is to accuse your opponent of the underhand things you are doing, or intend to do. The State Department, the public voice of the Reagan and Bush Administrations (as opposed to the "grey" or non public voices of the CIA and other agencies) kept up a steady drumbeat of accusations of human rights violations by the Sandinistas, of using terror tactics to frighten the Nicaraguan populace and killing or imprisoning anyone who spoke against them. Certainly there were acts of bad judgment and over zealousness by certain officials of the Sandinista Party, many of which led to trials and imprisonment. As in most propaganda it is often impossible to determine where truth ends and lies take over. But if the Sandinistas were half as skilled at manipulating the truth and hiding really bad deeds as the United States insisted they were, then they could give lessons to the best of the world's PsyOps warriors.

American propagandists were often crude compared to the Sandinistas. One of the more blatant examples of United States efforts to undermine the credibility of the Sandinistas and to shake the faith of their sympathizers was a slick booklet distributed in 1986 by the Department of State. It was a product of the department's "Coordinator of Public Diplomacy for Latin America and the Caribbean (See Chapter Eleven). The pamphlet, titled "Inside the Sandinista Regime: a Special Investigator's Perspective," was an illegal use of American taxpayers' money to persuade the American public of the villainy of the Sandinistas. United States law forbids use of federal funds to propagandize its own citizens.

The entire pamphlet was devoted to telling the story of an idealistic young Nicaraguan, one Alvaro Jose Baldizon Aviles, who is described as "formerly Chief Investigator of the Special Investigations Commission of the Nicaraguan Ministry of the Interior." Baldizon said he fled Nicaragua in 1985, disillusioned with the direction the Sandinista revolution had taken. As an investigator, he said, his reports were designed to avoid bad international publicity about Sandinista human rights abuses and were the basis for cover stories aimed at hiding the truth from the rest of the world. Baldizon seems to have been a busy fellow until his defection; the booklet, which hints that some of its information comes from other sources, is a twenty-page indictment of Sandinista duplicity, special measures (assassination), skullduggery and attacks on the Catholic church to ridicule it and lessen its influence on unsophisticated Nicaraguans. It says foreign visitors, especially those on herded tours, were duped by skilled Sandinista manipulation and steered past evidence of atrocities such as three hundred farmers it alleged were killed in the Jinotega and Matagalpa departments prior to 1984. Visits with police disguised as average Nicaraguans were staged for foreign visitors, Baldizon told the State Department propaganda specialists who prepared the pamphlet. I sought witnesses to the murders of the farmers but could never find anyone who had even heard of them.

Among the booklet's appendices to the pamphlet was a To Whom It May Concern letter identifying Baldizon and ordering that "civilian and military authorities present all necessary collaboration that comrade Second Lieutenant Baldizon requests." It may have sounded sinister to the State Department but it is the same wording and format as a press safe conduct letter I was given by the national press office so I could go into the "conflictive" zone in the north, in Nueva Segovia near the Honduran border.

As in most propaganda, there are grains of truth in Baldizon's stories. Where truth and exaggeration part company is impossible to say. I traveled, without escort, in Nueva Segovia a number of times and I met many people who had lived there for years, both Nicaraguans and foreigners, primarily missionaries and others trying to help the poor of Nicaragua and I was never told of any of the atrocities Baldizon mentions. I don't doubt that some Sandinistas, suddenly given power and guns to match, overstepped their authority. Latins, like other peoples who have never enjoyed the rudiments of democracy at home, in school or in local government, tend to abuse authority when it comes to them too quickly or too easily and without close supervision. I saw many instances of it in my travels not only in Nicaragua but elsewhere in Central America. I saw it in the rural Koreans with whom I lived for a year.

Another defector, Major Roger Miranda Bengochea, told lurid tales of debauchery among the Sandinista heirarchy and of their plans to invade neighboring countries. A secret plan Miranda supposedly took from the Sandinistas represented their intention to create "a new Cuba," according to Elliott Abrams, undersecretary of state for Latin America. Miranda, supposedly an aide to Nicaragua Defense Minister Humberto Ortega, was sequestered in Washington for a month after his defection before he was presented to the press, just as the Administration geared up for another attempt to persuade Congress to approve money to continue the war.

Miranda's charge that the Sandinistas planned to invade Costa Rica served the Reagan Administration two ways: it emphasized the alleged Sandinista threat and it bolstered efforts to force Costa Rica to organize an army in the face of the country's determination not to have one. Some Administration officials thought Miranda was more wind than substance[2] but they were afraid their careers would be damaged by speaking out, an assumption Abrams took pains to inculcate throughout the State Department.

Checking complaints of human rights abuses was difficult. I had heard enough of them, long before I saw the

---

[2] Richard Halloran, The New York Times, Washington, D. C. Dec. 18, 1987.

Baldizon and Miranda reports, that I was concerned that perhaps I was missing something. In 1985 I went to the office of the Permanent Committee for Human Rights in Nicaragua, which I suppose could be called the "opposition" human rights organization since there was another one, called by some the "official" group although it was run by an American nun, Mary Hartman. The Permanent Committee published monthly reports on alleged human rights abuses, disappearances, unjust jailings, tortures and deaths of Nicaraguans. I have no doubt that some of these occurred although documentation of the kind maintained by a similar organization in El Salvador, Tutela Legal, did not exist.

I talked to Marta Patricia Baltodano, director of the committee who had her office in a large house in a rundown middle class area of Managua. Baltodano is a lawyer, bright, dedicated and obviously sincere, but I got very little from our conversation of several hours beyond a series of vague charges. She gave me a batch of monthly reports, with names of people who had been jailed unjustly for political offenses but none included addresses or any other information that would allow me to seek them out, or to find their families, to hear their stories. She made no accusations of killings as Baldizon had reported. She said the Sandinistas interfered with her work at every step but she admitted that outside of surveillance of her office, which I could see no sign of when I left it, there had been no physical harassments.

When I was there a number of very depressed looking people sat in the lobby of her office. Baltodano said they were petitioners seeking news of their disappeared or imprisoned family members. None of them wished to speak to me and I didn't press them. I assumed that they would have been willing to speak to a foreign newsman unless they feared retribution. Whether that sort of retaliation was real or only in their imaginations I don't know.

I took Baltodano's accusations to the Sandinistas for their rebuttal and ended up still not sure who was right. I don't believe either side was telling lies; both were giving a version of the truth as they saw it. Rafael Solis, secretary to the Council of State, said those who Baltodano called political prisoners were actually Contra captured either in battle or in some clandestine activity supporting the invading Contra. They were tried by Popular Tribunals and most were sentenced to prison. Some may have been secretly killed, I suppose, although I never saw any proof, not that anyone could likely have produced any. And, in spite of what Baltodano told me, some were acquitted, Solis said. The only persons who could be considered political prisoners, he said, were members of the Somoza National Guard who had been tried on specific charges for crimes before and during the revolution and were serving out their sentences.

I went to a prison one day and sat with ex-guardsmen as they ate lunch, mostly beans cooked in an enormous pot by a prisoner. It seemed a show place opened at certain times to visiting foreigners. The prisoners seemed in good health and they said they were not mistreated. No guards were listening as I talked to them but it did occur to me that one or more of them might be plants, informers. I've visited enough American prisons to know that no matter how good conditions are prisoners are likely to have complaints; these men seemed to have none.

They answered questions briefly and simply and volunteered nothing. I asked several prisoners when they were to be released and each gave me a specific date. Often, political prisoners are kept as long as it serves their captors' purpose and one of their agonies is not knowing when they'll be freed. The United States Embassy in Nicaragua estimated in 1987 that the Sandinistas were holding some eight to ten thousand political prisoners, of whom about twenty five hundred were former Somoza guardsmen who had either been convicted of heinous crimes or refused to admit their guilt as guardsmen or otherwise cooperate with their captors. Solis, on the other hand, said some two hundred were being held, all of them convicted of collaborating with the enemy.

Baltodano, incidentally, left Nicaragua not long after our meeting to work for the State Department in its effort to curb the murderous human rights abuses of the Contra in Honduras. Contra leaders saw her as just a part of what they considered a "larger Communist conspiracy,".[3] She quickly found evidence within Contra ranks and mostly in their camps in Honduras, of the murders, sexual abuses, corruption and lies that others with less authority had been reporting for years. She was so harassed and blocked from doing her job that she was able to investigate only a few reports of abuses by the Contra in their raids and ambushes against Nicaraguan civilians. Mostly she was ignored and, at the end of the war, returned to Nicaragua to again monitor the Sandinistas.

The right to strike was suspended in Nicaragua in the early 1980s as Contra depredations increased. Ironically that restriction was often cited as evidence of Sandinista disregard for normal human rights by people who never blanched when Somoza jailed, tortured and murdered labor union members merely for their memberships. In spite of government denials the Sandinistas did keep a tight control over unions, both in urban and rural areas. They saw unions as the key to close supervision of the population and to educating people in social goals.

I attended a huge labor rally in Managua one evening in 1983 organized to commemorate a 1979 retreat from Managua to the city of Masaya during a battle with Somoza's National Guard. Thousands of people assembled in a large field to listen to harangues by Sandinista leaders. High points of rhetoric set the crowd to chanting *"No Pasaran,"* they shall not pass, a Sandinista slogan against the Contra borrowed from the Spanish Civil War. Each shout was accompanied by thousands of fists thrust into the night sky. Vendors of ice cream and soft drinks wandered through the crowd and children ran everywhere, giving the rally a county fair aspect. It also had something to it of the mass rallies of Nazi Germany, and standing in the middle of the crowd, I felt a disturbing sense of manipulation around me.

Outwardly, it was on the social-political level that the

---

[3] Comando, The CIA and Nicaragua's Contra Rebels, Sam Dillon, 1991, p. 199.

Nicaraguan Contra war was fought. Of all the distortions leveled at the Sandinistas by the United States, an alleged refusal to hold elections promptly after the revolution came as near as any to being bare-faced lies. According to State Department press releases and official speeches, the Sandinistas had promised their neighbors in Central America and the Organization of American States right after the 1979 revolution that they would immediately hold elections. No evidence was ever produced beyond a blandly worded telegram from the Sandinistas to the Organization of American States in which elections were promised, but with no time table.

In 1980, less than a year after the revolution, the government announced that elections would be held in 1985. "No one ever said elections would be before that," Solis, the Council of State secretary, told me when I asked him about elections. Ernesto Cardenal, a poet, priest and Nicaraguan minister of culture in the Sandinista government, reminded me that it was eight years after the American revolution before our first national election was held. Nicaragua had no tradition of real elections, Solis said, and it didn't even have a countrywide precinct system.

After repeated badgering by the United States the Sandinistas did call an election, a year early as far as they were concerned, for 1984. That prompted State Department accusations that the speeded up timetable was a trick to deny opposition parties time to campaign.

As one American in Nicaragua suggested, only mass suicide by the Sandinista commandantes would satisfy the United States that any action they took wasn't designed to deceive the world. The 1984 election followed a long and windy campaign of propaganda one-upmanship. The United States attempted to prove to the world that the Sandinistas were liars; they, in their turn, tried to show they were moving ahead with a peace plan devised by their neighbors which the United States was secretly trying to scuttle. That overture, known as Contadora for the Panamanian island where it was devised by Panama, Venezuela, Colombia and

Mexico, failed in the end, I believe, because the United States undercut it at every turn in a twisting diplomatic road.

The plan called for, among other things, the removal of foreign troops from every country in the region. When in mid-1984 the Sandinistas agreed to sign a draft of the peace agreement, obviously seeing either an end to the Contra bases in Honduras or a propaganda victory or both, the United States balked. That gave the Sandinistas their public relations triumph and the United States looked foolish and, worse, two-faced in calling for peace and then rebuffing a peace proposal.

The United States position was that the treaty would leave Nicaragua with a large army which would constitute a threat to its neighbors. At about that time United States intelligence suddenly discovered that Nicaragua had an army of more than one hundred thousand (some estimates said six hundred thousand). The figure included regulars but also reservists, inactive and active, which Nicaragua relied on primarily to fight its war, as well as local militias, and did not reflect strengths as they are normally calculated. By mid 1992, incidentally, the Nicaraguan Army strength was twenty one thousand, the smallest in the region with the exception of Costa Rica which has no army.

The United States said the Contadora proposal left open the question of "verification," how the rest of the region, and the world, was going to know if the Sandinistas were keeping their part of the peace bargain. It didn't include any verification for the United States, either, which was at that time in the process of fuzzing up explanations of why private American groups and mysterious foreign sources were financing the Contra war in what would several years later become known as the Iran-Contra scandal.

Congress, nervous at reports of atrocities committed by the Contra that Reagan was calling "Freedom Fighters" and "the moral equivalent of the Founding Fathers," was engaged in an intricate political dance, now bowing and voting for money for the Contra, now backing away. The Sandinistas may have been as devious in a pretended acceptance of the peace plan as the United States was but they clearly won that round of the propaganda battle. The Contadora countries continued for a while to try to bring the United States and Nicaragua together but eventually, in the face of United States resistance, the group dissolved and no more was heard of it.

One of Contadora's provisions was free elections in all the countries of Central America. When Nicaragua set its election ahead a year, to 1984, it drew a rebuke from the United States which was backing Arturo Cruz, a Sandinista ally in the revolution who had broken with the government. Cruz, who had lived for years in Washington as an employee of the World Bank, wouldn't have time to campaign, the United States said. Then, as the date drew closer, it accused the Sandinistas of obstructing Cruz' efforts to campaign, accusations that happened to be true.

I know that obstacles were put in Cruz' path, such as making radio and television time hard to obtain. But he ran a poor campaign, marked by elitism and a refusal to mix with the voters. He wasn't capable of telling his side of the story, to explain what he would do if elected, and finally he pulled out. Again, both the United States and Nicaragua had propaganda ammunition to prove that the other side was not sincere. While the Sandinistas almost certainly made conditions tough for the opposition, I am convinced that the election itself was fair and as honest as any ever held in Central America. The Sandinistas got sixty seven percent of the vote.

The rest of the world barely knew an election was going on, however, thanks to the Reagan Administration's success in keeping it out of the news. On election day, when thousands of international observers and hundreds of American reporters were on hand to watch for fraud and ballot-stuffing, the big headlines in the United States focused on a "leaked" report that a Soviet ship was unloading MIG jet fighter planes at the Nicaraguan Pacific Coast Port of Corinto. That story turned out to be wholly a lie, a fabrication by the PsyOps warriors in the Pentagon or at the CIA propaganda factory in Langley, Virginia. The United States media, newspapers and television, gobbled it up without question.

Mild "corrections" by the State Department a few days later never received anywhere near the press exposure that the MIG story did. It was a bald, contrived fabrication and no one was ever called to account for it. It had served its purpose, however, to blot out press coverage of the election, the first honest one in Nicaraguan history. Five years later, when the next election rolled around the United States was spending millions of dollars backing the opposition and making non binding explicit and implicit promises of vast American aid if Nicaraguans voted correctly. That election was billed by the United States as the first honest one in Nicaragua's recent history, ignoring the 1984 vote.

In the second election even the State Department was caught off guard, sharing a delusion with the Sandinistas that they would win. People at the United States Embassy, who had been predicting massive Sandinista voter fraud, seemed almost disappointed when the elaborate election system set up by Mariano Fiallos, the election supervisor, produced an upset. Daniel Ortega and the Sandinistas lost control of the government to Violeta Chamorro and UNO, a wrangling coalition of fourteen political parties ranging from the Communists to the far right whose only unifying ingredient was hatred for the Sandinistas.

The Sandinistas never received the credit they deserved for adopting and putting into effect a constitution created in the largest public participation project in the history of all Latin America. All political parties were invited to participate and most did, at least at first. They ranged from the Communists, through the Popular Action, Maoist, party, on the far left, to the Social Christians, the Liberals, which had split off from Somoza in the 1960s, and the Social Democratic Party. Only Somocistas were excluded.

"We wanted a constitution and courts free of foreign intervention," Solis told me. "It shouldn't be pro-United States or pro-Soviet Union. It (the constitution) calls for a mixed economy, of public and private enterprises, and political plu-

58

ralism (a mixture of capitalist democracy and socialism), with our parties not allied with outsiders."

A vast network of citizens was established to review a series of proposals for a national government. They studied systems as varied as France's and India's, arguing the benefits and drawbacks of each. Should the country be divided up into districts, or should everyone run for office (to the National Assembly) at large? The decision was for districts. They decided, as some other Latin American countries have, to make elections a fourth branch of the national government.

Every effort was made to strengthen the judicial branch and make it independent of the executive and the legislative branches. The Sandinistas, indeed everyone in Nicaragua, knew that democracy means nothing when judges can't judge without fearing for their lives. They instituted a one-person, one-vote provision and brought the voting age down to sixteen, a recognition of Nicaragua's youthful population and the fact that most of the fighters in the 1979 revolution were teenagers. Freedom to join unions, and the right to strike, in peacetime, were guaranteed. Freedom of the press was also guaranteed. Solis insisted that the censorship of La Prensa and some radio stations would be lifted once the threat of war was ended. Political parties could be recognized by petitions of one hundred people, and they were guaranteed freedom to say what they liked. At the time, I went to rallies to listen to opposition party leaders denounce the Sandinistas openly even though the Reagan Administration was accusing the government of stifling opposition.

Women had emerged as leaders during the revolution and the rights of women also were fully guaranteed in the constitution. A unique feature was a continuation and institutionalization of the "face the people" meetings Sandinista leaders were holding unofficially around the country, both to sound out public sentiment and to explain governmental actions. "It will continue to give the people an opportunity to present complaints to their government which will try to follow up with answers," Solis said. "We want people to feel they can denounce the government, and the bureaucracy and something will be done about their complaints." Freedom of religion was also promised but the new constitution made the government secular, completely removed from any religious faith. All of this and more was debated in meetings all over the country before it was finally adopted nationwide. Almost no one in the United States ever heard of it.

The Sandinistas, probably because they were young and not yet hidebound and ossified in their thinking, showed an unpolitical penchant for listening to new ideas that many observers found refreshing. Vice President Sergio Ramirez told me in 1989 that Nicaragua had not only preceded socialist countries around the world in modifying their central, command economic ideas but had been an example to the Soviet Union's satellite nations.

"I believe that we have been able to show here that a socialist model can be pluralist, that it must break with old-fashioned rules," Ramirez said. "We have never proposed a one-party state or a closed society."

"We are the origin of perestroika,"[4] Daniel Ortega told a reporter. "We proposed a mixed economy and non-alignment."

The Sandinistas imported the idea of local defense committees from the Cubans who had in turn copied it from the Soviets. To their critics, they were Big Brother, state spy gangs created to keep the people under control. Committee stores did handle distribution of the essential items the government said should be available to everyone, beans, rice, cooking oil and soap. For a long time everyone was entitled to buy these items, at low fixed prices with ration cards. Persons not in the good graces of the government, so the critics said, were not given ration cards and thus had to buy the same items in regular private stores at much higher prices. Perhaps, but I visited a number of those committees in various towns and I never saw anyone turned away until late in the war when there was often nothing on the shelves for anyone.

Members of the committees denied to me that they

---

4   Anne Marie O'Connor, Reuters, March 14, 1989.

were used to intimidate their neighbors and I never talked to anyone who said they had been harassed. I did, however, hear a number of second hand stories of discrimination against those who were considered enemies of the state and thus of the people. And I knew one family whose front garden wall was painted with graffiti, most of it calling family members *traidors* because they criticized the Sandinistas. That was harassment but when I asked about it the family never reported anything worse. The committees engaged in local defense drills, and some people may have been coerced to join. Such organizations do lend themselves to oppression by small-minded bosses and I don't doubt that it happened. But I still think that kind of behavior was the exception rather than the rule and, as important, that was not the intent of most of the sincere people who headed the committees. They encouraged people in rural and urban areas alike to dig trenches in their backyards against the day of the expected invasion by the United States.

Nicaragua's economic growth was rapid in the years immediately after the revolution, I was told by Xabier Gorostiaga, a Jesuit economist, at a Managua dinner one evening in 1985. "It was six percent last year," he insisted, to my doubtful look. He conceded, however, that it was starting to decline, punctured by the Contra war and the economic embargo Reagan had imposed on the country despite the opposition of twenty five Latin American nations. Only El Salvador and Honduras, obligated to the United States for weapons and domestic aid—in El Salvador's case $6 billion by 1990—supported the United States embargo.

By 1986 and 1987 it was apparent to all but the most die hard Marxists in the government that the planned economy that had intrigued the idealistic Sandinistas was not going to work, even if Ronald Reagan had called off his economic embargo. In fact, the embargo became an alibi for failures. Verdant Nicaragua couldn't even feed itself, partly because produce couldn't get to market. Terror in the countryside, especially in the north where much of the country's grain is grown, was also to blame.

The economy might have collapsed entirely had it not been for the Russian and Bulgarian trucks the Soviet Union was giving to the government. Also from Russia came wheat and oil. The trucks, about as inefficient as could be imagined and so heavy they broke up the fragile Nicaraguan roads, nevertheless were sturdy and got produce to market. Many of the country's buses were used as street barricades during the 1979 revolution's final violent July and most of the rest were breaking down under incredible loads. Argentine technicians who accompanied gifts of new buses tried to persuade transportation officials, and bus drivers, to limit the number of passengers but it was a hopeless task.

Once a bus's door was open it couldn't close again until every possible passenger was crammed in somewhere. I once got on a bus in Managua for a short trip and carelessly allowed myself to be pushed further and further into the middle until, when the bus came to my stop, I couldn't get off. By the time I was able to fight my way to the door we were further away from my destination, in the opposite direction, than we had been when I got on. Mexico also sent buses but the supply from all sources couldn't compete with the crush.

Suddenly one day in 1987 there was a national shortage of chicken feed for the farms, small and large, that supplied Nicaraguans with their main source of meat. Coffee growers cut back on their planting for future crops in a protest of the government's pricing policies. Dollar earnings thus slumped. A lack of spare parts, for buses, trucks and private cars, kept many of them inoperative. Nicaraguans showed genius in coaxing these machines back to life, and backyard mechanics were some of the more affluent working men in the country. But slowly the economic life of Nicaragua was strangling and it hasn't yet recovered.

Socially, Nicaragua made great progress in the years after the triumph and into the early 1980s. Only by contrast with El Salvador, Guatemala and Honduras did the sight of off-duty soldiers strolling the streets in Nicaragua with their weapons seem bizarre. These men, and women, walking in the evenings with their girl friends and boy friends were a symbol that most of those in uniform in Nicaragua were a part of a genuine people's army. Even traffic police did not carry weapons, the only place in this hemisphere that I know of where one could see that. As the war continued, the Sandinistas instituted a draft, highly unpopular and probably as critical in their eventual defeat at the polls as any other single factor. Mothers protested and young men fled the country. They had good reason to; at the height of the fighting in the late 1980s the Army was losing more than a hundred men a day, many to crippling land mines. It was a nasty, genuine war.

4

Some Questions of Real Estate

THE WARS IN NICARAGUA AND EL SALVADOR, AS WELL AS Guatemala's long agony, were, like most wars, at bottom conflicts over real estate. Who owns the land? If those countries revert again to open civil war it will be because the landowners continue to deny access to those who work it and, in many cases, were its previous owners.

No one could ever satisfactorily explain to me why El Salvador was so grossly overpopulated compared to its neighbors. Certainly it couldn't have been that mortality rates were lower. Land reform was supposed to be the key to ending El Salvador's social conflicts but it never really had a chance to prove itself. While the dense population made land reform an imperative, it also apparently made it an impossibility.

Before the 1800s, according to one study, Salvadoran peasant Indians grew grain and other staples on communally owned *ejidos*, while the larger landowners' *haciendas* raised indigo and cacao for export.[5] Then along came coffee, an export earner, and the big landowners manipulated the country's laws, in the name of economic development, to require that two thirds of ejidal lands be planted in coffee. From that it was only a short step for the oligarchy to "abolish communal ownership altogether" through legal trickery. The communal owners became day laborers on land that

---

[5] Dr. Michael L. Wise, USAID/El Salvador, Agrarian Reform in El Salvador, September, 1986, p.3.

had been their own. "The trend of concentrated land ownership and increased political power of the few continued into the 1900s, surrounded by a growing number of landless poor."

In 1932 the campesinos revolted, under a communist named Farabundo Marti, and some twenty thousand of them were killed in a massacre ordered by General/President Maximiliano Martinez, a crazed mystic. Marti was executed and when peasants again took up arms in the 1970s, they took his name for their umbrella group. An agrarian reform effort grew out of the 1932 slaughter but it amounted to little, even though in the 1970s a group of idealistic young Army officers attempted to bring about a distribution of some larger landholdings to the people who worked it. From 1960 to 1975, a United Nations study said, the landless increased from twelve percent of the population to forty percent. Two percent of the top families owned sixty percent of the land. Even those peasants who were able to rent land, as rental became a fixture of Salvadoran life, were nearly always in debt to loan sharks for seed money.

The land reform under way in El Salvador when I looked at it in 1982 was largely a fraud. Efforts were made, by sincere Salvadorans and North Americans, to divide up the large and often unproductive land holdings owned by the oligarchy that generally lived in Miami or elsewhere in the United States. Mostly those efforts were futile.

The government of El Salvador had glowing reports of land reform in the early 1980s and I'm sure some of the people who made those claims really believed them. Landowners had been paid, in government bonds, and land was supposed to be distributed to the campesinos who had been working it, some of them for many years, even for several generations. But everyone, the government bureaucrats and campesinos, all lived with the threat of a visit from a death squad if they pushed too hard. Consequently, when distributions were actually made most land titles were only temporary, provisionary, they were called. While I was there President Alvaro Magana ceremoniously awarded ten permanent titles, bringing the total to eight hundred, according to Roberto Torres, El Salvador chief of AIFLD, the American Institute for Free Labor Development, sponsored by the United States AFL-CIO. Twenty nine thousand titles still were being "legalized" by FINATA, the national land reform ministry, he said. An official of FINATA told me that his budget was exhausted and he could no longer process the titles.

Those titles that had been granted were often canceled by private armies dispatched by the ousted landlords within weeks, or even days. "You can get a campesino killed for one hundred colones," Torres told me, about the price of a six pack of beer. AIFLD, which almost certainly had links with the CIA, nevertheless was more diligent in trying to make land reform work than its detractors ever admitted. But it got most of its money from the United States Agency for International Development and was too obligated to that banker, and the banker's notion of the sacredness of private property, to do what was in any case a hopeless job. "Education is our biggest problem," said Torres, an American citizen of Puerto Rican descent, a comment that I began to appreciate only after touring some of the land that had been taken. Everyone needed education, the government bureaucrats who handled the program, the landowners who gave up their property and especially the poor who supposedly got the land.

Here's how one effort worked: In 1982 the government took a 7,000-hectare *hacienda* from its owner, one of El Salvador's "fourteen families," and gave it to five cooperatives composed of the campesinos who had been growing fibers for a factory making rope and sacks for export coffee. The oligarchical family also owned the factory and it set the prices for the fiber it bought. Thus the farmers continued to work as they had before, for the same factory for no greater income. Now, theoretically, they owned the land, but they had a debt, which they could never pay, as compensation to the previous owner. As synthetics replace the natural fiber they grow they will soon have no market for their crops.

Torres turned me over to Tania Papke of Iowa, a twenty-nine-year-old with a masters degree in business administration from Columbia University and a patience that was sorely tried as she attempted to teach the new farmer-owners how to keep their books. If they don't know where their money is going they'll never know how best to use their resources, mainly the seeds they planted and the fertilizers that were supposed to help them grow, she said. After visits to several cooperative farms with Tania I begin to see the immensity of the problem.

Blonde Tania towered over the dark little *jefe* of one co-op in the Department of La Libertad and tapped her finger on the blank pages of the account books in the granary-office where bags of seed were stored. He had pulled the virgin ledger from between two bags and now stood smiling shyly, like a puppy that knows he has made a mistake but is not sure just what it is. "Why haven't you kept the numbers?" she asked, gently but without smiling back.

He knew he should be keeping columns of figures lined up in the book but he was not sure why. So Tania reminded him. "You cannot know where your money is spent unless you keep the accounts," she explained slowly, and, the *jefe* knew, the farm would not receive more bank loans for seeds to plant unless he could explain how previous loans were spent.

He probably knew better than Tania, I surmised later, that bank loans were going to be tough to get no matter how nicely he maintained his books. Salvadoran banks and the big landowners are close, often in fact, the same people. But he assured Tania with his puppy-dog smile that he would keep the books up from now on. I wondered. Did he even know how to enter figures in the books? Could he read them if they were there? But I kept my mouth shut; I was trying to understand land reform, not become a participant. Tania told me later that the little man was literate and that he did know addition and subtraction. He could do the books if he really thought it was worthwhile. He reminded me of neighbors of my father's when I was a boy in Wyoming. They scorned him for his "town ways" when he kept a ledger to balance his income and his expenses for seeds, for cattle and sheep feed and for gasoline and parts for the farm machinery. Peasants here and in other parts of the Third World look down on people who don't work with their hands, who scribble with pencils in lined notebooks. Often they have good reason for their scorn; if a pencil is in one hand, the other may be out for a bribe.

Tania and I rode to the farms at La Libertad, near the ocean, in a Jeep Cherokee, a four-wheel drive vehicle with half-inch-thick bullet proof glass and an extra steel plate under the passenger compartment to deflect the explosion should we run over a mine. Steel plates had also been inserted into the car's doors. In the front seat, literally riding shotgun, was a young man with a pistol and a 12 gauge pump shotgun who looked left and right at each intersection as the driver slowed. It was not a situation that lent itself to examining the beautiful countryside.

Although that automobile belonged to AIFLD, I learned later that others like it, usually with darkened windows, were the vehicles of preference of the death squads. Often they were openly identified as such on the streets of San Salvador, their darkened windows hiding the inhabitants or, parked, with pot-bellied men wearing dark glasses lounging on their fenders. As we drove away from the co-op in our armored car I wondered whether the little *jefe* was most intimidated by Tania or by the former owners of the land. He was definitely sticking his neck out by even taking part in the land redistribution, let alone assuming a leadership position.

During a mid day break on one of our tours in La Libertad we went to a beach resort for lunch. It is one of the hotels built either by the Salvadoran Government or promoted by it that was supposed to take advantage of the tourist trade that government and United States economists touted in the 1970s. That was why the country's national airport was built nearby rather than near the capital forty miles away where nearly all arrivals were headed. The resort we visited still functioned, after a fashion.

I bought a beer for myself, Tania and the driver and guard, but I balked at the only food available, a seafood bouillabaisse that didn't look fresh. The place was rundown. Walls were crumbling, walkways were cracked, windows were displaced and it had been a long time since the floors were swept. The beach was a hard shingle, with no soft sand in sight and not conducive to either swimming or sunbathing. I saw no umbrellas of the type that adorn beaches in Mexico, Honduras and elsewhere that tourism is taken seriously. My hobby is marine biology but I could find no crabs or other tidal life along the water's edge.

A single employee, an uncommunicative woman of about twenty, served us. She was dirty and we did not stay long. I didn't visit any of the other resorts along the coast but from the road they all looked equally ill kept. And yet the Salvadoran government continued to advertise the country's beauties in tourist publications. The national airline, TACA, carried lavishly illustrated and tempting stories of El Salvador, including its beach resorts, in its in-flight magazine.

Land reform was probably doomed in El Salvador no matter how sincerely it was tackled, as long as the country was economically depressed by war and American trade policies. There is, in addition, an inherent force against land reform in any backward country and, indeed, in such progressive countries as the United States. Consolidation is inevitable as long as land is seen as a commodity and "property rights" are held to be inviolable. Where land is dealt out to peasants unschooled in real estate dealing and unskilled in modern farm techniques and mechanics it will soon fail. The land will quickly revert back to the previous land owners or be consolidated by new owners. Co-operatives will split asunder as older member-owners wish to retire and sell their shares to cushion their old age.

Thus redistribution, first by government fiat, recurs again and again through an evolutionary economic process and with each repetition land is gathered into the hands of fewer people, the ever more politically powerful. Owners, or their children, revert again to the status of hired hands or they move to cities, usually to slums. As long as the ethic of private property prevails, and ownership is the ultimate respectability, the title to land will gravitate to larger and larger holdings. Tax policies could alleviate this trend, but the people who write tax laws are nearly always those who own the land, or their hirelings. Land reform, over the long term, will never work in a economically backward capitalist society.

It was the special conceit of the United States Department of State that El Salvador's land reform was a success. Otto Reich, who held ambassador rank as head of the department's Office of Public Diplomacy, told United States newspaper editorial boards that reform had "turned one fifth of the land of El Salvador back to the hands of the people who are working the land." Even if true once, that statement could have applied for only a very short time. Land reform and its failure was the chief issue dividing El Salvador long after most of the shooting stopped.

Neighboring Nicaragua is an agricultural country and will remain that way as long as United States business interests get their way, which is likely to be a long time indeed. The Somoza family and its cronies and the families allied with them owned about twenty five percent of everything in Nicaragua and much of that was seized by the Sandinistas after the revolution. Farm land was distributed to those who had worked it, mostly in cooperative arrangements, although many individuals also got plots of land of their own. As conditions worsened with the war, more Nicaraguans fled the country and they were considered to have abandoned their land and other property and it was taken over and distributed also. With the defeat of the Sandinistas in the 1990 election and the return of many Nicaraguans from exile in the United States, ownership of that land became an explosive issue. It is not likely to be settled for a long time.

Nicaragua is relatively sparsely populated, and a caring government, supported by sympathetic international lending organizations, could defuse the explosive land conflicts if they were so disposed.

Some large private holdings became state farms under the Sandinistas and from what I could see they were reasonably well cared for but inefficiently managed. I drove up to one large dairy farm in a taxi one day, unannounced, and asked to see the manager. He was gone and not expected back that day, a number of loungers in the farm office told me. None of them were authorized to give tours to stray gringos. Neither were they versed in any of the farm's statistics, or at least they weren't going to give me any information. I walked around the farmstead for a while and saw little work being done by a crew that must have been close to forty where five would have sufficed. Several men were repairing farm machinery and one was puttering around the stalls where cows would be milked that evening, but the rest sat around doing nothing, not even reading or playing cards or otherwise idling away their time. They were merely enduring the work day.

That farm, which had obviously been well run and maintained previously, illustrated all that was wrong in the Sandinista version of a "plural economy," not least its bloated bureaucracy. But that bad example was not the norm, so far as I could see. Sandinistas claimed that seventy five percent of the farm land was in private hands and I believe it. Critics, however, accused the Sandinistas of a monopoly hold on such farm products as coffee, cotton and sugar through state-run marketing organizations. But I saw well-run private farms throughout the country, as prosperous as one could expect in a country as beleaguered as Nicaragua was.

One farm I visited was a polar opposite to the flabby state farm. Owned by Rene Montoya, an energetic young farmer, the place near San Dionisio in the central hills of Nicaragua's cattle country could be a model for any 4-H project in the United States. He defended the government when I talked to him as a tiny daughter clung to each leg. "If being a communist means wanting to have a decent life and freedom, I guess that's what we are," he said. His farmhouse was more like a series of separate rooms than what an

American farmer would call a house. But the place was nearly self-sufficient, in appearance much like United States farms of seventy five or a hundred years ago. Garden vegetables and locally butchered meat supplied the table, with butter churned at the farm and fruits canned in the open-walled kitchen. Pigs and chickens were kept out of the kitchen, unlike many Nicaraguan farms. Montoya had a large freezer, and a television brought him news and entertainment from the city. And Sandinista propaganda.

Nicaraguan dairy farms are mostly large, like their counterparts in the United States, and mostly in private hands although at least one of the larger ones was taken over by the government in a dispute with its owner, who remained in the country, a vocal critic. About sixty percent of such industry as Nicaragua boasted, clothing manufacture for example, was in the government's hands together with forty percent of the shoe factories. Most food processing was in small private operations while chemical industries were owned by the government.

Many cooperatives were small. They emphasized, among other things, planting gardens in backyards, behind farm houses and in vacant city lots. One co-op still operating in 1993, at El Corral, in Chontales Department, made strong and tangy cheese, providing local farmers their only source of cash.

Relations between the Sandinistas and private business were poisonous from the very beginning. Although the Sandinistas proclaimed their intent to build a "mixed economy," and did indeed try to do so, their actions were resisted and exaggerated. In their usual manner, so at odds with their political skills, they made the situation bad for themselves by high-handed methods that could easily have been avoided. In 1985 the Sandinistas seized the large cotton lands of Enrique Bolanos, a vocal critic of the government but who represented no real threat to it or to its officials. That seizure took on the aspects almost of myth among government critics and made Bolanos a martyr and the Supreme Council of Private Enterprise (COSEP) which he headed a magnet for visiting foreigners looking for tips on hoped-for evidence of Communist influence.

Less well known, and shakily justified as a national security measure, was the seizure of the lands of a banana farmer named Gurdian because of his public assertions that the United States was within its rights to cut off Nicaragua's historic preferential sugar import quota. But except for those hardly legitimate cases, most small producers and retailers, automobile dealers, hardware stores, pharmacies, grocers and the like, were left in private hands. So were most of the larger industries, the company that produces Tono Beer and Flor de Cana rum, for instance, as well as the two North American-owned oil refineries, Texaco and Exxon, and most sugar refineries.

A tour of the hundred-year-old sugar refinery San Antonio in Chichigalpa owned by the Palos family gave me a clue as to why the government had not taken it over as well as the condition of Nicaraguan industry; it was run down, inefficient even in my nonexpert eyes, and probably the most dangerous work place I have ever seen. Huge flywheels, pulleys and gears gnashed away only inches from workers' walkways. It reminded me of the omnivorous machines in Charlie Chaplin's "Modern Times."

The town was in court with the sugar mill over taxes; before the revolution, Mayor Carlos Garcia told me, the factory's wealthy owners never paid any taxes to the city. Now the city was trying to collect a tax partly, he said, to help buy the three thousand desks necessary for the schools it was opening. The town needed a sewer system; the water system was old and in disrepair and there was little water pressure. Roads were crumbling. That reference to taxes is a clue to what the Contra war was all about. The Contra leaders, the ones in Miami recruited by the CIA, were the owners of Nicaragua, its big estates, its meat packing plants, its factories, refineries, breweries. They didn't want to pay taxes; let the people pay a sales tax to finance government, they said.

Mayor Garcia epitomized to me the best of Sandinismo.

Are you a communist, or a Marxist? he was asked by my traveling companion, Judge Charles Cone of a Washington State district court. "I don't consider myself a communist or a Marxist," Garcia replied. "Not many people in Nicaragua are communists. The Communist Party's small vote in the (1984) election shows that. I can't see that communism has any significant attraction here.

"If we redistribute land, build schools, have freedom of religion and an equal distribution of wealth and resources, eliminate the abuses of the great landowners of the past and abolish corruption of public employees, if that is communism, well..." Garcia, like many of the emerging middle class, cited Somoza misrule for their militancy. The community civil defense committees, so often mentioned by critics as Big Brother interference in Nicaraguan private life, were one such response. They were set up, Garcia said, "by those who refused any longer to tolerate the abuses of the dictatorship. Previously only those with money had access to education, for example. We channeled the energies, the aspirations of the people for a better life."

Nicaragua's people are losing the environmental war. The Sandinistas had plans to salvage Lake Managua, which fronts on the capitol and is so foul with sewage that only some small, hardy scrap fish can survive in it. That effort, like so many others, was put aside as the war grew in intensity.

In addition to land reform the Sandinistas were making determined efforts to reforest the country until the Contra depredations and embargo drained away all the money for any but short-term, stop-gap programs. Guiding the tree planting and restoration of eroded hillsides caused by forest plundering under the Somozas was an American missionary. Howard Heiner, a rawboned, rangy Methodist who towers over everyone in any crowd he is in, was an Air Force fighter pilot in the Korean War who decided after that and a stint as a lumber dealer in Washington State that he would put his training as a forester to use doing The Lord's work in the world's misery spots.

Heiner and a few Nicaraguans attempted to repair the devastation wrought by the Somoza family and their friends who gave away logging concessions freely. The Contra deliberately targeted the foresters working with Heiner and I often found him downcast at the death of an assistant. The country was in such bad shape in 1989 that it couldn't even harvest the vast stands of trees blown down by a hurricane that swept through the Nicaraguan east coast jungles. The trees were left to rot, which Heiner said would take only two years in that climate. A member of the Nicaraguan National Assembly, Ray Hooker, attempted to find some North American company to salvage them but there were no takers.

Heiner's son, Dan, was following in his father's footsteps in the 1990s.

Rio San Juan Department, the vast rain forest of southeastern Nicaragua, where Lake Nicaragua drains away toward the Caribbean via the San Juan River, is the "agricultural frontier" the government is hoping will absorb some of the fast growing population. (Nicaragua's people have doubled in numbers in twenty five years, according to Donna Vukelich, a freelance writer formerly with the University of Central America).

Some Nicaraguans, especially in the still scenic southeast, hope "ecotourism" will be their salvation. Perhaps. But they have a long way to go. The country is astonishingly beautiful and the wildlife seen from canoes on the San Juan and its tributaries is colorful and diverse. Howler monkeys taunt visitors, anhingas, egrets, and various herons take wing as a visiting boat approaches. Alligators and turtles abound as do some of the tastiest fish in the world. Flocks of parrots, increasingly rare in nearby Costa Rica, fly overhead chattering to each other. A genuine European-type fortress dating from 1676, complete with moat and drawbridge, looks down over the river at El Castillo. Quaint (but poor) farms add color to the scenery. The area is remote, however, reachable only by water or by air.

By the early 1990s, Nicaragua's forests, which thirty

years before had covered the country, were largely gone. Unrestrained logging and burning by farmers and ranchers for pastures and crop lands had reduced most of the country's forests to a few parks and reserves. Even they were going fast by 1993 as forest wardens, their pay below poverty levels, looked the other way when timber rustlers offered bribes, or threats.

Poor as Nicaragua's neighbors are, some trees still stand in the forests of El Salvador, Honduras and Guatemala. To the south, in more enlightened and affluent Costa Rica, the story is the same as in Nicaragua; the forests are going. Even that country's justly famous national parks are being nibbled away around the edges. Outside the parks the land is raising cattle for North American hamburgers.

"Poor farmers are clearing land to grow food and the soil is eroding away inch by inch," Cirilo Otero, a sociologist and director of the Nicaraguan Environmental Movement, told me in 1993. "A model of agro-export has been forced on us," says Otero. "We must export cotton, coffee and corn and destroy our natural resources."

Why, then, does Nicaragua obey the IMF and World Bank strictures? The answer is because it is dependent on foreign aid. Some Nicaraguans and their foreign friends believe the country should defy those imperial mandates, especially since most of Nicaragua's trade earnings go to pay off debts going back to the Somoza days. "The debt is unpayable," says Vukelich. "Economists say Nicaragua should emphasize smaller scale farm enterprises. If everyone planted beans they could be sold to all of central America, as Nicaragua did to Costa Rica in 1988." (See Chapter Five). "Nicaragua should say to the IMF, `we will agree to earn dollars through traditional crops instead of export crops such as melons, cashews, macadamia nuts and the like'."

That scenario would be feasible in a rational world, especially since the United states is leaning on all the other Central American countries to shift production from home consumption to a low wages manufacturing economy geared to imports. United States agricultural trade policy, on the other hand, is driven by exports, especially in Central America and Mexico, as an outlet for American farm surpluses. United States farmers will supply the corn and rice, the staples Central Americans have always produced for themselves. Such a situation guarantees perpetual dependency and indebtedness.

Ranchers say they are losing thousands of cattle to rustlers but laws are weak and courts impotent. "We know who the rustlers are," said Carlos Carranza Lazo, an agronomist with the Catholic Church at El Corral, "but it is better to lose a cow than to complain and lose one's life."

Pablo Sierra, of the Chontales Cattlemen's Association, estimated that 40,000 stolen cattle were herded over the borders to Honduras and Costa Rica in 1992, equal to the numbers exported legally by their owners. Cattle growers talk nostalgically of the "golden decade" of the 1950s when the rapid expansion of cotton plantations and cattle ranches was Somoza policy. They, like small ranchers and farmers, lament the lack of credit. And, as anti-Sandinista as they are, they concede that under the previous "communist" government, credit was available to them.

Even prosperous peanut farmers, who have shifted their cotton lands to goobers, complain of a shortage of credit although they talk expansively of markets and harvests. They seem to be not concerned that they must sell their peanuts in Europe and are blocked from United States markets because of tariffs won by American peanut growers. "Maybe with free trade it will be different," one said, a reference to the North American Free Trade Agreement. He spoke just before NAFTA was approved by the United States Congress and he wasn't the only Central American who apparently believed that although the pact applies only to the United states, Mexico and Canada, it will open up big markets for them.

They had a somewhat strained precedent to support that fantasy. During the Reagan-Bush Contra war the United States embargo forbade import of any product of Nicaragua. So Nicaraguan ranchers were forced to sell their butchered beef carcasses to Mexican middlemen who naturally took a cut for putting Mexican labels on the meat before selling it in the United states. In such manner did the United States embargo hurt those, the cattlemen in this case, nearly all of them anti-Sandinista, that it was supposedly trying to help.

Members of the Chontales cattlemen's association, generally large ranchers although they evade questions about how many head of cattle they own, say the United States must resolve Nicaragua's problems. "The United States won't help us while there is no peace in Nicaragua," said one rancher wearing a Jordache shirt in 1993. "Which means that with the present political situation we won't get help." He and others were waiting for Violeta Chamorro to give up the presidency and turn the government over to her vice president, Virgilio Godoy, a hard line rightist.

"The United States should take direct action, as it did in Panama" in 1989 and "as it did in the (Nicaraguan) election in 1990," another rancher said.

Lack of credit is hurting smaller farmers and cattlemen even more and driving them off their lands.

"Credit to the campesinos (under IMF rules) has been cut by two thirds which means that many peasants who got land under the Sandinista land reform can't now buy seed and fertilizers to farm it," according to English economist Trevor Evans, who has been working in Nicaragua since 1986. "The countryside is devastated. Peasant farmers can't afford to farm and small businesses can't buy inventory."

The lucky farmers and ranchers are those able to function on a subsistence or even barter basis. Some co-operatives are surviving that way, at least temporarily. A goal is to set up co-op owned banks, but without capital for a start that is a near hopeless dream. To many wealthy Central Americans co-op is equivalent to communist and government economists are not sympathetic.

The Eddy Alonzo Rivas co-op in Chontales Department near Juigalpa created a relative prosperity by hard work. It has milk cows, a fruit orchard and its women and children members have planted two thousand trees grown in a co-op nursery along the banks of a river flowing through the farm. But although it sells its meat, tomatoes, onions, bell peppers, cabbages, asparagus and other vegetables in markets as far away as Managua there is another problem. Although its fifteen heads of households, all of them veterans of the war in the Sandinista Army, receive no pay, they can't compete with imports from neighboring Costa Rica. Co-op members are hazy about land ownership. Some of the land they farm was owned by a wealthy doctor before the revolution. It is theirs now, "but it (ownership) makes us insecure," Co-Op President Pedro Jose Martinez told me. Said another member: "We defended the land before and we will defend it again." Land tenure could yet explode into a genuine civil war.

Tourism promises wealth for those with capital to build hotels, restaurants and fishing camps. And it creates opportunities in such relatively noble occupations as guiding fishermen and conducting rafting trips down scenic rivers. But it dooms most of its employees to jobs as dishwashers, bed makers and toilet swabbers in hotels and restaurants financed by outsiders. Tourism has, however, saved some of Costa Rica's natural wonders and could help Nicaragua curb the plunder of its resources. Businessmen quickly become environmentalists when green dollars blossom.

Among projects being discussed are such things as a trail to follow the route along which economic pirate Cornelius Vanderbilt hauled "49ers" in last century's California Gold Rush, from Greytown on Nicaragua's Caribbean Coast, up the San Juan, across Lake Nicaragua and north along the Pacific Coast to San Francisco.

An interpretive center was planned by a Peruvian scientist on the Bartolo River, a San Juan tributary near where a small hotel and restaurant with a French chef served the occasional adventurous guest. Most accommodations were far too primitive for all but the most nervy tourists, however. The hospice Aurora at El Castillo was charging only $2.50 in 1993 for a night's lodging and breakfast, eggs, beans, steak, fried bananas and pineapple. But it offered little more than half a dozen hard bunks and a single toilet hanging over the river under which the town's urchins swim. Up the hill from the river and the city's main street (its only street, actually) a pair of vociferous parrots greet guests at a new hotel, El Albergue, with fine second floor rooms for $15 a night. There was only a single guest bathroom, however, downstairs on the first floor.

Roger Miranda lives in an immaculate home with a wide veranda fronting on a river at the Los Guatzos wildlife refuge on Lake Nicaragua. There he paints primitive landscapes and wildlife scenes of a remarkable luminosity which he sells in galleries in Managua. Miranda is also a spokesman for the Committee of Production and Development of the South Coast of Nicaragua. In its efforts to bring sanitation, roads and schools to the region it receives no help from the government, he said. He complained of sprayed chemicals drifting from Costa Rica across the river and onto the forest.

The official outlook for Nicaragua is cheerful. And for those in command there is indeed prosperity. To read the Nicaragua Economic Report, a slick publication produced monthly by a New York public relations firm for the Central Bank of Nicaragua, one would think the country is on a fast track to economic health. The bank's report, which not coincidentally reads much like the official country report put out by the United States Embassy, plays down the bad and accentuates the good. Like the embassy's report, the bank attributes Nicaragua's disastrous economic situation to the Sandinistas. Only glancing mentions are made to the ten-year Contra war financed by the United States and its economic embargo as contributing causes.

An example of the distorted views presented to the world by both the Nicaaaraguan government and the United States is coffee production. One of Nicaragua's chief dollar earners, coffee output dropped from 180 million pounds on a quarter million acres in 1977 to 90 million pounds from 170,000 acres in 1989, a bank report said. The figures are probably correct but they fail to point out that the Contras, in their raids into Nicaragua from their sanctuary in American-bribed Honduras, burned coffee plantations and killed coffee workers in a deliberate terror campaign to cripple harvests.

Many coffee growers also cut back on production when the Sandinistas required all coffee to be sold abroad through a state organization. Which hurt production most, terror or Sandinista interference, is hard to say but certainly terror was a major factor never acknowledged in two U.S. administrations' efforts to find money for the Contra.

New banks were approved by the government after the Chamorro election and a new foreign investment law allowed repatriation of 100 percent of profits after three years. A duty-free zone near Managua's airport quickly attracted eight manufacturing firms, and American jeans were soon produced by cheap Nicaraguan labor. Generous tax breaks are offered for exports of dollar earning products. Under American AID guidelines, if the experience of other Central American countries holds, those products will replace the subsistence corn and beans that Nicaraguans grow for their families. Those export products often run head on into tariff walls in importing countries. Farmers who converted their fields, often under credit pressures from their banks, suffered.

Before the Contra war began to disrupt their activities, the Sandinistas had embarked on a developmental program which, while it might have been too centrally oriented for efficiency, at least had as its goals helping the people. It included tree planting, pushing new roads into farming areas reachable only by horseback and building housing for the poor and middle class. Cooperatives springing up all over were bringing a beginning of consumer availability to Nicaraguans. They also ignited paranoia in the United States Embassy which had been programmed to equate co-ops with subversion of the capitalist status quo and, by Reagan Administration illogic, to Communism.

5

Roses and Beans

"I spent 33 years...being a high-class muscle man for Big Business, for Wall Street and the bankers. I was a racketeer for capitalism...I helped purify Nicaragua for the international banking house of Brown Brothers...I helped in the rape of half a dozen Central American republics for the benefit of Wall Street."
—Major General Smedley Butler,
U.S. Marine Corps 1881-1940

SHAWLED AND SILENT WOMEN HUDDLE ON THE SIDEWALKS in every city in Latin America, displaying for sale on blankets in front of them farm produce or chewing gum or collections of junk, ball point pens, knives, notebooks. They wait with what seems the patience of time itself for someone to buy something. So at first I didn't pay much attention to the San Salvador street vendors offering beautiful dark red roses, in precise bundles of a half dozen each. Shameful as it is to think of them that way, those women eventually seem little more than street furniture, annoyances, although they almost never importune a passerby directly to buy. They are almost oblivious to customers. But these roses and their tired sellers in the holiday season at the end of 1986 were different. For one thing, there were so many of them; they were on almost every street corner near the Alameda Hotel where I was staying. Finally my attention was forced. All those roses, where did they come from? Why so many now, just before Christmas?

The women weren't sure. They had purchased the roses, cheap, at the central market. They weren't grown in El Salvador, they were certain. Finally one, more curious than the others and with a higher quotient of indignation, said they were Costa Rican roses, grown for El Norte, the United States. For some reason, she said, they had not been allowed entry there just as they were cut for the holiday season. The Yanquis, she had heard, had urged the Ticos of Costa Rica to plant the flowers as a money crop, to earn dollars. Then something happened and they could not be sold in the United States. So the Costa Rican growers had been forced to ship their roses all over Central America, she said.

Could the woman's story be true? The word-of-mouth grapevine functions well in Latin America, as it does in most of the undeveloped world, but it is not always correct in details. And if her version was accurate, what was the purpose of this apparent set up and betrayal? The answer, I found, was in the United States Embassy in San Salvador, the fortress whence come most policy decisions for El Salvador. The information officer was young, earnest, well educated, just in from an early morning game of tennis, and eager to answer my questions. Had he seen the roses? Yes, he thought so, he said, obviously relieved that with the war, death squads and scandals linked to that year's earthquake relief supplies, I was interested only in why so many women were selling roses on San Salvador's street corners. He expressed doubt, on hearing the woman's explanation of the Costa Rica connection. But after a little urging he agreed to make some phone calls.

His earlier eagerness to be of service diminished as he listened and then passed on to me across his desk what he was learning about the roses mystery. Yes, they had been grown in Costa Rica and yes, it was a recent development, a response to suggestions by the United States that Costa Rican farmers shift from subsistence crops to dollar earners, for export. Roses for the North American market, for the

Christmas holidays and other special occasions, seemed a good solution for everyone. Costa Rican farmers would plant, tend and harvest expensive roses and, with their profits, would buy corn and beans for their families and still have money for other necessities they previously couldn't afford.

They would become part of the world economy, consumers as well as producers. And banks in the United States, creditors to Costa Rica's foreign debt, one of the largest per capita in the world, would have their loans paid, or at least see payments on the interest. Just to make sure the farmers understood their patriotic duty, I learned later, they had been told by the bankers, through local banks, that credit to buy seeds for planting might be scarce if they were stubborn about giving up their bean and corn crops. For roses, no problem.

Economists call this "export substitution."

L. S. Stavriano, in his book Global Rift, chronicled this shift from subsistence to export crops, citing the vast difference in return in Colombia between corn or wheat, 12,500 pesos a year, versus one million for flowers on the same acreage. The best land goes to grow carnations, roses and strawberries. Scarce dollars are spent on importing corn and beans. Profits go to multinational corporations and peasants are reduced to poverty or driven to the cities to look for low-wage jobs. The result is a "massive peasant exodus." In 1950, Stavriano says, Latin America's urban population rose from 40 percent of the total to 57 percent between 1950 and 1970. As peasant numbers decline governments have less incentive to reform land laws."[6]

And Americans cluck cluck and wonder why Colombians kill each other in drug wars.

I had a preview of this global economic thinking a few years earlier on my first visit to El Salvador, in the days when I was willing to believe that the United States really wanted to help the people of the country. As I sat in on a briefing for visitors by the economics officer at the embassy

---

[6] L.S. Stavriano, Global Rift, William Morrow Co., 1983.

I began to question, not only whether El Salvador could ever find a social balance reasonably fair to everyone, but also whether we—the United States, represented by our embassy officials—knew the practical consequences of their actions. I had not yet begun to doubt or question the rightness, the morality, of what we were doing.

El Salvador is too small, too densely populated, the embassy economist said, to ever be able to grow all its own food. On its surface that analysis makes sense, but it ignores the fact that a great deal of El Salvador's land lies idle, ignored by its absentee owners, while campesinos clamor for plots to grow beans and corn to feed their families.

"We have decided," the economist said, "that the only solution for El Salvador is industrialization." We? Yes, we, the United States, had made the decision that El Salvador would no longer be a nation of farmers; it could buy its food elsewhere to feed its people. They would earn wages on assembly lines, putting together high tech components, although in reality those manufactures that have been developed are mostly on the order of "assembling" pre cut clothing, stitching shopping bags and other cotton products for big United States department stores.

The solution for Costa Rica was similar. Farmers were urged to grow roses, if they wanted any bank credit, rather than their traditional corn and beans, and use the profits from roses to buy food and the other things their families wanted and needed. It's a neat package. But why were women of San Salvador sitting on street corners all over the city trying to sell Costa Rican flowers that should have been sold for dollars by florists in the United States? Just a simple matter of economics and politics; American rose growers, faced with sudden competition from Costa Rica for the Christmas market, squawked to their elected officials in Congress. This was an emergency, they said; the holiday season was here, cheap foreign roses were crippling sales, depressing the market. Something had to be done, quick. The answer, the embassy tennis player explained hesitantly, visualizing how this might play in a newspaper, was an emergency order, prompted by constituent pressures on Capitol Hill, from the United States Commerce Department, blocking import of the Costa Rican roses. It would be only temporary, of course, while the political economics were worked out.

Everybody was supposed to win. But the winners didn't include the poor women who bought the flowers and couldn't sell them. The farmers who grew the roses and sold them at a loss weren't winners. They had neither their rose profits nor their accustomed corn, beans and rice. Indeed, the country's plight was even worse, the debt solution even further away. It's hard to see how even the North American banks came out ahead on this one. Their loans went unpaid because the Costa Rican farmers didn't make any money on the roses.

Outside the embassy as I left that day, roses spread on the sidewalks in the blazing sun were wilting and turning black as dried blood. Many were discarded in the gutters. Most of the silent women still sat there, still waiting for someone to buy their unwanted flowers.

Such policies, not thought out to their illogical ends, have skewed economies, not to mention tradition and custom, all over Latin America, almost always as a result of pressures by whatever United States administration is in power or who is in charge in Congress.

It wasn't only roses that the United States had touted as new crops for farmers to score big money, aides to Costa Rican President Oscar Arias told me on a later trip. Broccoli is a good crop too, experts at the Agency for International Development decided. And so Costa Rican farmers were urged to grow it, in competition with farmers in Mexico, and in Florida and California. Which is probably why every meal served in every American restaurant from Miami to Seattle and from San Diego to Boston includes broccoli. American asparagus growers also demand tighter limits on competitive imports from Latin America in spite of a 25 percent tariff already on fresh asparagus. Labor is cheaper in Latin America, they complain, which must be interesting news to the migrant workers in California who bend over all day to cut asparagus at 20 cents a pound.

I learned the final sad chapter in Costa Rica's forced roses industrialization two years later. Because so many farmers had switched to roses and other cash-export crops the country was forced to import corn to make tortillas to feed its people, including its farmers. And where did Costa Rica buy the corn? From poor, miserable neighboring Nicaragua, which could scarcely spare it but which desperately needed the Yanqui dollars because of Ronald Reagan's trade embargo. Indeed, that corn trade was a breach of the embargo, via a back door commerce with other nations that enabled beleaguered Nicaragua to survive at all. Thus that foolish and ill-prepared rose experiment not only hurt Salvadoran street vendors, Costa Rican farmers and bankers and American bankers, but it also helped to undermine the embargo, a key element of Washington's war on Nicaragua. What would Ronald Reagan have thought, had it all been explained to him?

United States economic policies toward Latin America seem always spiraling out of control, clashing with and undermining our stated programs for political reform as well as leaving our collaborators in the field empty-handed and embarrassed. Why did members of Congress, rather than accepting obvious misinformation from the Reagan and Bush Administrations, never seek answers from the people who had them? The Central Intelligence Agency, or at least that arm of it that is not creating clandestine armies and arranging assassinations, produces some of the best analyses of economic trends in the world, a capability not really put to use until after the Soviet Union crumbled and the Agency needed a new mission.

Many people in the State Department would be willing to report on past blunders if given assurance of protection for testifying before congressional committees. Even that immunity wouldn't be necessary to prompt many retired foreign service officers to tell what happened during their tours in Latin America and what they knew, from contacts still on active duty, about current situations. All Congress need do is ask them. Surely committees don't avoid bringing these issues to light in public hearings out of delicacy about the separation of powers. Even a press cowed by the Reagan mystique would have been forced to report revelations thus made public. Perhaps Congressmen are dispirited by the press's failure to keep watch on other issues of national import. Coverage of Senator John Kerry's hearings on CIA involvement in drug dealing in Central America never got the attention one would have expected from a news media breathless over everything else concerning drugs.

Even when the information was shoved under its nose Congress was still too cowed by the administration to ask questions. A General Accounting Office report on United States economic boondoggling in Central America, although distorted by journalism school "on the one hand and on the other hand" objectivity, at least put the blame on the International Monetary Fund and USAID, both of which wrote indignant dissenting responses to the study's conclusions. In its assessment of United States attempts to "achieve economic stabilization and structural adjustment," the report had this to say: "Progress in El Salvador was hampered by United States and Salvadoran unwillingness to risk political instability arising from major economic reforms, and extensive damage caused by the guerrillas and the 1986 earthquake." Among those unaddressed economic reforms was the failed land reform, the most significant cause of political instability in El Salvador.

Lest Europeans be too sanctimonious about the contrast between their enlightened approach to Latin America and the United States's interventions, consider the case of bananas. One thing Central Americans do well is raise bananas; what they don't do well is sell them. Such giants as United Fruit, Chiquita in its latest disguise, get their bananas into American supermarkets, but they've had problems with Europe. Why? Britain, France, Spain and Portugal, to maintain the economies of former political colonies and present economic dependencies, slap duties on Latin American bananas which boosts their cost as much as twenty percent.

Apart from meddling and blundering by the United states and other outsiders, why have the Central American countries, indeed all of Latin America, never been able to pull themselves together and nurture a decent existence for their millions of people? I was not alone in wondering what made them so different from the Japanese and the South Koreans who had created powerful economies out of the devastation of war, to be followed by the "little tigers" of Singapore and Taiwan and even Malaysia. Former Arizona Governor Bruce Babbitt, later interior secretary, cited South Korea's economic miracle in urging liberalization of trade with Mexico as an example of how quickly a country can transform its economy.[7] In 1960, he said, South Korea's per capita income was $145; in 1988 it had reached $2,690.

When I left Korea in 1954 it was a basket case. Armies fighting up and down the peninsula had destroyed nearly everything standing; children starved to death in Seoul's alleys or in winter froze to death. Most of the country's trees had been cut for firewood, "slicky boys" would snatch the watch off your wrist on the streets, miserable prostitutes so licited American soldiers openly and whole families scavenged army mess hall garbage for their meals. Truck drivers wore respirators to cope with the clouds of dust that literally hid the roads. It was a sad and desperate country.

When I returned for a visit thirty-five years later Korea had been transformed. The biggest problem was traffic, although many affluent Korean commuters preferred to sit in their Hyundais in near gridlock rather than be seen riding to work in Seoul's magnificent new subway system. Dusty roads had been replaced by broad paved freeways lined with banks of flowers. Troops of laughing children raced through the streets of Seoul and other cities on their way to school, their homework in shiny backpacks. You could leave your briefcase by the door of a tiny diner on a Seoul street and find it there when you came out after lunch. Thirty-five-year-old trees were growing everywhere, at street corners,

---

7 Bruce Babbitt, World Monitor, March, 1988.

in backyards, along roads.

An amazing change, certainly, but no mystery. Koreans are endowed, through their Confucian heritage, with a work ethic that demands striving. The poor of Latin America work just as hard, maybe harder, although often to less purpose. Koreans almost literally worship education; Latins, especially their governments, too often pay it little heed. The driving spirit behind the Korean economic miracle was an authoritarian dictatorship determined to achieve economic parity with rival Japan, at whatever social cost. Well, Latin America has had more than its share of authoritarian military dictatorships and nearly every one has been more harmful economically than beneficial. Argentina, a country with more than its share of natural resources, a homogeneous society and plenty of space for its population, has never been able to function rationally.

But before we bear down too hard on the Latins in our comparison with the tigers of Asia, there is another factor largely overlooked in the miracles out of the Far East. The United States' wars in Asia pumped billions of American taxpayer dollars into Japan and South Korea. American "offshore" purchases of goods during the Korean War of 1950-1953 afforded Japan a healthy capital boost. Techniques and skills perfected in repairing American trucks and other war materiel for the fighting on the Korean peninsula gave Japanese manufacturers their big break. United States troops blew millions of dollars in leave pay in the fleshpots of Tokyo during their shopping sprees on seven-day rest tours from the Korean battlefields.

So, in largely the same sense, our war in Vietnam gave South Korea a jump start. In addition to the manufacturing experience gained from us as we floundered through ten years of that war, South Korea also earned dollars by renting its soldiers for the war itself. Receipts from those services and goods rippled through the Korean economy and, while not a lot of it trickled down to the people very rapidly, it did lift up the nation's gross wealth and fueled an amazing boom.

Our Latin aggressions, unlike our Asian wars, are

cheap and easy and not much rubs off on the locals. Proxy warriors of Low Intensity Conflicts do not cost much and their wounds are painless to us. Some Central Americans, chiefly the CIA's top Contra stooges, made good spending money off our war in Nicaragua, but most of it ended up in Miami bank accounts. The billions we poured into El Salvador likewise disappeared into the free-spending oligarchy. Most of the relative pittance Uncle Sam gave Nicaragua to help it recover from our devastating Contra war was spent the same way, on consumer goods, on cars and electronics gadgets, on apples from Washington State, grapes from California. Capital needs were ignored and little of the money went into productive investments.

That was a sharp contrast to the examples of Japan and South Korea where imports were limited to those contributing to national wealth as every bit of capital was poured into factories, machine tools and the like. Again, United States policy was a key factor, but in Central America's case with a backward twist; USAID is a political tool, geared first to finding outlets for United States products and, in the Reagan years and later, to providing clandestine financing for our wars. Programs were often so poorly handled they invited a "grab the money and run" attitude for local elites adept at manipulating complex rules for loans and grants. USAID, the IMF and World Bank talked tough about investment but never bore down hard on spending for consumer junk.

Even poor bribed Honduras hasn't benefited greatly from its forced hosting of the Nicaraguan Contra. The money was spent mostly in Miami. Agency for International Development funds are largely targeted to American suppliers, through credits to the recipient country or its businesses. That's the reason a conservative Congress can justify appropriating taxpayers' money for foreign aid; most of it stays at home in the pockets of the companies whose lobbyists support the aid.

I got a Nicaraguan intellectual's view of this foolishness from Dr. Gustavo Parajon, a founder and head of CEPAD, a Protestant church-based coalition devoted to education and development that is probably the most successful organization of its type in Central America. Parajon, who received his medical training in the United states (see Chapter Twelve), is scornful of North American policy toward the region.

"If the United States wants to oust the government of another country..," he said with a shake of his head, "that's what AID does. The Chamorro administration is just a pawn of the U.S."

Nicaragua needs tools and training in such basic community improvements as water works, sewer systems, windmills, solar ovens and computers, Parajon said. "The politics of the (Chamorro) administration is neoliberal. Everything should be privatized; we can't have water, electricity, telephones, unless they are in private hands.

"Nicaraguan farmers try to sell chickens here but someone will fly three or four planeloads of chickens from Miami," he said. "The wealthy supermarket owner will sell the Miami chickens cheaper than local chickens. Irish butter is cheaper in San Carlos (a remote area in Southeast Nicaragua) than local butter. It's the same with apples, grapes, pears."

Parajon is by nature cheerful, a devout Christian, and a man of ideas. But in late 1993 he was near to despair. Central America, he said, "has disappeared from the (United States) media.

"The world moved into the 21st Century when the Berlin wall fell." But "the collapse of socialism was devastating to the south (southern hemisphere). The north's control is stronger. Never before in history have so few controlled the rest of the world so completely, politically and economically," Parajon said.

"Structural changes made under United States policy, through the International Monetary Fund and the World Bank going back to Bretton Woods right after World War II, join to bleed these countries (the southern hemisphere) to death. Debt is the most effective instrument of neocolonialism.

"Seventy percent of United States aid to Nicaragua has gone to pay the internal debt, to finance the wealthy families here," Parajon said. "Only a little has gone to small farmers.

They get no loans, no aid to raise their rice and beans. Unemployment is 65 percent on the Pacific Coast and 90 percent and more on the Atlantic side. Poverty is everywhere. Land reform is only a memory."

Much of what employment is available is "largely informal," according to English economist Trevor Evans. "Half the working population is performing a whole range of activities such as making tortillas at home to kids wiping car windshields at stop lights. They're all self-employed."

Living standards in Nicaragua rose from the 1979 revolutionary triumph through 1985, Evans said, "partly due to a massive investment in public health and education. But at the beginning of the 1980s the bottom fell out of the Nicaraguan economy. From 1980 to 1982 exports fell by half.

"No matter what else the Sandinistas did or did not do, they would have faced major problems," he said.

Nicaragua's economy worsened in the last half of the 1980s because of the world economy, the war and the United States blockade, Evans said. "The Sandinistas made errors, too. Inflation undermined the value of wages, and social standards deteriorated."

Chamorro's foes in her own political coalition urged the National Assembly to get rid of all government controls and give all resources to the private sector to develop.

Under the Sandinistas farm produce was subsidized; crops were purchased and stored by the government at harvest when supplies were abundant and prices were low. Later that food was sold at stabilized prices as shortages drove them up in private shops. The UNO government "virtually eliminated" the program, according to Evans. As her advisers saw it, if the state got out of the picture prices would rise and farmers would benefit. Planters would produce more food, bringing prices back down. A balance would be achieved by Adam Smith's "invisible hand."

"It hasn't happened," Evans said. "Now big firms buy crops at harvest time when there is a lot of corn and beans for sale and prices are low. They store these foods and sell them later, when they are in short supply and they can charge higher prices for them."

If any country should have benefitted from a United States war, our proxy war in Nicaragua, it was Panama. But it too, even its pro-United States elites, wound up on the short end of the economic stick. For two years before George Bush ordered an invasion of Panama at the end of 1989, the country had been under an economic blockade more strangling even than the one imposed on Nicaragua. And Panama, conditioned far more to trade than Nicaragua, suffered more. Shortly after the invasion unemployment there was in the fifty percent range. Even that was deceptive since street vendors like the women selling roses are counted among the employed. Unemployment is always actually higher than figures calculated by Latin governments would indicate.

If it weren't for the "parallel economy" of the streets, countries such as Honduras could hardly be said to have an urban economy in the modern sense.

The original banana republic and still its best exemplar, Honduras was ripe for a United States quid pro quo for sanctuary for the Nicaraguan Contra. The country was bribed into renting space for the Contra and, in turn, learned to shake down the United States for more aid as the undisciplined Contra became increasingly unpopular within the country and demands for their ouster increased.

During the late 1980s the United States pumped nearly $400 million in direct payments into the Honduran military, an infusion that should be measured against a gross national product for the country in 1980 of $2.4 billion and a foreign debt of $1.5 billion. More than 1,000 American servicemen and women were stationed in the country. In addition, a steady stream of transient American units, including many state National Guard organizations, passed through Honduras on maneuvers or other training exercises designed to intimidate Nicaragua.

If American economic policy toward Central America has been inept, the efforts of American business has, with some exceptions, been just as constipated and bureaucratic.

Once upon a time, before World War II, the Singer Sewing Machine Company was a model for United States firms doing business in Latin America in competition with Germans and Britons. Singer liberated thousands of Latin women from some of the drudgery of their lives, but in recent years most of the sewing machines in the region seem to be made in Eastern Europe. American automobiles one sees on Central American streets these days are mostly 1950s and 1960s vintage. Japanese, German and Eastern European cars have squeezed later American models out of the market.

In 1978, on a river cruise in Brazil's Amazonia, I noticed that all the new outboard motors propelling dugouts and other canoes in that watery world were from Japan. The old ones, on the decrepit canoes, were American Johnsons and Evinrudes. A few years later, at a fishing camp on Costa Rica's Caribbean coast, I saw the same thing. In both places, when I asked why, I got the same answer. The manager of the fishing camp took me to his shop and showed me half a dozen American motors of various ages, all laid up, he said, for lack of parts.

"It takes months to get a replacement," he said. But when one of his newer Yamahas or Hondas broke down, "the dealer in San Jose will fly a part out the next day."

American motors were as good as the Japanese, he said, and the price about the same. But he wanted service and the Americans either couldn't give it or didn't care. Central Americans lust for many consumer products from the United States, from blue jeans to ghetto blaster radios, but in almost every case once a fad takes hold, Asian or European copies—usually improvements—replace it.

Latin Americans in recent years have been doing just what the economic missionaries of the IMF have been preaching: growing a crop for the export market. The trouble is the crop is coca or its by-product, cocaine, and, as with the roses, the United States objects to its import. It leaned on the countries involved, Colombia and Bolivia especially, but also Panama and Honduras, to attack the source. For these entrepreneurs, drugs seemed to be the only thing the United

States consumer wanted from Latin America aside from bananas. And they were willing to provide them. So, while the United States was coaxing Latin farmers to turn their bean fields to roses and asparagus for the North American market we were waging a war, mostly a futile one, to eliminate crops farmers are raising with the greatest export value of all. Latin Americans see this as just more Yanqui hypocrisy. Why, they ask, should Latin farmers work themselves into early graves growing beans for family subsistence, or even broccoli for Yanquis, when they can make much more money growing coca for an avid market?

In spite of all the bombast about Noriega and his drug dealings, Central America's role in the drug trade was primarily as a conduit. Few drugs originate in Central America or are used there although that is changing.

"Poverty and economic inequities continue, in some countries at levels worse than a decade ago," says a 1989 General Accounting Office report on Central America for the Senate Foreign Relations Committee.[8] "Development progress has been hampered by slowed economic growth, armed conflicts, weak host government capabilities and their failure to implement needed policy and institutional reforms, natural disasters, a poor investment climate, and administrative requirements of United States aid programs."

The study suggested many changes, including one that is most revealing of how much its consultants know about their mission and the region they're discussing. Wherever possible, the report says, the United States should encourage Central America's movement toward democracy by supporting "programs to strengthen both civilian and military institutions with the aim of increasing accountability and reducing the corruption and inefficiency that undermine public confidence in democratic governments."

Suggesting strengthening military institutions, even though the statement apparently refers to their human rights attitudes, is not what Central America needs. It

---

[8] Central America, The Impact of U.S. Assistance in the 1980s, General Accounting Office, July 1989.

needs less military institutions, period. And that means a new attitude in the United States, an emphasis on building up a free and equitable trading system not tilted in favor of multinational corporations and less on selling American guns, tanks and planes.

United States efforts to help Central Americans improve their economies and their democracies may have been successful in some cases. But I never found any in more than a dozen years of searching. Embassy personnel loaded me down with country reports and analyses on each visit. Everything was just about to happen; no concrete results ever appeared. An example of self-defeating American economic policies was the two-year attempt to drive Manuel Noriega from power in Panama (See Chapter Nine). United States sanctions were costly to American business interests, which weren't consulted about them in advance, as well as to Panamanians innocent of any involvement with or support for Noriega. One panelist at a GAO workshop on Panama nearly a year before Bush's invasion described the economic sanctions as "the most brutal ever applied." Sanctions did no harm to Noriega but just about everyone else suffered. Within two months after the invasion the country was in a near state of anarchy.

United States economic policy in Central America is as confused and as contradictory as its political policy. Officially, we have never established just what our intention is for the region. Is it to insure the widest penetration of markets for United States business? Is it to create stable societies, economically healthy enough to care for the needs of their own citizens without perpetual reliance on Uncle Sam? Is it to curb the pressures of their growing populations on our borders?

Whatever the stated goal, we fail in each of those objectives. By supporting local elites that oppress their own people we are preventing the emergence of middle classes likely to be able to afford our manufactures. By encouraging needless militaries that draw to themselves political as well as economic power we help destabilize democratic efforts to be self-sufficient, and by tolerating and encouraging ruthless local governments we invite desperate peoples to flee their homelands and come to ours. In the absence of a firm vision by government, foreign policy is being made elsewhere. American bankers have long filled the gaps and after the Arab oil shock of the early 1970s they had more money available for lending than their traditional customers could absorb. Young loan officers, fresh out of eastern Ivy League business schools, invaded Central and South America, signing up unsophisticated, or corrupt, government officials and local bankers with loans far into the future with no collateral and only vague ideas of how they were to be repaid.

Who got all that money? Who has it now? Some joined the capital flight of native money being squirrelled away in foreign bank accounts. Some, I am sure, was well spent, although it was hard to prove and intent and results often diverged widely. On a visit to Honduras in the early 1980s, I examined a freeway interchange being constructed near my hotel. The concrete in the curbs and traffic structures was still green, and already crumbling. Apparently there were no quality inspectors to assure that specifications, sand-to-cement-to-gravel ratios, were followed. If there were inspectors they may have been on the take from contractors who themselves were paying off government officials letting the contracts. Within two years that road was falling apart.

Much of the money in the big loans by banks never got to the debtor countries long enough for skimming. It remained right where it was and, presumably, purchased goods to be used in economic and social development. That in itself is not criminal, but too often the purchased goods never got to those countries either. And few of the dollars loaned to Central American countries ever trickled down to the small business people who really needed it and who could have put it to use helping to expand the local economy. Much of it bought weapons, even beyond direct United States military aid, with which the rulers of those countries keep their citizens in line.

In 1992, as political temperatures of all Latin America

subsided and even Nicaragua and El Salvador were presumably at peace, the United States was hustling its southern neighbors to buy new weapons. Even before George Bush in his desperate run for reelection promised renewed arms sales to Taiwan and Saudi Arabia as jobs programs for defense workers, the Pentagon was sending its salesmen to Argentina and Chile, long-time rivals, with deals on fighter aircraft. "The United States will satisfy the legitimate defense needs of our friends," said Defense Secretary Dick Cheney.[9]

From the United States side of the equation, the chief villains are the bankers who risked not only their own stockholders' investments, but knew, if they thought of the future at all, that most of those Latin loans could never be repaid and that the consequence would be chaos. Why should the people of those countries sacrifice to pay back loans taken out by coup leaders of illegitimate governments who stole most of it? Especially when much of the money wound up in banks in Switzerland, the Cayman Islands or Panama, or, in many cases, in United States real estate schemes from Texas to Connecticut. Latin leaders who came along after the loan deluge rejected calls by Fidel Castro of Cuba for total defaults on the loans, primarily because they knew that full and formal abrogation would have laid the whole loan charade open for a world public view and that would have meant, to them, no more loans with which to pay interest on the earlier ones. Through the late 1970s and the Reagan years about all the United States had to offer Latin Americans were guns and other military toys and loans that on their face were impossible to repay.

Theoretically the debt burden began to lighten in 1991 and 1992, as Latin American borrowers were allowed, through a plan devised by United States Treasury Secretary Nicholas Brady, to pay off their debts at drastically marked down rates. These were agreed to by the banks, essentially, because they knew they'd never get a better offer. By 1991 the "debt service ratio"—the share of a country's export earnings going to paying off its debt—had declined from a

---

[9] El Mercurio, Santiago, Chile, Sept. 1992.

1986 high of 22 cents of each dollar earned to 14 cents. Growth throughout Latin America in 1992 was 2.7 percent, sufficient to show improvement ahead. All of that stemmed from a revival of investor confidence brought about by the debt reduction, according to Enrique Iglesias, president of the Inter-American Development Bank. The earlier capital that had flown the country had actually become a "savings account" of $300 billion to $400 billion, Iglesias said. It was now returning home.[10]

By 1994 Wall Street seemed to have forgotten the debts of Latin America. As the stock market boomed, Latin stocks were hot, especially as recession tarnished Japan's economic miracle. The North American Free Trade Act hustled through Congress by President Bill Clinton had bankers in euphoria although resistance in Mexico's poverty lands dimmed that miracle also. American investors in Latin America apparently never asked where the wealthy residents of those countries were putting their own money. Outside investors should have been examining the continued relationship of the military, the real rulers, with local businesses.

In the eyes of multinational corporations Central America is a resource warehouse. There is little demand for manufactures from those countries. Even basics such as Nicaraguan beef must compete with imports into the United States from Argentina and Australia as well as from Western American ranches. Fisheries are a relatively safe product but the resource has a limit and most of what is functioning is already in the hands of North Americans. An informal Central American market, not to be confused with the formal organization so often discussed, apparently has parceled out some manufacturing. Guatemala seems to be the designated catsup maker for the region, for instance, but the product is controlled by North Americans.

Nicaraguans make magnificent furniture, rocking chairs and tables. An American entrepreneur could do himself and the Nicaraguans some good by bringing them to the United

---

[10] Hobart Rowen, The Washington Post National Weekly Edition, May 11-17, 1992. p. 5.

States for sale. But what would New England and North Carolina furniture manufacturers have to say about that? Salvadoran cottons are some of the finest in the world, but bringing them into the United States, unless they have American labels on them, would be difficult. Global textile companies could do it, but that trade would afford little benefit to Salvadoran mill workers. Pants "assembled" in Honduras or Mexico offer more steady employment and a more assured market but they pay barely subsistence wages.

Tourism is a possibility, as it is in Mexico. Honduras has magnificent offshore islands and every seasoned American traveler knows about Belize. There are other places that could easily qualify as world class resort destinations. But the capital to develop them is not available except at the price of North American control.

Not all the blame for Central America's economic distortions lies with the United States. Latin leaders, usually military, their collaborators or their puppets, need no instruction from Yanquis in cheating and stealing the fruits of campesino labor. Rather than accepting the idea that prosperity grows its own wealth, many Latin social and business elites actively keep the peasant poor in poverty, even when it works to their own disadvantage, as it often does. Internal Latin economic policies are often subject to swings as wild as Latin politics, zigzagging from populist state-run endeavors to sudden privatization, with little thought of consequence for either. The vision of many Latin businessmen is as distorted as those of their governments.

The owner of a Tegucigalpa department store entertained me one afternoon with wails that Honduran street vendors in the nearby square were taking business away from him.

Surely, I said, they don't sell much. On the contrary, he said, "they do more business than I ever do, and they pay no rent for their stalls." His proposed solution was to have the police run them all out of town.

Later that day I stood in the square, pricing the nicknacks and watching the action. I saw few sales. And, some of the vendors told me, they did indeed have over-head, a slice of every sale to the police. These are the people of the Latin "parallel market," independent businesses eking out a living, often through the efforts of several family members. Street vendors, backyard repairmen, home tortilla makers are significant factors in Latin American economics.

The Peruvian Writer Mario Vargas Llosa regards that unofficial market or informal economy, operating illegally, paying no taxes, as vital to the economic health of many, perhaps a majority, of those countries.[11] Certainly these small entrepreneurs provide a large share of the jobs. Vargas Llosa, who ran for president of Peru in 1990 on a conservative pro-business platform but was beaten by Alberto Fujimori, may be exaggerating their influence, but about one thing he is absolutely right. Latin America's stifling bureaucracies surpass illiteracy, depletion of resources and probably even corruption as an obstacle to running a small business. Anyone who has queued in three lines in a Latin bank to cash a traveler's check has had a taste of what locals must endure to obtain a permit to build a house, establish a business or just sell something. Bribes are only a small part of that frustration; inertia takes an equal toll.

Foreign groups, from Europe and the United States, make small loans, very small, to some of those people, in the neighborhood of $50 to $150, to get them started in their tiny businesses. ACCION International loans money at low interest to shoe repairmen for leather and needles, to tortilla sellers for flour, to house cleaners for soap and brushes, a whole world of genuinely small business people who would otherwise be perpetually in the clutches of loan sharks. Repayments are nearly one hundred percent, allowing funds to be recycled rapidly.

None of Central America's woes are new; only the figures are larger than they when General Smedley Butler, one of America's most illustrious soldiers, was pacifying Central America for Wall Street bankers.

---

[11] Mario Vargas Llosa, In Defense of the Black Market, The New York Times Magazine, Feb. 22, 1987, P. 28.

6

Censorship There, and Here

You cannot hope to bribe or twist,
Thank God, the British journalist,
But, seeing what the man will do unbribed,
There's no occasion to.
　　　　　　　—Humbert Wolfe, "Over the Fire" in
　　　　　　　The Uncelestial City.

THIS GOOD LOOKING BLONDE IN A SKIN-TIGHT WHITE SILK pantsuit parked her Mercedes in a no-parking zone on the shady street and sauntered with her spiraled hair-do glittering in the sunshine to where the men with dark glasses had piled signs on the sidewalk. She picked up a sign that read *Paz y Trabajo* (peace and work). Then she joined the march just getting underway down Franklin Delano Roosevelt Avenida toward the center of San Salvador. The street was already cleared of traffic by the men in dark glasses and civilian clothing and carrying the assault rifles.

One buxom beauty, about eighteen, wore a white T-shirt with a big red heart over her left breast. Below it, in English, was the message "I have a heart on for you." I was so fascinated I forgot my brand new camera until it was too late and she and her laughing, giggling group passed into the mass of marchers and I was unable to find her again.

I had just arrived in El Salvador that day in March of 1984 to watch the election still ten days off. "What's going on?" I asked Hugo, the lay Baptist church worker who picked me up at the airport.

"There's a women's peace march," Hugo said, in what I thought was a rather sarcastic tone. Another macho Latin chauvinist, I thought. But when we stopped at a church orphanage and the children literally climbed all over him I realized he was not that kind of person. He was tall and heavily muscled and broad in the shoulders as polio victims often are but limped badly on shrunken legs. Hugo told me the women marchers would set off at the Cuscutlan Park near the Alameda Hotel where I usually stay when I'm in El Salvador. The hotel is cheap, near downtown and not infested with *Norte Americanos* and the war junkies who were the bane of more than just the Salvadoran Army.

In the column I called in that evening to my newspaper in Seattle I suggested that the march for peace didn't represent the typical Salvadoran woman. I was cad enough to speculate that the blonde was probably a stranger to the work her sign proclaimed she was seeking, but I was sufficiently aware of my obligations to readers of a family newspaper not to mention the girl with the heart. The story of the peace march was heavily rewritten, considerably toned down by the copy desk and did not carry the usual admonition that I was a columnist and thus not to be taken seriously; in other words what was supposed to be commentary ran as a straight news story. So when it appeared in the next morning's paper back in Seattle many readers were enraged. Or so my editors said when I returned, although I never knew how many because they said all the irate letters had been thrown out. The nasty phone messages accusing me of everything from liberalism to Communism had been dumped.

"You weren't even in the country one day when you were making these judgments," the managing editor snarled. "What kind of objectivity is that?"

My reminders that I had been in El Salvador a number of times previously and understood the march's implications didn't placate him. He had been unnerved by references to differences between my version of the coercion that prompted Salvadorans to vote and the official, Ronald Reagan Administration view. Conceived and promoted by the United States, that version said, it was a heartwarming example of democracy in action. The same line was parroted by William Randolph Hearst, Jr., the owner of the paper and nominal author of mandatory Sunday columns applauding anything and everything the Reagan Administration did.

Those essays fawning on whichever Republican happened to be president, a cross of shame for all Hearst journalists, were "Junior's" ticket to White House functions. This was several years before the Iran-Contra scandal, and editors all over the country, in newspapers bolder and larger than the provincial Seattle Post-Intelligencer, were accepting the Reagan line that the United States was merely shoring up democracy in El Salvador and Nicaragua.

I had observed in the story that larger numbers of women left their homes or their jobs in downtown shops and looked on in silence from closed side streets as the modish marchers moved down the avenue denouncing *communistas* and Fidel Castro and singing the El Salvador national anthem. That too was not objective, the editor said. It wasn't up to me to make judgments of that sort. My mission was to tell only the facts; numbers of marchers, maybe some sexy words of the songs they sang, what their signs and banners said, laced with some "color" about the tropic heat or flowers. If I wanted assessments of what it all meant I should seek out "informed sources," El Salvador officials or United States Embassy spokesmen, and don't forget to attribute them. After some shouting and a few unkind words on each side I was told I was not to write any more about Central America. That ban continued for two years, while the paper was lamenting editorially the Sandinista censorship of *La Prensa*. Eventually that editor left for greener pastures. A new editor from outside the paper was a militarist and by flaunting my Army experience as a paratrooper and Green Beret, I managed to again report on Central America. Eventually, however, even he became nervous; my accounts didn't agree with Hearst's and the Bush State Department's.

Not challenging the administration helps to get published and it's sure easier on the nerves. Attend State Department press briefings and rewrite its press releases and editors won't fuss about objectivity. A safe message is that anyone who talks back to Uncle Sam or his surrogates is obviously a communist. A leading proponent of this go-along-to-get-along school of journalism is Georgie Anne Geyer, whose ego-tripping syndicated columns would be hilarious—"he told me a year ago in strict confidence," and "I was the only one to be told"—were they not so shaded by her admiration for fancy uniforms and tickets to official functions. Like Hearst, she kept an inside track by regurgitating the official line. It also got her fare paid, on foreign tours, by the United States Information Agency. The quid for that pro quo is that she writes nice about United States policy.[12]

Geyer quoted with scorn Senator Christopher Dodd, a Connecticut Democrat, that Nicaraguan President Daniel Ortega "is not a Marcos or a Noriega. He has a real popular base in his country." She said Dodd and other Democrats who had mildly deplored our war on Nicaragua were "revolution groupies."

Secretary of State George Schultz and his successor, James Baker, announced at different times that the Sandinistas were plotting to skew Nicaragua's 1990 election and, sure enough, Guyer's columns began warning the public that Daniel Ortega was plotting to steal the election. Another of these pundits with a foot in the door to the State Department was Ronald Radosh, who writes at times for *The New Republic*. Radosh and I attended one of Ortega's monthly "face the people" meetings in 1983 in a Managua barrio where a series of speakers denounced the government for food shortages and for planning to draft young men to fight the war.

Radosh, in a *New Republic* story, saw the meeting as manipulation by an unprincipled politician. Ortega was putting on a show, he said, and the Nicaraguans who sounded off were dupes. Radosh was surprised to see a politician acting like a politician.

---

[12] Fred Landis, Covert Action, Spring-Summer, 1983, p.25.

Geyer and Radosh and other writers defending the Yankee status quo in Central America constantly demanded of Nicaragua a higher standard of conduct than they did of any other country, including the United States. Ortega's openness didn't prompt further investigation by journalists primed to find Marxist skullduggery behind everything the Sandinistas did.

North American reporters and columnists weren't alone in taking a slanted view of what was happening in Central America, and especially of Nicaragua under the Sandinistas. "Sandinismo is the greatest hoax of the decade," a British writer said after a visit in 1988. Some of his report, exaggerating failures of management or other problems caused by Contra depredations, was so twisted as to almost defy analysis. "Most significantly they have not nationalized the 'means of production' as occurred in Cuba," the author wrote. Instead, "They manipulate the private sector through a system of licenses and monopolies."[13] No recognition there that economic control was a response to the United States embargo and the demands of the United States' proxy war.

Even honest journalists accepted the Reagan-Bush categorization of Nicaragua's Sandinistas as communists. Lou Cannon, whose coverage of Ronald Reagan was mostly balanced as well as revealing, followed that line. In one column he said the "Reagan Doctrine had sought to prevent the spread of communism by aiding anti-communist forces in all corners of the globe. This approach succeeded brilliantly in Afghanistan, failed miserably in Nicaragua..." He was wrong on both counts, but why would a responsible journalist express such sentiments when evidence to the contrary was easy to find?

After the collapse of communist governments in Central and Eastern Europe at the end of 1989, George Bush's invasion of Panama and the capture of Manuel Noriega, columnists across the country were predicting that Fidel Castro would be next. That's a logical assumption and it is examined elsewhere in this book. But I raise the point be-

---

[13] Ambrose Evans-Pritchard, The Spectator, London, Feb. 13, 1988. p.8.

cause Ortega was constantly being compared with Castro. That parallel, fostered by the Bush Administration, is laughable in its baseless assumption: that because Ortega relied on Cuba, and the Soviet Union, for help in his war with the United States he was their patsy. Ortega, unlike Castro, never lamented the downfall of the communist dictatorships across Europe. And he never stood anyone up against a wall and shot them.

Selective use of information in straight news accounts, supposedly totally objective, can tilt an article one way or another. A 1984 Associated Press story carried by the *New York Times* datelined Washington, D.C., just before the Nicaraguan election, discussed a large new airport the Sandinistas were building. All the comment was from a State Department spokesman who said the airport "did not appear" to be for use against Nicaragua's "armed opposition," the Contra, "as much as against Nicaragua's neighbors."

The spokesman, the story said, added that acquisition of high-performance aircraft "would alter the balance of power in the region." The story added that the Reagan Administration had said that "some 50 Nicaraguan pilots have received training in Bulgaria in flying MIG jet fighters. There have also been reports from defectors that MIGs are being stored in Cuba for delivery to Nicaragua after the Nicaraguan elections, scheduled for November." Another official said recently, the AP story continued, "that Cuban workers had been building the airport on a round-the-clock basis. President Reagan has estimated that 10,000 Cubans are aiding the Sandinistas in a variety of capacities."

That story, without any response from easily approachable Nicaraguan officials, could serve as a text in gray propaganda: an airport "directed (sic) against Nicaragua's neighbors;" the potential acquisition of high-performance aircraft and what that would mean; Nicaraguan pilots have been reported by the United States to be training in Bulgaria; "there have also been reports from defectors" of MIGs stored in Cuba to be delivered to Nicaragua after the elections; a report of Cubans aiding the Sandinistas.

This package of suppositions would seem to demand rebuttal or at least a reply. But no comment was sought even though the story said Nicaraguan officials "led reporters on a tour of the airport" a few days previously. Those same officials said the runways would be 4,400 and 3,900 yards long, the story said. It ended with this sentence: "American officials said either (length) could easily accommodate MIG jets." All this disinformation was groundwork for the phony story of MIGs being landed in Nicaragua just as it was holding an election later that year.

If many reporters were dupes, others were victims. Often, it should be acknowledged, they could be both. Reporters who would swallow distortions from dissembling presidents and report it without blushing would also go onto battlefields to get a story. Many of them found death there. "Attacks on the Press 1989," published by the Committee to Protect Journalists, a New York nonprofit organization, said fifty-three journalists were killed world wide that year, most of them in Latin America.

In El Salvador fourteen journalists died or were "disappeared" during the year. All, or nearly all, were at the hands of government forces, the army or its unofficial—and often identical—death squads. No one knows how many other Salvadoran journalists have been forced to leave the country in fear. I was confronted a number of times by a "what are you going to do about it?" look from the military and the burly men in the dark glasses in El Salvador.

The contrast between Nicaragua's treatment of the press, censorship of La Prensas, and the murdered reporters and editors in our client state, El Salvador, never made State Department press briefings. Neither, strangely, was it brought up at press conferences by reporters whom one would think might have a fraternal interest in the question as well as a professional curiosity. Nor, the New Yorker noted, have many newspapers, and none of the television networks, mentioned it in their news columns or broadcasts.

Some news people were killed in what the Salvadoran Army called "cross fire." Among them were four members of a Dutch television crew killed in March 1982 when they went searching for guerrillas. The Dutchmen had publicly asked questions in the Camino Real Hotel reporters' hangout as well as elsewhere for leads to the guerrillas' whereabouts. They were very indiscreet, other newsmen stationed there said, although the four may have thought their very openness would protect them. Most newsmen in El Salvador at the time believed the Dutchmen were deliberately killed as an example to others. "They were looking for trouble, and they found it," an American reporter said. "They just didn't believe this country is as dangerous as it is."

Linda Frazier, an American working for the English language *Tico Times* in Costa Rica, was killed when someone bombed a press conference called by Contra leader Eden Pastora just over the border in Nicaragua. Two Central American newsmen were killed also, and about twenty people were wounded, some badly. Another American killed in one of those cross fires was John Hoagland, who died in March of 1984 in El Salvador. It was the public execution style slaying of ABC News reporter Bill Stewart in 1979 on worldwide television during the Nicaraguan revolution that finally focused North American attention on that vicious but short war. Mexican dislike of the El Salvadoran regime was reinforced when a reporter for that country's Uno Mas Uno was killed when he was caught in a fire fight in San Salvador.

Another American, William Sullivan, a freelancer for the raunchy *Hustler* magazine, disappeared from his San Salvador hotel room in 1980 and was never seen again. Bones discovered along side a road three years later were tentatively identified as his.

Dial Torgerson, the *Los Angeles Times* bureau chief for Central America, and Richard Cross, a photographer working for *U.S. News and World Report*, were killed on the Nicaraguan border just inside Honduras near Las Trojes in 1983. Honduran authorities gave several different versions of their deaths, first saying their car had been hit by anti-tank grenades fired by Nicaraguan troops from their side of the border. Another story said it was a rocket grenade, another that it was artillery fire. I was in the area on the Nicaraguan side three days later and that section of the road was not visible from the Nicaraguan positions. Anti-tank rockets (I'm not sure what an anti-tank grenade is) are direct fire, line-of-sight weapons of short range. Later the Hondurans said the two newsmen, and their Honduran driver, died when their car ran over a land mine planted by the Nicaraguan Army.

I saw a picture of Torgerson's body, its upper half covered with a poncho, several days later and his legs, which would have been mangled by a mine powerful enough to have destroyed the car, were intact. Also, as the Spanish newspaper *El Pais* pointed out, the route was traveled routinely by Honduran vehicles and they hadn't run over any mines. My guess is that a trigger-happy combatant on the Honduran side, either a Honduran soldier or a Contra, killed them. A few days after their deaths a Honduran officer told another newsman that he had warned them not to go into the area because it was an active combat zone.

When I was there, on the Nicaragua side, I bantered with the Sandinista troops, who were sheltered in World War I type trenches, about going over the border after the Contra or at least shooting at them, and roused one of the few rancorous arguments I ever had with a Central American. A Sandinista lieutenant took my challenge as an aspersion on their courage and informed me grimly that they only wished they could go after the Contra in Honduras but the high command would not allow it. That proves nothing of course, one way or another, but the deaths of Torgerson and Cross look like either accidents or Contra provocations to me.

In Colombia the toll of journalists was at times higher than the killings of policemen by drug gunmen. Mexican reporters and editors are underpaid, harassed and often, out of poverty, forced to take favors from the people they're supposed to be covering with an objective eye. And they run serious risks, fatal often, when they try to do their jobs. Some forty Mexican journalists were murdered during the 1970s and 1980s, including a Tijuana columnist who trod on too many important toes, public and private. My treatment was benign compared to the persecutions inflicted on Latin journalists in their own countries. Reporters and photographers are regularly beaten up in Guatemala. My beating in Panama was probably not because I was a newsman; I was just another gringo, fair game for muggers.

The CIA took care of journalists differently, by bribery. A 1977 law forbids Agency personnel from posing as reporters or paying real reporters for slanting their stories. But it doesn't say anything about under the table payments to foreigners. At least eight Costa Rican journalists were on the payroll of the CIA during 1987, according to one report.[14] "Their job is to get into the press stories, commentaries or editorials attacking Nicaragua and sympathetic to the contras," said Carlos Morales, a Costa Rican professor of journalism. The Contra operating out of Honduras also had a fund to bribe journalists. Edgar Chamorro, a former Nicaraguan advertising man (for Tona beer and Flor de Cana rum) who was a spokesman and paymaster for the Contra, told the World Court in Nicaragua's case against the United States that he had bribed some fifteen Honduran journalists. "Our influence was extended to every major Honduran newspaper and radio and television station," he said.

Eden Pastora, a one-time commander of the Contra operating on the Southern Front, regurgitated CIA press releases, he told reporters after he broke with the CIA because of its close ties with members of Somoza's old National Guard. CIA operators persuaded both Chamorro and Pastora to issue CIA-written press releases saying they had mined the Nicaraguan Port of Corinto.

With the selection of Violeta Chamorro to head an opposition ticket in Nicaragua's 1990 election, the Bush Administration had a candidate to match its rationale for manipulating the voting. She was an attractive choice, the photogenic widow of Pedro Joaquim Chamorro, a national hero murdered on Somoza's orders in 1978. The nominal publisher of *La Prensa*, the long-time opposition newspaper,

---

[14] Martha Honey, Contra coverage—paid for by the CIA, Columbia Journalism Review, March/April 1987.

and matriarch of a vibrant and headstrong family, Violeta, as everyone calls her, was the most credible challenger to the ruling Sandinista party the CIA or the Bush Administration could have desired.

In the years following the revolution, La Prensa, under Violeta, had been the voice of the internal opposition, quick to attack the government's failures, whether in its inability to cope with an economy in shambles or for an early heavy-handedness in dealing with East Coast Indians. The paper was loathe to report Sandinista triumphs in health care, literacy and land reform. La Prensa always refused to acknowledge, as did its bankrollers in Washington, D. C., that the young and inexperienced government had the best human rights record in Central America (always with the exception of neighboring Costa Rica).

Chamorro's selection had proven, columnists and commentators said, how sincerely the opposition in Nicaragua wanted "democracy." That was undoubtedly true of some of the opposition, however they defined democracy, but others had no intention of permitting democracy in Nicaragua; after all, that's what they'd been fighting the past eight years.

The simple truth is that La Prensa was a disgraceful newspaper, selective, vituperative and dishonest. And, significantly to Nicaraguans, its polemics were financed largely by a foreign government, the United States. The National Endowment for Democracy contributed significantly to the paper's continued publication, $105,000 in 1984 alone, $800,000 in all up until 1989. The shading between the Endowment's above board contribution and the CIA's secret manipulations of their country were lost on most Nicaraguans. It was all Yanqui money. The Endowment is at least straightforward interference in another country's affairs, as contrasted to the CIA's secret terrorist war and campaigns of lies.

Among the most blatant of these were the recurring stories of international terrorists, Palestinians, Libyans and other assorted scrungy people, making Nicaragua their base while they plotted new misdeeds. "A terrorist country club," said United States Attorney General Edwin Meese. As one of Reagan's chief advisers in the Iran-Contra scandal, Meese should have known something about both terrorists and country clubs. Nevertheless, beyond the blathering of Meese and some tame columnists, there were never any details of this posh terrorist resort. No one I questioned in Nicaragua knew anything about the alleged terrorists, including officials at the United States Embassy who showed some redeeming embarrassment when I asked.

The Endowment for Democracy, plus other support a pliable Congress allowed Bush for the campaign, disconcerted some Nicaraguans, but not enough to overcome their desire for an end to the war and to get the economy back on track. So they voted for Violeta and the United States in 1990 even though Daniel Ortega played the time-honored, number one political card of all Latin America—reminding voters that the Yanquis were up to their old tricks. It was true, but it wasn't good enough. Jaime Chamorro, *La Prensa* general manager, told foreign news reporters that the Endowment money had no strings attached. "They don't tell us what to write," he said of the Endowment officials. "Ronald Reagan may like what we're saying but we were saying it before he was."[15]

La Prensa's chief claim to international sympathy was the heavy-handed censorship imposed by the Sandinista government for most of the years following the revolution and its closure for a year. It was back on the streets for a year before the 1990 election but had the Sandinistas not panicked and muzzled it in the first place, the paper's delinquencies would have been little noted outside the country or even within it.

La Prensa's two rivals, it should be noted, weren't much better. *El Diario* was headed by another Chamorro, Xavier, Pedro's brother, who took most of the *La Prensa* staff down the street in 1979 after the Revolution to found the new paper when *La Prensa* immediately attacked the Sandinista government. *El Diario* followed the Sandinista line in most

---

[15] Ibid.

things, offering more servitude than the sort of close scrutiny a truly independent newspaper would provide. It was definitely one-sided, but Nicaraguans could at least learn something about the war in their own country from it, news that appeared in *La Prensa* only when it reflected badly on the government.

The third newspaper, *Barricada*, had previously, in the years it was telling lies and suppressing the truth for Somoza, been called *Novedades*. The Sandinistas put Violeta's son Carlos in charge, renamed it and made it the official government organ. As such it exemplified the Sandinistas' skillful use of propaganda and public relations. It was written in an easy vernacular that even most newly literate Nicaraguans could read, unlike the ponderous prose of so many Latin newspapers. Its makeup was inviting, with lots of pictures, and its features were light hearted but informative, if ideologically laden. It published a weekly international edition, more moderate in its English than its daily Spanish version, mostly analysis and commentary.

Barricada also often could not be trusted and its stories of the war were many times difficult to confirm. I tried once to follow up an account it carried about two young men impressed into the Contra who one night shot to death their squad mates while they were sleeping and stole all their weapons which they turned in to the Sandinista Army. I was unable to find anyone who knew anything about it. But *Barricada* did also cover subjects embarrassing to the government, usually with more explanation of why things went wrong than what actually happened or how.

"They all lie," said an American who had long been a resident of Nicaragua.

Before the Nicaraguan 1979 revolution, when *La Prensa* was attacking the Somoza tyranny, other papers more friendly to the government were giving a black-and-white, one-sided view of events in and out of Nicaragua. *Novedades*, the pro-Somoza newspaper, was full of denunciations of Yanqui newspapers when I was first in Nicaragua in 1978. News stories from Washington, D. C. that reflected the

Carter Administration's disapproval of the Somoza government never saw print in Nicaragua although Carter's failures were fully covered. Articles criticizing Fidel Castro got big play. A *Novedades* story of that time accused American newsmen of "assassinating the character" of Nicaragua and of Somoza and his National Guard by their stories of murders, disappearances and corruption. In El Salvador ten years later the same theme, accompanied by the old background chord of anti-communism, was being played constantly in newspapers under the thumb of that country's Army to explain its atrocities.

Censorship, to my mind, is never justified, but *La Prensa's* stories were wrenched out of reality often enough to try the patience of the most ardent free speech advocate. Provocation is the only word for it. I argued with Nicaraguan friends that La Prensa's distortions would eventually be obvious to its readers and that censoring the paper was drawing attention to it and losing the government friends all over the world. They replied that most Nicaraguan readers are too unsophisticated to see through such blatant disregard for the truth. In that, of course, they're not too different from presumably more sophisticated North American readers who seem willing to believe almost anything put in front of them on paper or on television if it has a jingoistic hook.

The American Newspaper Guild joined the Reagan Administration in calling for an end to Nicaragua's censorship of *La Prensa*. "The repeated suspension of *La Prensa* serves only to stifle free expression and to erode the credibility of your government as one dedicated to democratic principle," the guild, a newspaper union, said in a 1982 letter to Ortega.

At the same time a group of American journalists who should have known better reported after a trip to Central America that foreign and Nicaraguan journalists were "profoundly threatened" by the government's state of siege. This was nonsense right out of the Reagan Administration's campaign of disinformation. I traveled in Nicaragua for fifteen years on my own, without hindrance, and I never was limited in what I could do or where I could go, and I met many other American and European reporters who had the same experience. Not one ever told me of intimidation by the government. Bumbling, clumsy bureaucrats perhaps, stiffly rigid in their exercise of their authority, but never a hint of a threat.

I was once told that it would be best if I had an escort when I visited troops in combat positions near the Honduran border and was assigned a young Sandinista lieutenant to take me wherever I wanted to go. He answered questions, some not as completely as I would have liked, but he allowed me to set my own itinerary and go where I pleased. He never interfered when I talked to troops who didn't seem to be intimidated by his presence.

Censorship of La Prensa was clumsy and probably self-defeating in the long run, certainly in the eyes of the world, but it was justified, so far as the government was concerned, by the war, which was very real inside Nicaragua. Legless veterans, hospitals full of maimed children and daily funerals of campesinos murdered in a campaign of terror were all testimony to that. Nicaraguans believed themselves under siege while La Prensa was using its news pages to run down the government and promote a war against it.

Nicaraguans repeatedly made a comparison with United States newspapers censored during World War II. "Would your government have allowed your newspapers to tell the German or the Japanese side and ignore United States' victories?" one Nicaraguan asked me. Many others voiced similar queries. Censoring La Prensa, so far as the government was concerned, was necessary for national security since the newspaper was clearly on the side of the enemy. When the Bush Administration talked about "democratizing" Nicaragua it failed to remember that democracy means more than elections, no matter how free they look to us.

Nicaragua's censorship of La Prensa was always a peculiar endeavor, erratic and sloppy. Similar stories were treated differently; one might be forbidden, one trimmed, another run entirely. Some excisions, such as the photograph of an elephant on roller skates, were just plain strange. Why was it cut? An embarrassed Sandinista official explained vaguely that the picture was a not so sly attempt to make the government look foolish. He didn't disagree that censoring it made the government look even more foolish. Another censorship anomaly: the government didn't interfere when *La Prensa* pinned photocopies of everything censored each day to a bulletin board along the sidewalk in front of the *La Prensa* compound. Anyone who wished could stop and read it. And the United States Embassy gleefully distributed sheafs of copies of the latest banned news stories and pictures to visiting journalists, or anyone else who could be persuaded to take them.

Foreign newspapers were hard to find in Nicaragua through the early years of the Sandinista regime and I was never able to determine for certain why. Sandinista spokesmen told me there was no restriction on newspapers being shipped into the country. Why then, I asked, weren't there any for sale at hotel news stands? The answer was that the cost was too great.

Another Sandinista admitted to me that the government imposed a heavy duty on the papers. I knew, during this time, that people were able to obtain United States newspapers by subscription. One friend got the *New York Times* each evening of publication day, delivered to his door. An embassy spokeswoman told me that American newspapers were seized by customs officials from passengers arriving at the Managua airport. But it never happened to me and I never saw or heard of it happening to anyone else. I think, however, that up until about 1986 the government was actively blocking papers from entering the country. It was crude and silly.

I've heard tales of distributors of *La Prensa* in Nicaragua being harassed by the police or the *"turbas divinas,"* the divine mobs of the Interior Ministry. Those tales probably contained some truth, but bad as they were, no one, so far as I know, ever accused the Sandinistas of murdering news reporters. *La Prensa's* editors complained of blockades of newsprint, of harassment of delivery trucks and other outrages by the government. They told of reporters being jailed, failing to mention that those jailings, as unjustified as they may have been, and I was never able to really obtain any information about them, had lasted only hours. Some editors left the country, but again the reasons were always vaguely linked to some "oppression." Those totalitarian actions hurt the government, in foreign as well as local eyes, more than they hurt the enemy. But compared to the official treatment of news reporters in El Salvador Sandinista dealings with La Prensa was benign. Its employees lived and they continued to complain.

News stories of Violeta Chamorro's trip to the United States to ask for help in her election campaign made it appear as though the poor woman was a stranger to these shores, a shrinking bumpkin in glittering Miami. Actually, she spent a great deal of her time there, according to knowledgeable Nicaraguans. In Managua she was frequently on the schedule of visiting tour groups, eager to ask about La Prensa, but few ever saw her. Especially after she became a candidate, she was "suddenly called away," her handlers would say when she failed to show up for appointments. The Chamorros, like most of the "high bourgeoisie" of Nicaragua, are as at home in Miami as they are in Managua and certainly more at ease there than they are in Leon, or Esteli or Matagalpa. The family is wealthy, with sugar mills, orange juice plants, rum distilleries and other holdings, most of it untouched by the government La Prensa accused of plotting to eliminate private enterprise.

La Prensa's coverage of the war was about as poor as it could possibly be. I was never able to see Violeta but after being rebuffed for years I did meet one of the paper's editors, Carlos Rodriguez. A friend had just returned from a memorial service for twenty two coffee pickers killed when the Contra ambushed their truck in an attempt to cripple the harvest of coffee, Nicaragua's chief dollar export. It was a terrorist attack against mostly women and children. According to reports in the other newspapers the truck had been shot up on the road and then, after a few of its occupants had fled into the jungle, the Contra had tossed the wounded back on the truck, doused it with gasoline and set it afire.

I told Rodriguez I hadn't seen any stories of the massacre in *La Prensa*. He was sure the paper had carried a story, he said, and rummaged through a pile of back issues on the coffee table in his conference room until he found it. The story was on the front page of the paper, below the fold, but the reason I hadn't noticed it earlier was that it was not about a massacre. It was a mass obituary of the twenty two victims, although it didn't call them that. In fact it didn't label them in any way; it gave their names, the ages of some, and a few details of the funeral. But there was no explanation of how those people died or what had caused their deaths. Nothing to indicate, without reading between the lines, that they had been murdered.

Why was that? Well, Rodriguez said, "you know about second day stories." Reports of the massacre had come in too late for *La Prensa*, he said. *El Diario* and *Barricada* had carried it the day after the massacre. Since his paper wouldn't have the story until the following day there was no reason to go into all the details, he said.

Three years later, at a luncheon at the United States ambassador's residence (Ambassador Andrew Melton had just been kicked out of the country for interfering in the coming election and the host was Chief of Mission John Leonard) I asked Jamie Chamorro, Violeta's brother-in-law and vice president of *La Prensa*, about the ambush story. Members of a congressional touring group I was with, sponsored by the Unitarian Universalist Service, were allowed to ask one question each after a lunch with a "representative" group of Nicaraguans the embassy had assembled.

I first told Chamorro that I had been entertained by a *La Prensa* story several years earlier about a woman who had given birth to a chicken. The paper gave the story two columns, running from top to bottom of Page Three.[16] Chamorro said *La Prensa* was forced to run the story because thou-

---

[16] La Prensa, Managua, Feb. 24, 1984

sands of people were flocking to the woman's home and threatening to make it a shrine. The Sandinistas had "turned it around" and were trying to peddle the story as true to the poor ignorant campesinos. *La Prensa* was only trying to set the record straight, he said. I wasn't able to ask him how the Sandinistas were spreading the tale since it hadn't appeared elsewhere. The story got plenty of play after *La Prensa* ran it, however; the weekly Nicaraguan satirical magazine *La Comica* ribbed *La Prensa* and opposition party officials about the chicken for weeks afterward.

Chamorro said he didn't remember the massacre story but he did not refute it. If it happened that way, he surmised, it was because the government made gathering news so difficult for *La Prensa*. So far as the incident and other massacres were concerned, he said, it was because the government often included children in the coffee brigades "in such a way that they form a military target." And, he said, the coffee pickers "often carry weapons." They were provocateurs, he was saying.

La Prensa was so oppressed by the government, Chamorro said, that its reporters were unable to get out into the combat zones to verify incidents or to reach military or local officials for comment. Our luncheon ended and there was no time for rebuttal and no critic of the paper present, in that supposedly representative Nicaraguan group, to point out that *La Prensa* had no hesitation in accepting without confirmation accusations that discredited the government. Nor did anyone point out that Chamorro continued to voice his criticism of the government without fear of arrest or harassment.

The Sandinistas did clamp down on the news media, even beyond *La Prensa*, through decrees limiting the kinds of items that could be reported. In one decree complaining of a "conspiracy against our people and their revolution, promoted by the current administration of the United States Government," the Sandinistas made their case. The conspiracy was "clearly proven by the plot to destroy the cement factory and blow up the refinery, the terrorist attack on an Aeronica (the national airline) plane in Mexico, the terrorist attack at the Augusto Cesar Sandino Airport causing the death of Nicaraguan citizens and the destruction of public property, criminal attacks by Somozist guardsmen—whose latest actions included the destruction of the bridge over Rio Negro in Chinandega Department and partial damage to another in the city of Ocotal—campaigns of lies and slanders against our country for the purpose of justifying terrorist destabilization actions, training of mercenaries for the purpose of overthrowing the Nicaraguan Revolutionary Government, maneuvers by spy vessels off the Nicaraguan coasts and flights of spy planes over Nicaraguan skies admitted by the United States Government itself."

For all these reasons, the decree said, a state of national emergency was declared which meant that "all radio and written media are hereby ordered to submit their daily programs or editions to the Communications Media Directorate to be reviewed before releases." It also suspended "all radio newscasts, political party opinion programs or those of any other organizations." Further, radio stations were ordered to join a network of the *Voz de Nicaragua* (the official radio net) four times each day for transmission of the newscast "The Voice of the Defense of the Fatherland." Most of that decree remained in effect throughout the war, only being partially modified just before the 1990 national election.

Among issues forbidden, so the opposition said, were references to shortages of food and other items and police matters. Yet I read news of those issues in all three newspapers over the years. A number of the country's radio stations were seized as government property, chiefly because they had been owned by the Somoza family or their cronies, shortly after the 1979 triumph. Other radio stations were closed down or shut for periods of time in the years afterward, and not always because of Contra activity. In its dispute with the church, reminiscent of the battle Mexico had with its *Cristeros* earlier in the century, the government shut down *Radio Catolica*.

The station was broadcasting comments by leading church officials, including Archbishop Obando y Bravo which were blatantly supporting the Contra. Opponents accused the Sandinistas, however, of specifically curbing mention of two biblical passages, Luke 19:41, in which Christ laments for Jerusalem, and Matthew 5:10 where Christ blesses the persecuted. It wasn't those gospels, or even their message, that was censored, but inflammatory comments by a bishop that accompanied them. The Sandinistas were accused of blacking out all news of the Pope's 1983 visit or even mentioning his name, which was nonsense. (See Chapter Thirteen on church relations.)

The press war of ideas extended far beyond Central America. United States newspapers gave their usual "objective" coverage to visiting defenders of the oppressors in the region, usually in a clumsy effort to balance the stories they published of the other side. When Young Americans for Freedom, a rightwing activist group that sporadically carried the word for the Latin oligarchs, brought an El Salvador editor to the country in 1982 he was given a respectful hearing of his views. The guerrillas of El Salvador are financed and trained by outside Communists, said Enrique Altamirano Madriz, editor-publisher of the newspaper *El Diario de Hoy*, a sorry rag that hid one-paragraph stories of major battles costing scores of dead inside the society pages. Those communists, Altamirano said, raise funds by "disseminating propaganda in their favor."

In one of his talks Altamirano said he had tried and failed to find the site of a massacre reported in United States newspapers, implying that it never happened. Twelve years later foreign forensic investigators unearthed hundreds of bodies with wounds clearly indicating gun shots. That was the Dec. 11, 1981 massacre at El Mozote in which perhaps one thousand men, women and children were slain. It was well documented by Ray Bonner, of the *New York Times*, and by Alma Guillermoprieto of the *Washington Post*.[17]

---

[17] Raymond Bonner, Weakness and Deceit: US Policy and El Salvador, Time Books, 1984.

Bonner's report on that atrocity, and some of his other stories roused the wrath of United States Ambassador Deane Hinton and the chief U.S. military advisor to El Salvador at that time. Bonner got into a shouting match with Hinton at an embassy party for the press and not long afterward *The Times* pulled him out of Central America and put him to re-writing press releases for the business page in New York. *The Times* has denied that Bonner's reassignment was the result of State Department pressure. "That's bullshit," A. M. Rosenthal, then executive editor, told one writer. "That just doesn't happen." That's not what Bonner told me but he hinted that it was done with more finesse, in a roundabout way. He soon quit and wrote a book.

Altamirano, who got his newspaper the way most American publishers do, by inheriting it from his father, offered the world a scoop on his trip that even American newspapers were not credulous enough to accept: communists in Nicaragua had claimed responsibility for the murder of El Salvador Bishop Oscar Romero in his pulpit, he said. Romero's 1980 murder was carried out by a Salvadoran right wing death squad, according to President Jose Napoleon Duarte who accused Arena Party Leader Roberto d'Aubuisson of being the instigator. Finally, Altamirano said changes forced onto El Salvador by former President Jimmy Carter, in banking and agriculture, apparently a reference to land reform, were responsible for most of the country's problems.

Other propagandists from Central America who toured the United States were a little more credible, but the views of Altamirano, a grandson of one of Anastasio Somoza's handpicked presidents of Nicaragua, were a reflection of the thinking of the oligarchy that still runs El Salvador. That his ravings were given space in American newspapers tells as much about them as it does about him. I don't know if the State Department clamped down or what happened, but I never heard of other Salvadoran editors touring editorial boards in this country after Altamirano's 1982 visit.

Another El Salvadoran newspaper, *El Mundo*, did at

least at times try to tell what was going on, but its attempts at truthfulness seem to have made it nearly invisible, even to the American wire services who normally pick up, re-write and distribute local stories world wide. In 1985 *El Mundo* carried what I thought was one of the most interesting stories to come out of that country's long war. It reported on the front page December 5 that a unit of special air troops had the day before captured a guerrilla medical aid station in Morazan Department. A French woman doctor was killed, "rifle in hand," holding off the attackers until six other foreign women, including two nuns, were able to escape.

In the women's knapsacks, the story said, the soldiers found items of women's clothing, cosmetics and other feminine articles. Also in the clinic's detritus were boxes of Marxist-Leninist books for reading by guerrilla fighters treated there. The identity of the French woman would be revealed later, an armed forces spokesman said. That was all. I was never able to learn if the armed forces did reveal the name of the woman, or the disposition of her body or whether she was buried there or returned to France. No mention of her appeared in any newspaper during the next two weeks I was in El Salvador. Neither was there any later speculation in *El Mundo* or any other papers, so far as I could find out, about what happened to the other six foreign women or whether the story was even true. None of the correspondents for American wire services knew of the story and as far as I could determine none tried to check it out.

Another time when I arrived in El Salvador I bought a newspaper, again *El Mundo*, and read a one-paragraph story of an ambush by the guerrillas in which twenty seven Army soldiers had died. I went to the office of one of the American wire services and asked to read the daily report, all that day's stories ripped off the Teletype machine and fastened to a clipboard hanging on a wall in the bureau's office in the Hotel Camino Real. It was a standard practice of mine, as well as other travelling reporters, in any of those countries. There was no story of the ambush and I asked the bureau chief, an American, why not. Apparently my question was couched in what seemed to be an accusatory tone or the bureau chief was embarrassed at not having filed a report on the incident. "I have a lot of other things to do," was the answer.

I shrugged and left, realizing that there was no point in making a case over the issue. But it seemed to me then, and still does, that few things could have been of more interest about El Salvador to the wire service's clients outside the country that day than another major ambush of conscript soldiers of the inept Army. So far as I could determine, neither of those stories was ever reported in the American press. It illustrates the sad truth that not all the sins of omission were committed by editors back home; some correspondents assigned to cover news in those countries also neglected their duty to readers. It may have been that the bureau chief knew that any story would have been trashed once it reached headquarters in New York. That does not excuse a failure to check it and pass it on.

One of the frustrations of covering events in Central America, or other foreign areas for that matter, is the coy attitude of the State Department. Interviews are almost always "off the record" or "for background only," no matter how innocuous questions, and their answers, might be. In 1982 I asked for an interview with Anthony Quainton, the United States ambassador to Nicaragua and got the "background only" restriction. I decided that if I couldn't quote him I didn't want to talk to him. Several days later I got a call at my hotel from the embassy information officer saying Quainton would like to talk to me but our conversation must still be off the record. I'd cooled off by then and had also talked to more people and had more questions, so I made an appointment. As I entered the embassy the next morning the metal detector just inside the door squawked about the small tape recorder I was carrying in my shirt pocket, a gadget I had purchased especially for my trip. "You'll have to check it, sir," said the Marine guard.

"It's just a tape recorder," I protested. "I certainly couldn't hurt the ambassador with it." The Marine summoned the information officer.

"The ambassador does not give interviews on the record," he said. "The ambassador won't talk to television crews."

"I agreed it would be off the record," I told him. "This is not a television camera. It's a note taking device. Surely the ambassador would want me to get my quotes straight."

"You can't take it in to the interview," he said.

"To hell with it," I told him. "I've already compromised by agreeing not to quote him." After a few more words, some of them even more rancorous, I left.

I learned later that if I had been part of a touring group I could have listened to Quainton on the record and taped his comments. *Sojourner*, an ecumenical religious magazine whose editor apparently had no instructions not to quote Quainton, reported what the ambassador was telling everyone who visited except the working press. Other Americans were doing it all the time and so I made the acquaintance of some of them and listened to their tapes and cribbed from their notes and wrote my stories. A Nicaraguan friend gave me a several weeks old copy of *La Prensa* which carried a very long interview piece with Quainton in which he freely discussed what the State Department saw as problems of dealing with the Sandinistas. I quoted from that. In later trips I did meet Quainton and found him to be a sensitive representative of this country. The dumb limit on quotes was not his, I realized even then, but came from a constipated bureaucracy in Washington, D. C. that was so afraid of the administration, any administration, and of Congress that it was unable to realize that intelligent people like Quainton were not about to reveal any national secrets.

Some newspapers and at times some television stations did significant work covering Reagan's wars. The *Miami Herald*, until Cuban fanatics in South Florida began their own version of censorship, showed great courage. But it was a reporter's war, not an editor's; the good coverage was often published in spite of editorial nervousness. Many great stories lie in city room computer dump files.

7

Cuba, Quickly

MY SOVIET AIRLINER ENTERED CUBAN AIRSPACE IN A TROPICAL storm, buckets of rain washing over the windows. As I looked at the flooded pastures below, the stewardess passed out customs cards and I was forced to a decision. What was I to be? As I filled out my card I paused at the space asking my profession. Was I a newspaper reporter or a sewing machine salesman?

I was preparing to make a swing through Central America in 1982 to see how the Sandinista revolution was progressing in Nicaragua and what was happening in the war in El Salvador. On my way home I would drop in on Fidel Castro. I had arranged to go to Washington, D. C. for several weeks first to do some stories for my newspaper, the Seattle *Post-Intelligencer*, on what the Washington State congressional delegation was up to. I could get a Cuban visa and pursue some Central American contacts.

The Cuban interest section (the Cold War euphemism for embassy) in Washington stalled on whether I could have a visa. Why did I want to go to Cuba? the *charge'e d'affaires* wanted to know. I told him of the stories I'd read about Cuba's progress. They were true, he assured me. I said I wanted to see for myself, so I could write about it in my newspaper. The *charge'* said I would have to submit a letter outlining my reasons, together with my planned date of arrival and how long I would be there and where I would stay. I wrote the letter although I felt I was violating my principles in bending to a news source's demands. Even then the answer was no. Sorry, but a big international conference was planned just then and there would be no accommodations for casual visitors like me. The real reason, I was sure, was that I was a reporter. Uncle Sam forbid me to go to Cuba; Comrade Castro didn't want me there either.

The *charge'*, perhaps stung by the scorn mustered in my daily visits to the gloomy offices of the interest section, had an inspiration when I told him I would be in Nicaragua. "When you get to Managua go to the Cuban embassy and we will have an answer for you, one way or another. There will either be a visa there for you or a message telling you that you can't go to Cuba." He was sure that six weeks from then my visa would be approved.

Near the end of my tour I hitchhiked to the Cuban embassy outside Managua which, of course, had never heard of me. But the much friendlier *charge'* there had a solution. If I would stay in Cuba no longer than three days, he said, a tourist card he could supply me was sufficient. Three days was better than nothing and he helped get my ticket changed from Iberia, the Spanish airline, to Cubano and was at the Augusto Sandino International Airport the next morning to help me get aboard.

Now, as the plane descended through the downpour, I pondered what to put down for profession. I thought of the possibility of spending the next five years breaking rocks on the Isle of Pines. Fear made me honest. I wrote *periodista* in the blank.

My concern was justified; I never got through customs at Jose Marti Airport.

◆ ◆ ◆

Fidel Castro's New Year's 1959 conquest of Cuba captured world wide admiration. The country, under dictator Fulgencio Batista had become an American whorehouse, with Cuban girls the livestock, and a Mafia gambling den for tourists. Castro's easy victory, with Batista taking the usual Latin tyrant's out and fleeing the country as his sorry army threw down its arms, was a heroic accomplishment.

The good feeling didn't last. Screams by United States rightwingers that Castro was a communist didn't turn me off; even then I knew that those people were ready to call anyone a communist who refused to genuflect to the United States. I doubted Castro's ability to undermine the western hemisphere but my view soured also when he began shooting anyone who differed with him. Some of Batista's thugs deserved punishment, but Castro launched a "people's tribunals" blood bath and stood thousands of Cubans, innocent as well as guilty, against the nearest wall. By contrast, it should be remembered, when the Sandinistas came to power twenty years later in Nicaragua after throwing out their own tyrant, Anastasio Somoza, one of their first acts was to abolish the death penalty.

Castro learned early that the way to solidify his hold on Cubans and gain stature with his neighbors was to give a hard yank now and then to Uncle Sam's beard. Denouncing Yanquis is always a sure crowd pleaser for Latin politicians. I doubt, in spite of testimony to the contrary, that Castro was a dedicated communist when he first came to power. He made his overtures to the Soviets after President Dwight Eisenhower, just before he left office in 1961, imposed an oil embargo on Cuba. That first preemptive strike of an economic war that continued into the nineties came two years after Castro's triumphant march into Havana. President John F. Kennedy, perhaps because he was a Democrat and felt he had to prove his anti-communism even more fiercely than the Republican Eisenhower, ratcheted up the pressure on Castro and made him a permanent enemy. I believe a calm approach to Castro would have avoided decades of conflict and many deaths and much misery for the Cuban people.

If Castro had contemplated an independent course in the world he soon learned it was impossible. The United States was not going to leave him alone and his only option was to seek a patron. The Soviet Union jumped at the chance to bedevil the United States in its own backyard. The price, for the Soviets, was cheap, a few billion rubles and some obsolete tanks and other weapons and a guaranteed supply of the oil that the Soviet Union had in abundance. As relations deteriorated, both the United States and Castro profited, in their own perverse demagogic ways, by each making the other the public demon responsible for their own stupidities.

Certainly Castro used classic communist techniques to keep the people of Cuba in line. At the same time, however, he brought vast changes to Cuba, many of them good, changes that would never have been inaugurated by the indigenous ruling class had a Castro not existed. Castro's rule has been totalitarian and in some respects flagrantly in violation of the civil rights of the Cuban people, perhaps worse than before. But except for the Cuban upper and middle classes, most of whom fled after Castro came to power, the average Cuban had few rights under Batista.

It was in trying to view Castro's beneficial changes that I encountered first hand his crudity that brooked no freedom of thought. My punishment was inconvenience, but had I been a Cuban I would have had to pay dearly for my crime. Cuba, from what I was reading in those days, was undermining the governments of its neighbors by "exporting revolution." I had been one of the first officers assigned to Army Special Forces (Green berets) when it was organized and I had learned, both in the Special Forces school and from practical experience in Korea, that guerrilla revolutionary armies are always home grown.

Castro was correct when he said revolution cannot be exported. Revolution is indigenous, rising from intolerable conditions, usually among conservative peoples, something those American Castros of the right have never learned. Too bad for his friend Che Cuevara that Castro failed to impress on him that truism before Guevara went off to free Bolivian tin miners who were not ready to die for a liberty they barely comprehended and certainly not on the suggestion of a stranger. While outsiders might capitalize on local unrest and even finance and arm rebellious cadres, revolution is always local. Lafayette and Von Stueben contributed to the

American Revolution, but they did not import it.

Castro certainly helped the Sandinistas when they were preparing to overthrow Somoza. But it is nonsense to think that his help was decisive, any more than the little aid Cuba gave to the El Salvador guerrillas made a difference in that long war. Soviet Union support for the Sandinistas, with weapons, munitions and helicopters, was likely decisive in their victory over the Contra, recruited, trained, paid and hand held by the United States. But Soviet help didn't bring the Sandinistas to power nor did Castro.

I wanted to find out the truth of Cuba in Cuba itself. I had already begun to understand that the Cuban export that was making the United States nervous was not guns and military trainers. It was in its example, in the idea that a Latin country could, if its people were sufficiently resolute, make their own destiny in spite of their rich uncle.

Most importantly, I also wanted to explore for myself the truth of accounts I had read, chiefly in obscure newspapers and magazines, of the immense strides Castro's government was making in health care and education. Was it true that he had wiped out prostitution and beggary? Did Cuban children, unlike those in all other Latin America, all get enough to eat? Were they all going to school? How was Castro able to send doctors, nurses, teachers, engineers and technicians of all kinds to other countries?

All we in the United States heard of in the general press were stories of the soldiers Castro was sending to Angola and Ethiopia and, supposedly, guerrilla organizers to other countries. Yet I knew he was sending those other, peaceful and constructive, people, too, and that Cuban builders were putting up houses for the poor in several countries. Cuban scientists were making real breakthroughs in medicine which other Latin American countries envied. I wanted to see how this small country was able to do those things that I believe my own country should be doing. Was it only Russian money that enabled Castro to educate his whole country? If it was, why hadn't the United States sent the money, adding its own tilt, rather than savaging whoever attempted to lift the eyes and hearts of Latin Americans?

I wasn't alone in wondering how Cuba had done what no other Latin American nation had accomplished. Robert McNamara, former Secretary of Defense under President John Kennedy and later president of the World Bank, at a meeting in Cuba in 1991 to discuss the 1962 Cuban missile crisis, praised Cuban advances in health care and education. Cuban infant mortality, he said, is less than that of Washington, D. C. "I spent 13 years at the World Bank trying to make similar progress (in other Third World countries) and I did not," McNamara said.[18]

◆ ◆ ◆

As I stood in the customs line at Jose Marti Airport a young man in a smart uniform tapped me on the shoulder and motioned me to follow him. In a small office to the side of the terminal a pudgy official of some importance asked for my airline ticket. I showed him the ticket for Mexico City on Mexicana Airlines. He took it and my passport and the tourist card and said "just a moment."

It was three hours before he returned. "I am sorry," he said, handing the ticket and passport back to me. "You cannot enter Cuba; you will have to leave on the next plane."

"But I have a tourist card," I protested.

"It does not matter," he said. "You have an open (undated) ticket. Cuban law says if you come into this country with an open ticket you must leave immediately, on the first plane."

"That's ridiculous," I said. "I travel with an open ticket all the time, to all kinds of countries. I have a ticket on Mexicana. Let me use your telephone and I'll get it dated for three days from now."

"That is not permitted," he said.

"I can't use your telephone to make a call?"

"No. You will have to leave on the next plane."

We argued for a time and I saw I was getting nowhere. This man had his orders and he obviously couldn't deviate from them.

---

[18] John Newhouse, The New Yorker, April 27, 1992, p.73.

"All right," I said. "When is the next Mexicana plane for Mexico City?"

"The next plane leaving Jose Marti is going to Managua," he said. "You must be on it."

"But I just came from Managua," I protested. I knew that he knew that, but my indignation was beginning to make me reckless. "I'm not going back to Managua. Surely there's a Mexicana plane to Mexico soon."

"I will see," he said, and again left the room, returning a half hour later. "There is a Mexicana flight in the morning," he said. "But you will need a Mexican visa."

"No," I told him. "I am an American citizen and I don't need a visa to get into Mexico." I mentioned something about Mexico being a civilized country.

"You need a Mexican visa if you come from Cuba," he said. "That is a Mexican law; it is not ours." He was almost apologetic.

"How can I get a Mexican visa?"

Again he left the room. When he returned in another half hour there was a half smile was on his face.

"We will get a taxi for you," he said. "You can go to the Mexican consulate. You can get your visa there. The driver will take you there and bring you back here. You will leave your luggage here."

Rain was pouring down when I ran out of the airport to the almost brand new red Lada, a small Russian car, that drove up to the curb. The taxi driver was friendly and I asked him to give me a tour on the way to the Mexican consulate which, it turned out, was not necessary since he didn't know where it was anyway. So we drove into Havana in the driving rain, through car-jolting potholes, past scores of Cubans with their thumbs out for a ride. That part of Havana had obviously once been a rather posh area but even through the sheets of rain I saw signs of neglect in the mansions that lined the street. Lawns were unkept, cement curbs and walls were chipped and scarred and trash lay in the gutters. It was five o'clock, quitting time in Havana, and hundreds of Cubans stood at bus stops holding newspapers over their heads against the rain. The few cars we met on the streets were all of 1950s vintage, a sight that has tickled the fancy of nearly every American writer visiting Cuba in the Castro era.

Eventually, after several inquiries, we found the consulate and I dashed inside through the rain. Indoors, the building was elegant with marble floors and statuary and a broad staircase. A beautiful young woman asked me, in English, for my business, and I told her I needed a Mexican visa. She looked doubtful but rang someone on the phone and then beckoned me into an office. The man there also spoke English and he listened sympathetically to my story.

"It would take me three days to get you a visa," he said. "But Americans don't need visas to enter Mexico."

"Tell that to the Cubans," I said.

"Yes," he mused. "They sometimes do not understand." He opened a drawer in his desk and took out a lined pad of paper and, opening my passport, filled in the lines.

"But this is a tourist card," I said.

"Show it to them," the consul said. "They will never know the difference."

So back I went to the airport through the rain and paid the taxi driver a United States $10 bill. No one ever asked to see my visa, or tourist card, and I am convinced that the only reason I was hustled out so quickly was that I was a reporter, a *periodista*. So I spent that night sitting in the terminal watching waves of passengers departing Cuba. What passed as a snack bar sold only American Coca Cola and some foul-tasting and heavily sugared candy bars, all selling only for dollars. I bought a copy of Granma, the official Cuban newspaper, certainly the most dismal paper in appearance and content I've ever seen, and had to pay for it with a United States dollar. And although I think that I and two Englishmen who passed through the terminal that night were the only English-speaking people there, all the announcements were in Spanish and English only. A duty free shop, which was selling American-made electric razors and other gadgets, also accepted only dollars.

My only entertainment that night was the running show put on by departing Russian families. The men all seemed to weigh three hundred pounds, the women two hundred and the children at least one hundred each. They came with enough luggage to stock a dacha and I wondered what they could possibly be carrying. Some of them wheeled hand trucks with boxes stacked eight feet high across the floor to the check-in counters. Most of the boxes bore vodka labels and I puzzled over the seeming paradox of Russians taking vodka home from Cuba.

For hours they came until finally the wheels on one hand truck jammed and the whole tower of boxes toppled to the floor with a hell of a crash. Then I found out; the boxes, having served as vodka containers when the Russians arrived, were now carrying Cuban rum back home. Many bottles were broken in the crash and all through the rest of that night newcomers to the terminal were lifting their feet in exaggerated, jerky steps off the sticky floor.

Even El Salvador, which made visas hard to obtain for the "internationalists" that plagued its army while it was murdering what it called subversives, didn't make access as difficult as Cuba did. But Castro had no need to be mannerly to American visitors, especially those he hadn't invited and would not agree to do their visiting in supervised tour groups. The Salvador Army, on the other hand, had always to look over its shoulder lest Uncle Sam might be watching, although usually he wasn't.

If Castro's refusal to grant any democratic opening for the people of Cuba was self-defeating, what can one say in assessing United States policy toward Cuba? It consisted of a trade embargo, extended illegally to bully other western nations as well, a ban on travel by Americans to the island and backing for some of the most virulent anti-democratic elements, in the Cuban exile community in Miami, that the United States has ever supported.

I wasn't alone in my belief that United States policy was the major factor in Castro's long hold on his people. "The primary effect of the U.S. economic blockade over the past 32 years, besides violating Cuba's right to self-determination, has been to bolster the internal solidarity of the Castro regime and build popular support for it in Cuba and Latin America...(and) has allowed Castro to rally Cubans by appealing to their nationalist sentiments and opposition to U.S. imperialism."[19]

Aside from its Cuban victims the United States policy's chief effect was on American companies denied trade with Cuba and those moderate Cubans in Miami who dared to speak reasonably. The policy seems to have been dictated as much by the personal ambitions of hard-right Cuban exile leaders as anything resembling a thought-out foreign policy. In the boiling intrigue that was and is Miami, Cuban exiles on the right, through browbeating and other tactics that would have made Castro envious, assumed a self-appointed role as spokespersons for all the exiles. The leader of this gang was Jorge Mas Canosa, a Miami contractor who intended to be president of a "liberated" Cuba if someone else would just liberate it, the United States Army, for instance.

Mas Canosa's radio broadcasts brought out Miami's own version of Nicaragua's *turbas divinas*, the "divine mobs." They smeared shit on news boxes owned by the *Miami Herald*, one of the most courageous newspapers in the country, and tried to cow the paper into writing only the views approved by the Cuban American National Foundation, headed by Mas Canosa. Death threats, even in the newspaper letters columns, were commonplace. The paper's publisher, Richard Capen, buckled under, however, in the 1990 election. He rejected his editorial staff's suggestion that the paper endorse Gerald Richman, a Democrat, but instead backed Republican Illeana Ros-Lehtinen, a Cuban-born state senator, for an open United States House seat. Capen said failure to endorse Ros-Lehtinen would result in financial losses for the newspaper.[20]

If there was any difference in the approach to the politics of Mas Canosa and Fidel Castro it was difficult to de-

---

[19] Samuel Farber, World Policy Journal, Spring, 1992, p.344.
[20] The Washington Monthly, February, 1990.

tect. Mas Canosa and his ilk made South Florida a reflection of the worst of Latin American intolerance of differing views, and their tirades against the *Herald* and other newspapers that tried to tell the truth of the struggles going on in that part of the world are chilling indeed. Freedom of the press has no place in their version of a democracy enforced at the point of a gun or by mob rule. The Cuban right in Miami has created "a political climate in which civil liberties have become seriously endangered. Given the Cuban establishment's record in Miami, we can only expect the worst if it were to take power in Cuba with U.S. support."[21]

While official America was raging at terrorists around the world through the 1970s and 1980s, the Bush Administration was protecting a Cuban who in 1976 planted a bomb in a Cuban airliner flying out of Barbados. Seventy three people died. Orlando Bosch has been accused of dozens of other bombings, yet in 1990 the Justice Department turned him loose after heavy lobbying by George Bush's son, Jeb Bush, and Senator Connie Mack. The United States has consistently refused a Cuban request for his extradition. That bombing prompted nothing like the media frenzies that followed the destruction of other airliners by what were believed to be enemies of the United States. In fact, it was barely covered. These omissions do not go unnoticed by resentful Latins.[22]

Many Cuban exiles did well in their Castro diaspora. A number of them teamed up with the Somoza family that ruled and misruled Nicaragua for so long. The last Somoza entered into a deal with Miami Cubans in the 1960s to consolidate into large tobacco plantations lands taken from peasants in northern Nicaragua. The Sandinistas took over that land after Nicaragua's 1979 revolutionary triumph and gave it back to the people. It was at least partly a desire to recover that property that energized the Miami Cubans to support the Contra, the very overt covert army organized by the United States to terrorize Nicaragua. Other Cubans went into government in the United States, many into the

---

[21] Farber, p.346.
[22] Jeff Cohen and Norman Solomon, Creators Syndicate, Inc., April 1992.

138

State Department where their influence was felt in embassies all over Latin America, but especially in Central America.

An example of the unthinking, almost hysterical response to right wing exile demands was an amendment proposed in 1989 by Senator Mack, a Florida Republican who usually jumped when the Cuban right snapped its fingers. The amendment was to forbid foreign subsidiaries of American companies from trading with Cuba, a provision removed from the law fourteen years earlier when its pernicious effects became evident. But Mack and others such as Senator Jesse Helms eager to curry favor with the extremist exiles plunged ahead in spite of warnings that the amendment would create serious problems not only for the companies involved but for such trading allies as Canada, Mexico and Argentina who would have been forced to choose sides in our spite war with Cuba. "Several (senators) subsequently acknowledged that they had been unaware of the executive branch's opposition, or of all the measure's ramifications. But the result was the same: It passed."[23]

For a time in the early 1990s a gradual shift in United States Cuban policy could be detected if one studied the political columnists who often purvey policy or trial balloons in exchange for inside tips. Suddenly there was a trend to recognizing that one way to neutralize Castro would be to relax the United States' persecution as many experts on Latin affairs had long advocated. Two years after the collapse of communism in Eastern Europe the United States began showing signs of a rational reassessment of its policy toward Castro, the idiocy of its position becoming evident even to earlier apologists. As one of them explained: "The United States has basically formulated no policy of its own toward Cuba because of fear of losing Republican votes in Florida."

Jeb Bush was for years the unofficial conduit between his father's advisers and the exile community where he is a

[23] Wayne Smith, one of the unsung stalwarts at the State Department who tried to report accurately on Latin America. At one time represented the U.S. in Havana in our interest section; The Christian Science Monitor, Oct. 20, 1989.

fixture, an ambassador almost with portfolio to the administration. He conducted the campaign in early 1991 that led to the United Nations placing a human rights monitor on Cuba.[24] He also lobbied the Immigration and Naturalization Service to grant political asylum to Nicaraguan refugees, thus keeping them from deportation at a time when refugees from El Salvador death squads were being sent back to their homes, and to death, they said.

Both Ronald Reagan and George Bush courted the extremist Cuban exiles for votes. Bill Clinton, notorious for his co-optation of Republican endeavors, also traded support to the Cuban exiles for campaign money. Clinton tightened the noose around Castro's neck, joining Helms in his grim crusade of viciousness. Would establishing normal relations with Cuba in the 1980s or 1990s have relaxed Castro's grip? No one will ever know, but if the drumbeaters of trade as a civilizing influence are correct, the United States could have long since have dried up support for Castro at home.

A series of administrations took the hard road, apparently never pondering any other course. None ever seemed to consider how their policy read in Latin America. Castro's defiance of the Yanquis had long made him a hero. Cheers went up from The Rio Grande to Tierra del Fuego when Castro in 1961 humiliated the band of exiles who called themselves an army and expected a walk over when they landed at Cuba's Bay of Pigs.

Veterans of that fiasco have been causing mischief for this country, under the auspices of the CIA, ever since. No one will likely ever know all the clandestine foolishness they and the CIA carried on after 1961, but it is known that there were attempts to assassinate Castro, probably by Mafia hit men. One effort to humiliate Castro by somehow making his beard fall out was appropriate to the effort. Did the CIA introduce biological agents against Cuban crops? I don't know, but some Cubans think so and given the CIA's record who can dismiss the idea?

Among other efforts unworthy of a great nation to

---

[24] Christopher Marquis, Miami Herald, March 26,1991.

keep up pressure on Cuba was Radio Marti, sponsored by the United States and named for a martyred 19th Century Cuban revolutionary hero and writer. It was a direct interference in Cuban internal affairs and so was its successor, TV Marti.

Enemies of Cuba were handed a triumph by Castro in 1989 when he accused his top general, Arnaldo Ochoa, the capable commander of Cuban troops in Angola, of drug running and corruption. Ochoa, apparently in a deal to spare his family, put up no defense at his trial and was shot, with three subordinates. If Ochoa was dealing in drugs and Castro didn't know it, El Supremo was losing his grip for sure. Most observers of the Cuba scene, whether detractors or defenders, believe there was another reason, probably that Castro thought the popular Ochoa presented some danger to himself. In any event the judicial murder of Ochoa further proved that Castro, in spite of his obvious ability and the truly impressive advances he brought to Cuba, was, under it all, really just another Latin American caudillo, ruling by fear and with his major consideration his own political skin.

Castro himself has denounced corruption in his Cuba although it is probably on a lesser scale than in many other Latin countries, Mexico for instance. He never learned that the only cure for the corruption that is always latent except for an initial euphoria following a revolution, is a press free to ask embarrassing questions. For Castro, any questioning was treason and so the Cuban people, and he also probably never knew who was stealing and getting away with it.

Accusations have been made over the years that Cuba, including Castro and his brother, Raul, were involved in the drug trade. These stories never seemed to jell and there was never any follow up, none of the hammering at an issue that two Republican administrations brought to bear on other drug alarms. In Cuba's case, the charges would be made and the accusers would move on to something else.

Castro was accused for decades of supplying weapons, mostly those he got from his Soviet friends, to guerrillas in Central America. But unlike the arms charges, which were persistent, the drug stories never went anywhere. United States drug police, whether in the Drug Enforcement Administration, the Customs Service or one of the other stumbling agencies assigned to the job, were better at dreaming up excuses for why drugs were flooding American streets than they were at catching the drug king pins.

One reason for the Bush Administration's slight relaxation of its hard line isolation of Cuba for a time was an increased prospect of trade by European and other nations, bypassing American companies. Cuba, said a *New York Times* business page story, with its strategic metals, rich croplands and pristine beaches "is seen by many corporate executives and academics as a country in need of almost wholesale economic reconstruction but also as a land of potentially bright opportunity." Hostility by the Miami exiles, the story said, gives pause to American entrepreneurs, but once lobbyists begin showing balance sheets and bar graphs that nervousness will be overcome. Castro had already signaled interest in doing business with American companies and he had angered some Cubans by opening up hard dollar stores for the tourist trade which were closed to Cubans themselves. He's not totally unaware of capitalist values.

The break-up of the Soviet Union meant Cuba would have to quit its oil thirst cold turkey. Cuba compensated, partially at least, by turning to bicycles imported from China, to the delight of many Cubans who found them better for commuting and handier for getting around. Macho Latin men have long scorned bicycles as beneath them, and introducing them into Nicaragua was difficult. But Cuba's Chinese bikes sold so well the country turned to bicycle manufacturing itself, a development that raises questions of why that sort of thing hadn't happened earlier.

Castro's greatest failure, from his own standpoint, may have been that failure to diversify the Cuban economy. There is no excuse, for instance, for a country with Cuba's rich soils running short of basic foods. But that is what happened. While sugar cane went unharvested in the fields, beans and corn were rationed for Cubans. Castro's Soviet buddies, with their generous gifts of oil and machine tools, lulled him into a dangerous complacency.

When I was kicked out of Cuba I never got first hand answers to my questions. But later I did get a glimpse of the results of Castro's positive achievements in Nicaragua where those trained Cubans who had piqued my curiosity were putting to use their skills in day to day good works that ignored international politics and intrigue. They were asked to volunteer for assignments abroad as a way of repaying the costs of their quality educations, they said.

It was difficult for me, an American reporter, to talk to the Cubans there but a friend of mine, who worked for years in Matagalpa, befriended a twenty seven-year-old Cuban doctor, who had extended his original two-year hitch in Nicaragua after marrying a local woman. "Your full salary is paid to your family in Cuba while you're away, and you're maintained completely by the government while you're on your assignment," Candido Barreto said. "It's a great program for us young people. We learn about the world and we give something to less developed countries. Lots of us take part in it."[25]

Some 600 Cubans were divided into teams of twenty five assigned to each of Nicaragua's twenty departments (states). "All of us work in town now," Barreto said, "since the countryside became just too dangerous for us. The Contra went out of their way to kill Cubans." When he arrived in Nicaragua, he said, there had also been about a thousand Cuban teachers there, "but so many of them were killed by the Contra out in the rural areas that the program was suspended altogether. There aren't any Cuban teachers in Nicaragua anymore."

Berreto said Cuba had some 800 military people, mostly technicians, in Nicaragua, but he scoffed when told that the United States set their numbers at 10,000. "Reagan is obviously distorting our presence here for his own purposes," he said, when told that the United States considered people like himself as soldiers too. Doctors, like everyone else in Cuba,

---

[25] Tony Equale, Unpublished, Philadelphia, March, 1986.

were trained to shoot a rifle, Berreto said. "I can handle a rifle but not much more than that."

From 1991 on, speculating on Cuba's, and Castro's future was a popular diversion for newspaper columnists and television pundits of the global kind. Most could barely restrain their glee in anticipating the kind of end sure to come to both very soon. One popular theme was that while older Cubans had come to enjoy their social safety net, cheap housing and health care, the youth were embracing American rock and roll and blue jeans and baseball, long the national sport. That doesn't mean, however, that they will welcome United States capitalism any more than the people of Russia, after the Soviet Union's breakup, were accepting it.

How will the Miami Cubans, entrepreneurs all, divvy up the country if their surrogates are the 82nd Airborne? Will they even have a role if island residents expel Castro? Who owns the properties taken over from the exiles and parceled out to Cubans who remained? Answering that question could make solutions to El Salvador's land ownership disputes tame by comparison.

8

Our Toad

ON ONE SIDE OF THE BROAD STONE SIDEWALK WAS A SEAWALL and beyond it the dark blue Bay of Panama, a shimmering chop as dazzling to the eye as a flamenco gown. On the land side a four-lane parkway bordered with palm trees and gleaming bank buildings was noisy with midday traffic. Tiers of pastel mansions and upper middle-class apartments climbed the hill beyond. It was hot in the mid-afternoon sun and when I heard behind me the sound of running footsteps I moved nearer to the seawall to let the runners pass.

A sudden blow to the middle of my back, just below the neck, knocked me to my knees at the same time a hand ripped my rear wallet pocket downward. I grabbed the outside of the pocket and attempted to rise, only to be kicked in the side and knocked flat. I tried to roll to one side as the mugger clung to my wallet from the inside of the pocket, while I held on from the outside. Four black teenagers, yelling and cursing, were kicking me as I got to my feet, only to be knocked down again, still holding onto my wallet. This time a foot caught me in the right ear.

"Policia, policia!" I yelled as a police car drove slowly by, its two occupants only mildly interested spectators to the Gringo beating. But after probably no more than a minute several civilian drivers on the parkway did stop and come to my aid. My attackers fled, dodging through the cars, across the street and up an alley. My shirt was spattered with blood, my own, and my left pant leg was ripped nearly off. Panamanians surrounded me, apologizing, denouncing the four hoodlums and offering help. I accepted a ride to my hotel where I washed the blood from my hands and face and staunched the trickle from deep inside my ear.

That mugging, early in 1978, could have happened anywhere, certainly in the United States, and I attributed no specific reason for it beyond a desire for quick loot on the part of the muggers. I doubt if it had any political implication although since those teenagers were black there might have been a racial aspect to it. Of more interest to me once my blood pressure came down was that it occurred just across the street from the doors of one of Panama's hundreds of banks, most of which line Avenida Balboa, the bay side drive. It was here, a decade before President George Bush sent my old outfit, the 82nd Airborne Division, into Panama to prove he was no wimp and to capture his former buddy Manuel Noriega, that I got my first personal lesson in United States foreign affairs, Latin American division.

Why, I wondered, did Panama have so many banks? Its population, while perhaps on average a bit more affluent because of the Canal payrolls than other Central Americans, certainly couldn't sustain so much commerce. Few Panamanians even had checking accounts. The answer came from three minor staffers at the United States Embassy there who told me, for "background only," as is the custom with embassy people, that those banks were money launderers. "You know the Mafia and drug kingpins hide their money in Switzerland, don't you?" they asked. Sure. "Well, this is where they put it when they don't want even the Swiss to know about it." This was even before drug imports from Latin America became a major social and political issue in the United States.

Americans with shady backgrounds could even purchase Panamanian diplomatic immunity for the right price, I had already discovered. Back in the late 1950s a Washington, D. C. wheeler dealer obtained a Panamanian diplomatic passport, countersigned by United States Secretary of State Livingston Merchant, to dodge a summons from a grand jury looking into a multimillion dollar dam construction scandal in my home state of Washington.

Panama is where smugglers of all kinds, from all over Latin America, come to make their deals and to stash their loot and make it legitimate elsewhere via bank wire transfers. Panama, I learned, is only secondarily the home of the isthmian canal; it is first a nest of corruption. I had already heard something of this earlier when I was in Paraguay and saw freighters swinging at anchor in the broad Parana River offshore from the seedy capital, Asuncion. Why, I asked, were ocean-going vessels anchored here a thousand miles from the sea, at a place where there weren't even wharfs big enough for them to dock?

This is the other end of a smuggling axis that runs through Panama, the embassy staff there, and others, told me. Japanese and German television sets, cars, cameras, outboard motors, and American whisky and cigarettes were all loaded at Panama's free zone, at Colon, onto freighters bound for Paraguay. I saw no activity on the river but I learned that at night small boats laid alongside those ships, took on their cargoes and then floated downstream to landings in Argentina and Brazil where they were unloaded without paying the high duties those countries imposed then on most imports. Police in all three countries knew about the trade, the embassy people told me, but the practice is accepted, along with the bribes that go with them. It's part of the custom officer's compensation.

At least half of Paraguay's gross national product comes from smuggling, they said. I never learned if anyone had made a similar estimate for Panama, but it is probably not as great there. Banks and the canal tolls make up a greater portion of GNP. Even so, sub rosa commerce is a major factor in the country's economic life. *Tio Sam* is the heavyweight on the board of directors of corporate Panama. More even than in El Salvador, the United States determines how Panama shall be governed, by whom and, especially, for whom. The refrain, during the 1977-78 debate over a new treaty giving Panama eventual control (nearly) of the canal that cuts it in two, was that "we stole it, we own it." President Teddy Roosevelt promoted a rebellion in 1903 in Colombia's province of Panama and then, when it came, recognized the new country with a bit of cash and quickly signed a treaty to build the canal.

Panama was a beneficiary or the chief victim of Roosevelt's "big stick" policy but through most of the rest of the century the United States kept its influence on Panama's internal affairs quiet. No one cared, outside of a few Panamanian hotheads, that Panamanians weren't in charge of their own destiny. And, especially in comparison with most of its neighbors, Panama was well off, relatively stable politically. Only next-door Costa Rica enjoyed a greater material and governmental equilibrium.

When President Jimmy Carter, listening to demands of Panamanian nationalists, proposed a treaty granting the country control of its chief asset, the canal, Panama suddenly came out of the shadows of Latin American neglect and assumed a temporary importance in world affairs. Americans in Panama, some of them the third generation to work for the Canal Company, were not alone in protesting this threat to their cushy colonial status. Right wingers in the United States howled that Carter was inviting seizure of the canal and a foothold on the American mainland by communists.

The man on the other end of that negotiation was Omar Torrijos, a general of the National Guard more charismatic than most of the Latin bullies who rise to the top of armies in the region and, unlike many of them, politician enough to allow his countrymen to share in some of the nation's wealth, which made him extremely popular. One of his more diligent subordinates was Manuel Noriega.

That Noriega was a thief and a murderer as well as a double dealer was well known to Americans in the country, and in the State Department at the time he was edging his way upward in the National Guard's intelligence apparatus. But he was our thief and murderer and if he did a little business on the side who was the Central Intelligence Agency, under then CIA Director George Bush or whoever, to deny him his chance to profit from his hard work in the trenches of intrigue?

My encounter with Noriega's soldiers occurred late one night on the Costa Rica border. I had long wanted to travel the length of Central America by bus and in 1987 I finally did it, starting in Mexico City and ending up in Panama. Night had fallen when the bus halted at the Las Canoas border crossing into Panama where the head of Dr. Hugo Spadafora, one of Noriega's most outspoken critics, had been found in a mail sack a year earlier. When we pulled up to the customs hut a soldier ordered all passengers off the bus. We were told to collect our baggage and bring it to a row of tables standing under a string of electric lights. I was one of the first ones to retrieve my bag and opened it on the table and watched as the customs inspector poked around in my dirty underwear and then told me to close the bag and put it back on the bus.

That done, I strolled out into the shadows away from the custom station's lights and the insects that danced around them and down the road as the inspectors went through the suitcases and boxes carried by the other passengers. It was a balmy night and the cicadas singing in the surrounding jungle made it a soothing one. As I walked along the road, taking big breaths of the night air, I came to a billboard standing at an oblique angle to the road. I stopped and read it, rather slowly in the dim light. Gradually I made it out: a paean of loyalty to Manuel Noriega, the maximum leader of Panama for whom all his subjects would gladly die. "Manuel," said the message from his loyal followers in the Defense Force across the middle of the billboard, "we will not allow them to do to you what they did to Omar."

I knew this was a reference to Torrijos, Noriega's onetime mentor, who had died in a mysterious airplane crash in 1981. I also knew that in some Central American circles there was a question whether the crash had been arranged by the CIA or by Noriega. Or, one variation had it, had Noriega done the deed for the CIA on whose payroll he had been for years? Or was he freelancing?

I took out my notebook and was copying the message

on the billboard, when I was grabbed by the shoulder and spun around by a man in uniform who also jerked the notebook out of my hand. He began yelling at me, accusing me of spying. Others came up and they all led me back to the bus where the luggage of the last of the passengers was being inspected. The soldier in charge ordered me to take my bag off the bus. I balked and, pretending to believe that he was a customs officer, told him that my bag had already been inspected. One of the actual customs men came up and told me, in English, that the National Guardsmen wanted to search my bag again. That alarmed me, because the customs people hadn't seen, or at least hadn't opened, all the compartments of the bag, including one that held newspaper clippings from Guatemala, El Salvador, Honduras and Nicaragua, many of which would undoubtedly raise the ire of troops loyal to Noriega who was still in his anti-communist phase.

I stalled, the soldiers shouted some more and one pushed me toward the bus. I decided a semi-tough stance was better with these macho types than humble acquiescence and resisted, shoving him back. That brought on more brandishing of rifles, shouts that I was probably a *periodista*, a journalist, and demands that I get the bag and quick.

I turned to the bus to do as they ordered when the driver came up to the officer in charge and said something I couldn't hear. But the customs man joined the conversation and I understood that the driver was saying that he had a bus schedule to keep and that if he left his only gringo passenger out here on the border he might be in trouble. The officer said something to the customs inspector who turned to me and said "get on the bus." That ended that interlude, but I could see how Panamanians were treated when they inadvertently rubbed the military the wrong way. We rumbled on across Panama through the night, and in Panama City I got a hotel room with a double lock on the door.

Most of the thugs the United States has supported overtly or covertly around the world have survived to enjoy the fruits of their subservience. So it must be especially galling to Noriega as he sits out his life in an American jail to know that his real crime was to be our toad at a time when American politicians were discovering that the country's streets were becoming the turf of drug gangsters and an element of the population was feeling threatened by drugs. For the moment, most of the drugs seemed to be coming through Panama although at other times, when political winds blew in other directions, the chief source ranged from the "Golden Triangle" in South Asia, to Marseille, to Columbia. It was also Noriega's misfortune to be in the world's eye as a chief of state tied to an illicit drug trade at a time when Bush was being taunted in newspaper cartoons and editorials as a wimp.

We will never know everything that happened in Bush's splendid little political war in Panama in December of 1989. Months after the invasion the United States Southern Command was still "adjusting"' its figures on United States and Panamanian military killed, and the innocent bystanders, the civilian dead.

Some Panamanians believe the casualty toll of American servicemen was actually much greater than the Pentagon's official figures of 23 dead and 324 wounded, cheap for the double reward of asserting American hegemony over the region and giving the president breast-beating privileges. That figure is probably correct, or nearly so, although confirming it, or proving it wrong, would be nearly impossible. That's one benefit of a professional army, it can keep its secrets much better than a military made up of conscripts.

That United States Command tally also says about 50 Panamanian soldiers died but it was certainly more than that. More pertinent to Panamanians, however, was the number of civilians killed in the invasion. The official United States figure is 202. Many Panamanians, and Americans living in Panama, said the number was far higher. Some, including former United States Attorney General Ramsey Clark, who questioned survivors, believe the civilian toll may have been as many as 7,000 dead.

"It can't be less than 3,000," said Diego Claffey, a Catholic priest from Philadelphia. Father Diego, who shortly after I talked to him left Panama after seventeen years service in the country, often ran in the early morning on a road alongside the enormous Queen of Angels cemetery two blocks from his home.

On the fourth day of the invasion he heard rumblings from the cemetery and saw, through the morning mists, American bulldozers gouging out enormous holes. That evening he inquired of the cemetery manager about the holes and was told that he must be mistaken, there were no holes. But on questioning a grave digger he learned that truckloads of bodies had been dumped there and the holes had been covered and re-sodded, all early in the day. He walked over the ground that evening and saw signs of disturbance where fresh raw earth still had not been washed away in spots. Other Panamanians reported that bodies had been stacked on the beach not far from Noriega's *comandancia* and burned there and the ashes later bulldozed into the water. I am more skeptical of that allegation.

The invasion and Noriega's comic book capture obviously gave a lot of satisfaction to American policy makers and to large numbers of the American public whipped up by Bush's drug war rhetoric. Noriega evaded American soldiers searching everywhere and turned himself over to the papal nuncio in Panama. Then, having endured days and nights of United States Army rock and roll blasted at him, he surrendered.

Noriega's capture changed almost nothing in Panama. When the invasion commander, General Maxwell (Mad Max) Thurman, arranged to have Guillermo Endarra sworn in as president inside a United States military compound he was not just exhibiting thoughtless Yanqui arrogance. One would think he might have hauled the ponderous Endarra out of the barracks and into Panama City proper, to a police station or a garbage transfer point, anywhere on "Panamanian" soil, to drape the presidential sash around his thick neck. The general, who seemed most outraged by Noriega's pornographic magazines, was making a point about End-arra: this is our boy and don't anyone forget it.

The press didn't cover itself with glory in the invasion. The Army's corps of public information officers, doing damage control in advance of criticisms of the type raised by the Grenada invasion, co-opted reporters. And the reporters, or at least their editors, largely liked it. By offering a stream of news releases and briefings, such as those sniffing at Noriega's red underwear and his pornography, Thurman's copy machine warriors headed reporters off before they could get too nosey about what was really going on. One can see the reporters now; hunched over typewriters in the air conditioned press office at the Marriott Hotel, Coca Cola at hand, batting out stories about brave Rangers jumping at Rio Hato.

Then here comes the press release about the mysterious powder, almost certainly cocaine, found in Noriega's private quarters. Each reporter looks at his colleagues out of the corner of his eye; "that guy's obviously sending off a story about the cocaine. The city desk will want to know why I didn't have it. I'll do it now and get the invasion story later." That's called heading 'em off at the pass.

Even back home, the foolishness continued. How could a columnist of David S. Broder's stature have written this in the Washington Post: "...Panama represents the best evidence yet that, 15 years after the Vietnam War ended, Americans really have come together in recognition of the circumstances in which military intervention makes sense. The elements of agreement have been in place for some time; Bush's contribution is to demonstrate that the new national consensus will survive when tested."[26] That was about as accurate as the story of the cocaine powder, which turned out to be tamale flour.

A later war, George Bush's victory over Saddam Hussein after almost inviting him to take over Kuwait, had an element of rationality to it, in a greedy sort of way. In spite of Bush's disclaimers that it was a United Nations action against aggression, and Secretary of State James Baker's sug-

---

[26] David Broder, Washington Post, Jan. 13, 1990.

gestion that it was for "jobs" for American workers, it was at least justifiable in a corporate (oil company) sense.

But the invasion of Panama? It was aggression, pure and simple, a bully kicking a weakling. Noriega was a thug and he had almost certainly sold out to, or at least connived with, drug dealers. He had certainly murdered or ordered murders. But he was only doing what Panamanian strong men had been led to believe by American proconsuls for years was acceptable behavior: use your office to get whatever goodies you can while you can.

Noriega got his start in the intelligence game through finking on fellow classmates in military school by reporting to the CIA those he thought had leftist tendencies. He beat the rap on a charge of brutally beating a prostitute and he was caught wiretapping American Army conversations. Yet the CIA, under George Bush and others, kept him on its payroll for years. Noriega sold out his colleagues in the drug trade, to American officials on the perpetual and eventually fruitless hunt for drug runners, and he sold secrets about his on-and-off friendship with Fidel Castro to the United States as comfortably as he apparently sold United States secrets to Castro. He offered to help the Sandinistas in Nicaragua and he offered to have the Sandinista leadership assassinated; anything for his American friends and bankrollers. He was a merchant, dealing with what he believed were merchants, in the commodities they had taught him to value.

Bush's war on Panama, a continuation by arms of Ronald Reagan's ineffectual but damaging economic embargo, was as senseless as Reagan's previous "war" on Grenada. Another coup would probably have taken out Noriega within months and, even if it hadn't, what was to be lost by allowing him to continue to rule like so many other thugs we've tolerated over decades past? Noriega's effectiveness as a front man for the Columbian drug lords ended when the United States fingered him as a traitor to those same business associates.

At first Bush, in the grip of common sense, refused to be panicked into going overt in support of a coup by some of

Noriega's subordinates two months before the invasion. The coup leaders, who had been encouraged by the running litany of condemnation of Noriega for weeks beforehand, held Noriega for a time, a development Bush failed to exploit. Then they turned him loose. The plotters, no more democrats than Noriega, but scenting their chance to replace him, lost their gamble, and their lives.

But when the editorial page cartoonists, as unoriginal as their print colleagues, launched their wimp attack, Bush did the only thing he knew how—he charged up the hill of public opinion and captured an 80 percent poll rating. America was standing tall and only a few thousand people died. What were the other rationales for the invasion? So far as George Bush ever took the nation into his confidence, it was a matter of American lives. A young American officer had been killed at a Panamanian roadblock, just one of a number of alleged provocations of the peace-loving Americans.

Any death is tragic. But all accounts agree that the dead Marine and three other officers had become lost while out late in Panama City and drove up to a roadblock near Noriega's command post where they were ordered to halt and get out of the car. Instead, they gunned off down the street and were shot at. Running roadblocks manned by armed troops or police anywhere is a foolish thing to do; in a tense, trigger happy Latin country it's tantamount to suicide, something any military officer should know without a detailed briefing. United States units had been running chip-on-the-shoulder tank patrols through Panama City for weeks before the invasion, something almost ignored by the American press. The shooting, and affronts to another officer and his wife at another roadblock, were the incidents Bush needed.

Bush also excused his war with the accusation that Noriega had declared war on the United States. It never happened, and again, the press shows up as accomplice. What Noriega actually said was reported in a Reuters wire service story in the *New York Times* on December 17–18, 1989.[27]

---

[27] New York Times, Dec. 17, 1989, p.5.

The story, which dealt with Noriega's comments regarding United States accusations against him, quoted him as saying to the National Assembly that, "the North American scheme, through constant psychological and military harassment, has created a state of war in Panama." Hardly a declaration of war, but that was the way it was reported in the United States, after first being almost ignored. *The Times* story went on to say that "the Bush Administration which did not recognize the assembly as a government said the assembly action was 'another hollow step in an attempt to force his rule on the Panamanian people'."

I prefer not to spell out names for fear of bringing trouble to people who trusted me, but I talked to a number of Panamanians who, while they greeted Noriega's ouster with cheers, were still saddened or angered by the damage done to their country in rooting him out. They all considered the invasion a case of massive overkill. A prominent restaurant owner told me that Noriega's "own friends would have taken him out before long. My business has been ruined," he said, gesturing around the large dining room where one other table was occupied, by two Gringo men.

I am certain that there was never an order, on paper or even verbal, that Noriega was not to survive the invasion. But whatever troop did do him in could certainly have expected some special attention, a promotion or some extra leave. The Bush Administration did not want a living breathing Noriega on its hands when the affair was over. Noriega fooled them. He gave himself up to the papal nuncio, and who would dare shoot him in that setting, even in the act of "fleeing from custody?" So we had the spectacle of the head of a sovereign nation being hustled onto a helicopter by American gunmen, on television for all the world to see. Eventually he was convicted with the testimony of some of the sleaziest characters ever to bargain a plea, for a certain price, their freedom or reduced sentences.

Syndicated Columnist Georgie Ann Geyer, who never misses a chance to suck up to an incumbent administration, said in a column that Noriega's conviction on eight counts of drug smuggling and conspiracy showed that Bush had been correct all along in his invasion. The end justifies the means. Noriega is a bad guy and probably deserves to spend the rest of his life locked up, if for no other reason than ordering the death and beheading of Spadafora. He wasn't charged with Spadafora's murder, however.

Panama's President Endarra and his banker cronies, and probably a majority of Panama's citizens, were pleased to have the United States remove Noriega, even if it had to kidnap him. After all, as long as he was in power *Tio Sam* was going to be unpleasant about trade and banks. And, it should be noted, Noriega was disliked for his own proclivities, without any subtle finger-pointing by North Americans. Thus few mourn his fate. But Americans should ponder whether it was worth it to bend our law to convict this miserable creature in the manner that it did. Noriega didn't get a fair trial and while it's likely he's guilty of the crimes for which he was convicted, there is, for lack of evidence from anyone but convicted thieves and liars, room for doubt. Had the same evidence been introduced in the trial of an American of no notoriety he would almost certainly have been acquitted.

Noriega the deal maker, who was "born again" as a Christian in his Miami prison, understands what put him in the pokey for the rest of his life and then some. He probably doesn't appreciate the irony but as an expert in not so subtle deals he can at least recognize a frame-up when he sees it. The prosecution in that long trial in Miami won by a series of agreements with some of the scurviest crooks ever to lie to save their skins in any American courtroom. Convicted drug dealers facing hundreds of years in prison were granted shortened sentences, like months instead of years, for their testimony that they had seen, or heard that, their former buddy Manuel was pushing drugs and using his armed forces to do it.

One of these was drug boss Carlos Lehder, who was also kidnapped, in Colombia, and brought to the United States for trial at which he was sentenced to 135 years in a federal prison. Lehder, a vicious crook, had admitted earlier that he had never met Noriega and said in his testimony at trial that he had only heard of Noriega's drug dealings from some of his pals in the Medellin cartel. Nevertheless, for his hearsay contribution he was offered his freedom.[28] He apparently has a pile of drug money stashed away and will live to enjoy spending it unless one of the other drug dealers he ratted on gets to him. Others of his ilk also got reduced sentences and will walk out of prison relatively young to recover their hidden drug fortunes.

When it is convenient, and they are doing their jobs as stewards of justice, United States prosecutors disdain the "tainted" testimony of convicted drug runners, pushers, even users. But not with Noriega. The right of discovery is fundamental in American law. The accused must be allowed to search through the evidence against him, no matter how embarrassing it might be to his accusers or damaging to the prosecution. But Judge William Hoveler went along with the prosecution's contention that national security would be jeopardized if Noriega's lawyers were allowed to introduce some federal records. Neither did Judge Hoveler lose any sleep over the taping by someone, no one ever determined exactly who, of Noriega's jail house telephone conversations with his lawyers, another violation of a fundamental right that roused little indignation in this nation.

Judge Hoveler also refused to let Noriega's attorneys mention the name of his one-time associate, George Bush, in court. He did allow the prosecutors to speak Fidel Castro's name in front of the jury, however, in their attempts to paint Noriega even more evil than he already was. Castro had apparently interceded in a dispute between Noriega and some of the Colombia Medellin cartel drug kings.

Bush hailed the verdict on his former pal as a "major victory against the drug lords." It sounded good to a public confused over why the government can't win its "war on drugs" but his conviction is otherwise meaningless. Since Noriega's kidnapping drugs have continued to flow through

---

[28] Mark Cook, EXTRA, January/February, 1992, p.17.

Panama, more, some say, than even before.

Since the invasion the United States has squeezed the Panamanian government, but not very hard, to tighten regulation of its banks. This is a losing proposition; the banks bring cash into Panama that the country badly needs. Opening the banks' books to international or United States inspectors would render them useless for the service they were created to provide—laundering money. The drug dealers and other world financial manipulators would immediately find somewhere else to put their money and the Panamanian banks would wither away. Panamanian bankers weren't worried, however, and neither were knowledgeable drug runners, or those with alert lawyers.

Most of Panama escaped any physical damage in the invasion although those who were in the path of the American juggernaut suffered terribly. Noriega's *comandancia* was located at the edge of a tenement slum called El Chorillo, whence came the muggers who attacked me in 1978 and just across the street from the manicured lawns of a residential area of the Canal Zone. Enormous firepower, beginning right at H-hour of the invasion, and some apparent deliberate arson, perhaps by Noriega's "Dignity Battalions," reduced the entire area to a smouldering ruin, inside which many of its residents were buried or incinerated. There was no damage on the other side of the street. My taxi driver at first refused to take me into El Chorillo and then, when I insisted, would only drive through without stopping.

Three months after the invasion the first agreement on United States emergency funds was signed after new President Endarra went on a well-publicized protest hunger strike which, in true comic Latin political tradition, coincided with his desire to lose a few hundred pounds before marrying his 22-year-old trophy bride. El Chorrillo was to be "redeveloped,"' a gentrification guaranteed to make someone rich. The place was urban renewal by cannon fire.

Chaos followed the invasion. Law and order had broken down and no one felt safe on the streets, except when American patrols were nearby. When I got ready to leave a restaurant one evening the proprietor insisted that I wait until he could get his car so he could drive me the five blocks up the hill to my hotel. "It is not safe out here for you," he insisted as we drove along the empty streets.

A part of the anarchy was directly traceable to the police, who were being recruited by the United States Southern Command. Some were members of Noriega's old Defense Force, and indeed, one of the new commanders was a top officer of the old Army, having sworn that he had always been, secretly, a democrat.

Policemen, miffed at their status reduction from soldiers, were especially angered that they could no longer carry automatic rifles. They were issued small pistols, which they insisted were not sufficient firepower to cope with the gangs of armed criminals running loose in Panama City and other cities. They may have had a point, but that was no reason for the Southern Command to put up with their obvious stalling to win back their right to carry heavier firepower. One woman told me that while she was halted at a traffic light a man walked up to her car, smashed the door window with a brick lying in the street, reached in past her and took her purse and walked away with it. All this, she said, happened while a policeman stood on the corner watching, doing nothing.

Violent crime was almost unchecked in the two years after the invasion and every criminal act was attributed to "terrorists." We armed Noriega and he armed the gangs of thugs he called his dignity battalions and then everyone lamented the wide proliferation of weapons in the society.

What's next for Panama? The canal is still a valuable asset but its worth diminishes with each new innovation in air travel and air freight. The largest tankers can't squeeze through its locks and neither can American aircraft carriers, hence giving our military establishment justification for a "two-ocean navy." The volume of talk about a new canal, probably through Nicaragua's big lake, is turned up periodically by news people on dull days, but it isn't likely. It would cost too much for the benefits it would offer and it probably would be an environmental disaster since, being nearly at sea level, unlike the canal in Panama which passes ships up and down a series of locks, it would allow a dangerous mix of marine species.

Rightwingers in Congress, their eyes alight with patriotic fervor, still insist that the canal is ours and that we ought to continue running it. For once they may be right, although for the wrong reasons. On my last trip to Panama, two years after the invasion, I was surprised to hear more Panamanians saying the same thing, that the United States should continue to operate the canal. Why? Because they don't trust their government to operate it efficiently or, more pertinently, honestly. They claim that already as the time nears for a nearly full Panamanian takeover the canal is showing signs of neglect, that maintenance is being shorted, needed repairs not made. The railroad paralleling the canal, on which I took a pleasant ride to Colon in 1978, is now a wreck, its locomotives and cars rusting and its tracks disappearing under new jungle.

"You should continue to operate the canal," one Panamanian friend told me, first obtaining my assurance of anonymity. "If you let our government run it the politicians will steal the revenues and it won't be long before the engines (that tow ships through the locks) will no longer work. The locks and especially the lakes between the locks, will silt in unless the dredges run constantly. The whole thing will come to a halt in just a few years. It is best that you run it and allow Panamanians to do the work."

Other Panamanians said the same thing, all without any sign that I could see that they were sorry to have to think that way. Corruption is so well understood, so much a part of Panamanian life, that discussing it is no cause for expressions of shame, only caution that the wrong people aren't listening.

Is Uncle Sam to blame for the corruption? Well, not directly. But we have winked at it often enough and dealt so cozily with the corrupters that we are seen by the people of Panama as actively encouraging the surface stability engendered by bribes and payoffs. More than in most of Latin America, Panamanians have rubbed shoulders with Yanquis. We are recognized as good hearted as individuals, naive as public officials, and indifferent and dangerous as policy makers. Panama is a beautiful country, its people are friendly and hard working, with the exception of those degraded by their ties to corrupt military and banking officials, and they could have a country genuinely to be proud of with a little help from those of us who profess to be their friends.

Panamanians themselves are hardly a factor in the back room debates about the future of their country. Most seemed almost unanimous in their desire that the country not have an army. They had seen the example of neighboring Costa Rica, which has so far successfully resisted United States efforts to militarize it, and they liked the idea. "Why do we need an army?" several Panamanians shot back at me when I asked them for their opinion.

"Who is it going to fight?" one asked. Not Costa Rica on its north, certainly; not Colombia, the country's only other bordering neighbor, which has its hands full for now and a long time to come with drug kingpins and guerrilla armies of various hues.

There was no justification for a Panamanian Army. And the National Assembly recognized that fact of life and abolished it. But that doesn't mean there will not be an army at some time in the near future. There is no justification for an army in Honduras, or Guatemala or Mexico or Nicaragua or El Salvador for that matter, but they all exist, either out front as the actual rulers or in the background shadows.

In spite of all that, it seems pretty certain that the average Panamanian would like to confine its armed officials to a national police force. Fortuitously, that also seemed to be the position, for local public consumption, of President Endarra, a rather foolish fellow who, despite the publicity campaign by the Bush Administration to present him as some kind of Latin Thomas Jefferson, is of the same strata of Panamanian society that created the social conditions that brought Torrijos to power and made Noriega possible. A revived National Guard suits Endarra and the people who pull his strings just fine. It doesn't, however, satisfy Uncle Sam and American arms makers so well. What kind of precedent would a disarmed Panama present to the world? Stubborn Costa Rica without weapons is bad enough.

9

Costumed Clowns

I WALKED OUT OF THE ROUGH SHACK THAT IS THE HONDURAN border customs post at El Espino into the burning sunlight and found the contents of my luggage in the road dust and a squad of soldiers pawing through them. They had taken my two bags from the taxi and dumped everything, underwear, shirts, socks, newspaper clippings, my camera, books and magazines. My four traveling companions, heretofore friendly, now stood to one side, looking away toward the Nicaraguan post on the other side of the border. One soldier was grinding into the dust with his boot heel a small socialist pamphlet I had bought the previous day in Tegucigalpa. *"Comunista,"* he said gleefully, looking at me with a mean smile on his face. The squad's leader held a large glossy paperback book I had been persuaded to buy that morning at my hotel. I held out my hand. He pulled the book back.

"Military secrets," he said.

I hadn't really wanted to buy the $8 book but a Honduran friend appalled at the American military presence in his country had suggested that if I wanted to know something about the Central American military mind, and specifically what enchants the Honduran Army, I should have the book. "It will tell you better than anything else where this country's priorities lie," he said.

The text was short, polemical and full of errors, but the pictures, by a French photographer, were well done. They showed Honduran soldiers in camouflage gear, as carefully made up with brown and black paint as any chorus girl, their machine pistols, Uzis as well as the ubiquitous AK-47, fondly displayed. There were pictures of Americans, with their names, although soldiers of my old outfit, the 82nd Airborne Division, were identified as Marines, a real gaffe in United States military circles. The Americans were shown jumping from airplanes and on maneuvers on the ground, with their radios, brand new vehicles and a variety of weapons.

Other pictures were of dead men, Nicaraguans, Sandinistas, the captions said, killed by the Contra.

The soldiers wanted the book and national security was their rationale for taking it even though I explained that its printing was subsidized by their own army as a public relations effort and that I had bought it on a public news stand. "It contains military information," the leader said. I demanded a letter of explanation for his seizure and he refused to discuss it. I asked his name and he turned his back on me and ordered his men to stuff my clothing and other gear back in my bags and said I was free to walk across the border into Nicaragua.

Among the atrocities committed by Fidel Castro and his Soviet sponsors in Central America was the enhancement of the legitimacy of the military. Exploitation of the perceived threat of communist take overs, seized on by the peacocks who pose as soldiers in those countries and with naive incomprehension by Ronald Reagan and cynicism by George Bush, added to the economic and physical misery of the region.

The Honduran Army is probably not the worst. That honor would go to El Salvador's more experienced cut throats, although many Honduran soldiers are just as thuggish. Understanding who runs Honduras doesn't take long. You want to visit Palmerola, the American air base later called Soto Cano? the American woman at the United States Embassy asks me. "You'll need press credentials." And where do I get them? From the Army, she says, as though that is obvious. And it is. I go the next day to the Army's intelligence office and get a press card, primarily to add to my collection of souvenirs. It isn't difficult, just fill out a form and hand over a $20 bill and two passport sized pictures (which I had learned long before always to have available).

With armies that must report to no one, the countries of Central America are in a perpetual state of occupation. Laws are flouted, corruption is everywhere although few ever know the details because no one is allowed to discuss it in print. The courts enforce only the laws that the oligarchies who own the countries see fit to obey. Judges, if they should reject bribes and try to render justice, find themselves in trouble.

The proprietor of my hotel in Tegucigalpa and an American friend of his joined me at breakfast in the hotel dining room the day I left for Nicaragua. The hotel owner regaled me with a tale at the expense of his friend, whom I will call Bill Johnson. "He came here chasing pussy," he said, and Johnson nodded in smiling agreement and then told me his story. A retired technician for a United States federal agency, Johnson came to Honduras on vacation and met and married a local woman. They soon broke up and she obtained a divorce. But before that conclusion, Johnson said with his tired smile, "I spent nine months in a Tegucigalpa jail before my (divorce) case came to trial." There is no bail in such cases and he didn't have enough money to bribe the judge. He still lives in Honduras, but wiser now, on his Social Security.

Such travesties, duplicated in these countries all the time, occur only because their militaries will not allow normal democratic rule. A free press and a free judiciary would threaten their enterprises and their hold on their countries' treasuries.

During my first trip to El Salvador, in 1981, I was told at the United States Embassy by the military attache that the Salvadoran army had at last learned how to cope with the guerrillas. The officers were no longer going to Miami on weekends, leaving their conscript troops to defend themselves in inadequate fortresses. "It's no longer a nine-to-five army," he said.

A year later I got the same briefing. The Salvadoran Army had at last been convinced to operate in small patrols, seeking out the guerrillas instead of waiting for them to attack, he said. The Army had learned to fight at night. All those were basic to counter guerrilla warfare, learned the hard way by armies through history. In 1984 another American colonel was still insisting that "the Salvadoran leadership is beginning to deal with the problem" of the death squads.[29]

Years later his successors were preaching the same sermon. And the Salvadoran Army was still operating in battalion and brigade sized units, in daylight. In 1988 I followed a company of one of the elite battalions on an approach march in Cabanas Department. They bunched up, had no flankers out and left a spoor of ration cans and food wrappers a Cub Scout couldn't have missed. They were ripe for another of the disastrous ambushes that occurred again and again in that war. Earlier that same day, in the garrison at La Victoria, I was given an impromptu show of physical skills by another company. Those soldiers pumped out pushups, chin ups, sit up and knee bends in a blur of motion. They were thin and wiry, with sinews hard as rubber tires. What they lacked was leadership.

Shortly after the supposed end to the military conflict, in early 1992, near the town of El Paraiso in Chalatenango Department I rode past the fortress that had just been completed to keep the Army's 4th Brigade safe from guerrilla attack after a series of defeats. No expense—to the American taxpayer—had been spared in building a ten-foot-high concrete block wall that marched over hills and across arroyos like the Great Wall of China. Alongside that wall is a razor wire fence, the whole thing reflecting a bunker mentality. Inside the enormous walled area, which must cover nearly a hundred acres, were concrete buildings, barracks, offices, mess halls and other structures necessary for an army in garrison. The assistant driver of the van I had hitched a

---

[29] Col. John D. Waghelstein, New York Times op-ed page, Aug. 9, 1984.

ride in pushed my arm down as I raised my camera to get a picture. The Army was still capable of bad things, he said. No pictures from this van.

Milgroup commanders were saying in 1987 that "the war has just turned a corner." The good guys were winning. Then came the guerrilla offensive of 1989 and suddenly the tune turned discordant. Guerrillas infiltrated the whole capitol, even into the exclusive Escalon area where the United States ambassador lives behind high walls like his neighbors in their mansions. Probably more than anything else, that penetration into the heart of the oligarchy's domain helped bring about talks that led to the final peace accords; the rich of El Salvador had never before been exposed to the war and it frightened them. No longer were the guerrillas nameless Indians in the countryside, they were men and women with weapons and they were there, inside the gates.

It was while the guerrillas were showing up the Army that its soldiers did the kind of work they did best. They went into the University of Central America in the night and executed six Jesuit professors and their housekeeper and her daughter. Since they couldn't defeat the guerrillas they sought scapegoats for their inadequacy, priests who dared to tell their students they had rights.

Usually the Army was more subtle in its murders but I assume they considered this an unusual case. Normally a soldier who became part of a death squad took off his uniform. The Army's involvement seldom came to light; people knew the death squads were operating only because mutilated bodies were showing up regularly alongside roads . But in 1989 a Salvadoran corporal who claimed to be fleeing from a special group of the 1st Infantry Brigade turned up in Washington to tell United States officials and newsmen that his job had been to kill captured or suspected leftists in El Salvador.

Cesar Vielman Joya Martinez said American advisers knew what he and others in his unit were doing. The Salvadoran high command denied Joya Martinez' claims, as did the Pentagon which described the very idea as "patently absurd. We know of no instances in which United States military personnel have been even remotely associated with such morally repugnant activities," a Pentagon statement said.[30]

Joya Martinez, who said he took part in eight killings, told reporters the orders came to his unit on one-page sheets of paper and once the killings were carried out, reports went to the commanders of the brigade, Colonels Juan Orlando Zepeda and Francisco Elena Fuentes. In a four-month period, he said, seventy-two persons were "brought to justice," the Army's euphemism for killing. Joya Martinez said two American advisers attached to the unit did intelligence analysis and he didn't know if they actually endorsed the unit's mission but "obviously they had to know what was going on."

I was given a history lecture, along with a couple of members of Congress, on one trip to El Salvador, when we met with Colonel Emilio Ponce, the Army chief of staff, in his bunker-like quarters at the Estado Mayor, the Army headquarters. Ponce is a small man, rather handsome with a smiling face, erect and trim. He wore a United States Army-type field uniform, his sleeves rolled up in a business-like manner. His office and his briefing room could have been any brigade headquarters in the United States Army. Two swivel chairs behind the table facing an auditorium of about fifty chairs were upholstered in mottled green and brown silk camouflage material. Military gadgets, grenade cigarette lighters, models of Huey helicopters, lined the forward edge of Ponce's desk, and behind it, next to the Salvadoran national flag and unit guidons was a shield ringed with bayonets. A large group picture was of Ponce's graduating class at an American military school.

"You are here to find out for yourselves what is happening in this country," Ponce told us in concluding a briefing on the progress of the war. "So often the news you get on the outside is intentionally or unintentionally wrong." He asked for questions.

---

[30] Associated Press, Oct. 27, 1989.

"Is the Army outside civil control?" asked Congressman Jim McDermott, a Washington State Democrat. "It seems the death squads are back again."

That was when Ponce, still smiling, said we needed a "little history lesson, to understand the evolution of our Armed Forces." He then related events leading up to the military coup of 1979 when some young officers threw out a corrupt general and decreed land reform for the campesinos as well as other changes in the country's civil life. After the coup leaders themselves were overthrown, Ponce told us, "we realized the need for us to be on the sidelines and to support the will of the people. The military comes from the middle and lower classes," he said. "We come from the people and we need to serve the people." An election was coming up, he noted, and "I assure you the Armed Forces will stay away from party politics.

"There has been a subordination of the Armed Forces to the civilian government." As proof, he said, "we have had to sacrifice military security because of political requests," apparently by the United States Congress. "Soldiers have died while trying to capture terrorists, yet they (the guerrillas) are given amnesty for political reasons. These are political decisions and we must carry them out. The battle is not only military," Ponce said, "a great percentage of it is political. We are learning quickly the role of the Armed Forces in a democratic society."

I interrupted to remind Ponce that McDermott's question was about death squads. "Unfortunately, yes, and when anyone hears about the death squads, what immediately comes to mind are military people," Ponce said. "I think the death squads began when public officials were not capable of coping with crime and prostitution and people took the law into their own hands. Yet I can assure you that they are not a part and parcel of the security forces. We do not have in our organic structure as an armed force any place for death squads."

"You could define the FMLN (guerrillas) as death squads," he said, "because they battle outside the law. It is our responsibility to search them out and combat them and that seems to create a negative public opinion against the Armed Forces. So we are very interested in finding out who is responsible (for the death squads).

"We can't end the war with bullets and guns," Ponce said. "We are struggling with the support of the people. And the country has not fallen because we have the support of the people."

Ponce told us that guerrilla strength had dwindled from twelve thousand men and women under arms in 1983 to six thousand then, six years later. Salvadoran Army numbers were fifty four thousand, he said. The guerrillas, he said, used hit and run tactics, blowing up bridges, then disappearing, setting off explosives at the bases of power transmission lines and then running for the safety of the hills.

He had his concepts right, but didn't the Armed Forces have uncontested control of the air and didn't they continually bomb suspected guerrilla locations, not to mention civilian communities in conflictive zones? I asked. Ponce was patient with me; eighty percent of his army, he said, was tied down protecting bridges, power dams and communication centers. Of the remaining twenty percent many were recovering from wounds "and that leaves us with only twelve percent" to run down the guerrillas.

When asked how many guerrillas the Army had killed, Ponce said he had no figures and he made a polite dig at his American handlers: "We don't keep body counts."

Ponce complained that he was not getting the weapons the Army needed from his United States benefactors. And some of what they did get, he said, "were not of the correct types." He told of the wrong ammunition for grenade launchers and of being sent anti-tank weapons they didn't need while not receiving enough assault rifles.

Elections were coming up in two months and Ponce was asked by Congresswoman Louise Slaughter, a Democrat from New York, what kind of negotiations with the FMLN the military would accept. The military, Ponce replied, had written "an open public letter" to six political parties pointing out that the military was "the only authorized armed forces in the country and any party elected within the constitution would be respected."

Before we left Ponce he told us that the Army "will continue to protect democracy in this country and we will continue to protect human rights of the people. It is also our desire to improve our combat proficiency and our professionalism. Our concern is Salvadoran security; we don't want to be another communist satellite in the Americas."

Probably the best public analysis of the Central American military, aside from some most likely classified in Pentagon files, was a piece in *The New York Times Magazine* on the corruption that is the Salvadoran Army.

The mission of the members of its officer corps, the story said, is to make money. Not to whip the guerrillas, not to defend the country from foreign invaders. Just to position oneself and one's friends for lucrative business deals after retirement, although according to the story most of the top officers were deeply involved in business while still on active duty and presumably fighting the enemy.[31]

While most of the graft was related to military activity or affairs in some way, some of it was plain old banditry. From 1982 until 1986 a group of military officers collected as much as $4 million in ransom from families of wealthy Salvadoran businessmen they had kidnapped.[32]

American soldiers advising the Salvadoran Army soon understood where the loyalties lay of the men they were supposedly helping fight a war. Major Eric Buckland, who learned of the planned murder in 1989 by the Army of six Jesuit priests before it happened, told an interrogator afterward how the system works. "When you made colonel you got a phone call from the oligarchy and somebody basically bought you. You made good bucks and you looked out for that guy or whatever it was that was going on. Human rights was not a discussion. It's not an issue.

"The military still to a great extent now, but for sure

---

[31] Joel Millman, New York Times Magazine, Dec.13, 1989.
[32] Lee Hockstader, Washington Post, May 28, 1990,

before, before America got involved in this civil war, was above the law." In talking to his Salvadoran bodyguard, Buckland said, "As an officer you don't get (traffic) tickets. When the police stop you, they don't ticket you. You carry a pistol wherever you want to, you can do pretty much whatever you want to, you're above prosecution. My bodyguard asked me (if) in the states I could run red lights. I said no, I'd get a ticket. Well, you carry your pistol around with you? I said no. Can you beat women up? I said no. There in the United States the military is almost, has less rights because people look at us so much harder."[33]

Rumors floated through Central America for years that one source of weapons for the guerillas of the Farabundo Marti National Liberation Front were men and officers of the Army. "One billion dollars in American military aid seems to have bought an army big enough to survive its own mistakes, and powerful enough to resist any effort to reform it— to end pervasive corruption or weed out corrupt officers," the Times article said. "Instead of fostering reform, the American money has been absorbed into a network of corruption and patronage that has grown up over half a century, and has made the Salvadoran military an empire unto itself."[34]

Officers steal from their unit's funds, The Times story said. They rent their men out to landlords, they shake down businessmen and insist on the kind of "taxes" that the mob collects from victims in North American cities. Officers pad unit rosters and pocket the salaries of their "ghost soldiers." The Army has no central roster, the story said, and thus padding is almost invited. Enlisted men are charged for their food, clothing and other supplies. At the top of this pyramid of corruption is a social fund into which every soldier pays. The money was invested through the Army's own bank in all kinds of enterprises until the fund had grown to $100 million in 1988, the article said. While the country was receiving $1.5 million a day from United States taxpayers,

---

[33] Transcript of FBI interview with Maj. Eric Warren Buckland, U.S. Army, San Salvador, Jan. 12, 1990, p. 5
[34] Ibid.

The Army was using its slush fund to buy real estate, an ocean-side resort, a 500-lot housing development, a funeral home. That financial clout allowed the Army to make alliances with developers and contractors, invading financial markets, making mortgage loans and buying a thirteen-story office tower for its bank headquarters.

Why did the United States tolerate such conduct? After all, without American money the Salvadoran government, and the Army, could not have continued to function for more than a few weeks. "American officials in El Salvador and Washington acknowledge the endemic corruption, but argue that improving battlefield performance has necessarily been a higher priority."[35] A core reason was that the colonels were "fighting communism," meaning people who talked back to their *padrone* or refused to accept their place in life as peons tied to some rich family's land.

"The U.S. equated a professional armed force with democracy," the piece quoted Ruben Zamora, an opposition leader who fled the country when his brother, the Salvadoran attorney general, was killed. "They're not synonymous," he said. "What the U.S. has done is teach the Army it's better to be owner of the country than a landlord of a building. Instead of their own party, they control the whole political system."

The communism card always struck immediate sparks in American administrations. Nothing else need be said. Skeptical reports to the contrary, from American soldiers, diplomats and, I suspect, CIA analysts, went unheeded, indeed served as black marks in personnel files and probably ruined some careers.

Many Latin American officers went to United States military schools such as the School of the Americas in Panama, later moved to safer Fort Benning, Georgia, or the command and general staff colleges. If they learned nothing else, or listened to nothing else, they did come home knowing that an allegation of communism against an opponent was like turning on a spigot to the United States Treasury.

---

[35] Ibid.

Pay for El Salvadoran enlisted men was meager and their lives rough. So was their induction. Often they were impressed in the same manner the British once "recruited" American seamen, at gunpoint while on the job. A standard tactic in El Salvador was for an Army recruiting squad to hold up a bus, order everyone out and then march able bodied males from fourteen to forty off to the local jail where they were held until they were sworn in as soldiers, with suitable threats of what would happen to them if they attempted to desert. In Zaragoza, a little town not far from San Salvador, a local priest told me of another recruiting technique. The mayor arranged dances some Saturday nights at the city hall for the youth of the town and the surrounding countryside. Every few months at the height of an evening's gaiety a cordon of soldiers would surround the building. The girls would be told to go home and all the boys who could not convince the soldiers their families had clout were marched away to the nearest Army garrison where they started basic training the next morning.

That didn't happen to every youth. One day as I was having a hamburger and a beer in one of the many fast food franchise restaurants that lend a North American air to San Salvador, I noticed a group of about fifteen young people, in their late teens and early twenties, male and female, at several nearby tables. "Why aren't those men in the Army?" I asked my companion, a church lay worker.

He looked at me in mock surprise. "Look at them," he said. "Look at their clothing, see their gold chains, see their cars out there." He pointed to the open window. "They are rich men's sons. Rich men's sons do not go into the Army in El Salvador." They were a laughing, attractive and carefree bunch and one would never have known, by their loud laughter and banter that not twenty miles away on the slopes of Guazapa Volcano two armies were busy killing each other. Nor would one have believed that less than two miles away was one of the foulest slums in the world, a refugee jungle of cardboard shacks and open sewers where daily children died of diarrhea and malnutrition.

Latin Americans to a degree deserve it. War and its alleged glories pervade the cultures of those countries. From Mexico to Argentina, war toys predominate at Christmas time. Books on war, lavishly illustrated treatises on World War II battles, often glorifying the Nazis, cover tables in many book stores. German uniforms are especially admired. This seems to me to be more wistfulness than a reflection of individual Latin macho; since the series of revolutions that separated Latin America from Spain and Portugal, the region hasn't had many real wars. Mexico's 20-year revolution killed more than a million people and was every bit as bloody and nasty as our own Civil War. Paraguay fought the armies of Argentina, Brazil and Uruguay for five years in the 1860s, as awful a war as any addict of bloodshed could ask. It killed most Paraguayan males over age ten and created a matriarchy whose overtones continue to this day: I once saw a strapping six-foot blonde Amazon cop pistol-whip a scrawny male bus driver who ran a stop sign in a narrow Asuncion Street. She never even worked up a sweat before she literally dragged him off to jail. My fellow passengers barely paid attention except to lament the need to find another bus with a driver.

The chief purpose of Argentina's 1982 adventure in the Falkland (Malvinas) Islands was to cover up the disastrous mess the generals had made of the economy of one of the world's naturally richest countries. The farcical war proved they weren't any better at modern warfare, real combat (they were good at murdering people snatched from their homes at night), than they were at running an economy.

But with those exceptions Latin wars have been more on the order of comic opera coups by one military faction on the outs seeking its turn at the trough. Others, such as the 1969 "soccer war" between El Salvador and Honduras, were mostly bluster. Supposedly that four-day skirmish erupted over a disputed score in a game between the national champion soccer teams of the two countries. Actually, however, it was, as most wars are, a squabble over real estate. Honduras has empty land and El Salvador is one of the most densely populated countries in the world. Salvadoran squatters had for years been moving into Honduras seeking plots of land on which to grow their corn and beans and that slow and gentle invasion alarmed Honduras. During the Reagan wars of the 1980s the two countries were both bribed by United States money to not only cooperate, but serve as proxies for our paranoid obsession with communism.

Yanqui efficiency and management brought an end to these inept and relatively bloodless conflicts. Ronald Reagan's wars were the real article, but since they were fought under the rubric of Low Intensity Conflict with few American body bags, they didn't much impress the United States population. Nicaragua lost some 30,000 people dead, a majority of them civilians, during the eight years the Contra were fighting against what they were told was communism. The number of maimed, mostly by land mines, was enormous. All that was on top of the 50,000 dead in the 1979 revolution. Our war in El Salvador had cost probably 75,000 lives as the 1980s came to an end. Guatemala's death toll from a long, dirty war is even greater. For countries with populations from three to ten million those are enormous casualty rates. But with a few exceptions the militaries of all those countries escaped death; it was the conscript soldiers and innocent civilians caught in between who paid the ultimate price.

Military action often masks other problems and not only by Latin Americans. Just as the Falklands war was intended to divert attention from Argentina's economic problems, so Ronald Reagan's conquest of tiny Grenada distracted public opinion from his bloody debacle in Lebanon; George Bush's invasion of Panama helped dispel his wimp image, at least for a time.

The military is often the only hope a bright kid from a poor family in Central America has of bettering himself. Manuel Noriega, who became a CIA "asset" as a top officer in the Panamanian Defense Force, began his climb up the ladder of successful graft and corruption via a scholarship to a Peruvian military school.

For some Latin military, education meant other things; Somoza, who attended the United States military academy at West Point, tried to comply with a demand by his American mentors that his National Guard officers have a certain proficiency in English before they could attend military schools in the United States. Most of them managed to fudge and they were as little proficient in English when they were running the Contra as they had been before the revolution. If we were to spend a fraction of the money we wasted on fancy guns and uniforms on educating those young men and their sisters in peaceful pursuits we would be doing ourselves as well as them big favors.

What possible rationale can the United States offer for arming these people? The answer, of course, was to fight communism. It never made much sense, but whole careers, political and bureaucratic and journalistic, were created under its banner. Absent communism some other ideology will suffice. The Monroe Doctrine was President James Monroe's message in the early 1800s to Europe that the Western Hemisphere and specifically Latin America was our economic preserve. In the later 1800s it was Manifest Destiny, the near devine obligation of Americans to carry democracy, and capitalism, to the less enlightened.

President Jimmy Carter's human rights campaign, which most significantly affected Latin America, alarming every dictator from Alfredo Stroessner in Paraguay to Anastasio Somoza in Nicaragua, was accompanied by a cut in some of the more outrageous and ridiculous military aid. Military assistance to Guatemala was ended entirely in 1977, and it wasn't until 1985 that the Reagan Administration found an anti-communist rationale to resume sending weapons to Guatemala's Army, one of the nastiest in the hemisphere.

The generals who call the tune in Guatemala said they were fighting commies, who were actually poor Indians resisting relocation from their highland homes in a campaign of "pacification" that really was paving the way for more private takeovers of communal lands. Genocide better describes it. The Guatemala military, like the Army in El Salvador, is a class to itself. It has its own housing, its own schools, clubs and its own bank. It is unaccountable to the country's series of window-dressing governments supported by the United States. Its leaders are paranoid about "subversives." And they should be; they've created conditions for subversion with a brutality that El Salvador's Army might admire.

Guatemala's Army, although it took lessons from New York public relations firms in how to smile at tourists, had neither American military advisers looking over their shoulders or the sort of attention by the press that put El Salvador's agonies on front pages around the world for a time. Not that it made much difference. In Honduras the press is more free than in most of its neighbors, but even there it dares not ask hard questions of its military, such as where does government money go?

On my bus trip from Tegucigalpa to the Nicaraguan border, passing through pastoral farm lands and colorful Honduran villages, I saw a Honduran Army officers' club, guarded by soldiers with assault rifles strolling over the manicured lawns under palm trees. At the gate perched a Huey helicopter, still in camouflage paint but apparently past its prime and now a mothballed decoration. Down the road, in this country where many never get enough to eat, was another billboard advertising an American brand of dog food.

Most of these armies are worthless as fighting units although not because of substandard manpower. Any American who has fought beside or commanded Latins in the United States Army is well aware that they make superb soldiers. But in Central America, especially in El Salvador, Guatemala, Honduras and Panama, the purpose of the army is not to guard against foreign invasion. It is, first, the suppression of the country's civilian population, and secondly the enrichment of its officers, with fighting a war always a distant and unlikely third.

Retired United States Army Lieutenant Colonel Edward King, in a 1984 report for the Unitarian Universalist Service, made frequent references to the distaste younger Salvadoran officers had for the graft and corruption that pervades their military. Perhaps, but that may have just been what those officers thought their gringo guest wanted to hear. Certainly King's quotes from Colonel Domingo Monterrosa, in 1983, that the guerrillas were less eager and growing tired of the war were shown by later events to be wildly inaccurate.[36]

Monterrosa, one of the rare officers in that Army willing to fight, was the Salvadoran Army's "golden boy" in his advisers' eyes. He was also one of the few higher ranking Salvadoran officers to be killed in the war. Fellow officers said mechanical trouble caused his helicopter to crash but it was almost certainly shot down by guerrillas as it lifted off a battlefield in Morazan Department. Monterrosa was an engaging guy and a candid one. I attended a press briefing he conducted shortly after he returned from a sweep by his brigade at which he casually mentioned that several women and children had been killed in the action. Salvadoran newspapers the next day mentioned the military casualties, guerrillas and soldiers, but did not report the colonel's story of the women and children killed.

Colonel King's confidants may not have been altogether blowing smoke. Not all soldiers were killers of unarmed civilians and women and children and not all accepted their roles as puppets to officers who plundered their own troops. Some Salvadoran officers were appalled by the misconduct and criminality of their superiors. I have a copy of a "Letter sent by young officers of the armed forces to the Executive Committee of the National Unity of Salvadoran Workers"[37] listing names of officers involved in death squads during 1989 when they were supposedly no longer operating. These young officers told the trade unionists that "the blood we have shed gives us the moral authority to attempt to bring

---

[36] Lt. Col. Edward King, UA (Ret), Out of Step, Out of Line, U.S. Military Policy in Central America, Unitarian Univeralist Service Committee, Sept. 11, 1984. P.10
[37] Alliance for Latin America Update, January 1990. I do not know where this letter came from but I know that at least a portion of its content is true and I therefore give a qualified credence to the remainder.

the conflict to a political solution favorable to the people. Still, in the minds of some commanders, the dollar holds sway, and so they will not permit an end to the current state of war." The broadside went on to say that "we have come from the people, and our duty is to the people. We are in disagreement with the concept of Low Intensity Conflict, even though we received our early training in the United States."

I had heard similar sentiments in 1982. Embassy people and some Salvadorans told me that some of the young officers were a moderating influence in the country, and they may have been, in 1982. "The Army believes its honor has been tarnished by the killing of women and children," one Salvadoran told me. "Most of that killing has been at the hands of the civil guards, the rural police, whose first allegiance is to the oligarchy, and the National Guard and the National Police, the Treasury Police and the Air Force." That was probably so, certainly the Treasury Police and the Air Force seemed to be most feared by the people. But the Army, had it wished, could have restrained those other elements. Perhaps some of the young officers would have liked to end abuses but by the time the war came to at least a temporary halt in 1992 few of them were untainted. Everyone was implicated in the atrocities that came to light again and again as the war progressed. Peer pressures are hard to resist, especially when one has guilty baggage of one's own.

In Nicaragua, the government's strategy called for keeping most of the Sandinista Army regulars in strategic reserve while civilian reservists, called up for periods of three to six months, did most of the fighting against the Contra. That program, holding back the better trained regulars and letting the greener reserves do the fighting made a lot of sense militarily. It kept the Army ready to move forward to cope with any major invasion rather than getting tied down in the two bit battles the Contra presence provoked. But it also angered many Nicaraguans, especially the parents of the reservists and the reservists themselves. Some of them did four or five tours of a few months at a time chasing the Contra through the hills.

The Nicaraguan Army that most visitors saw, reservists in neighborhood battalions at home or in their camps or on patrols in the *selva*, was an unsightly lot. If any of them ever used boot polish I never saw it. Their hair was long, their combat uniforms sloppy, torn and patched. Guitars seemed to be almost as much a part of their equipment as their rifles, a mixture of old American weapons, newer ones salvaged by arms dealers from Vietnam (or sent by communists via the Soviet Union via Cuba, United States officials said) and others of the world's castoffs.

Cuban military advisers were in Nicaragua, a cause for great alarm for the Reagan Administration. But the Cubans were technicians; the Nicaraguans didn't need the handholding by foreign advisers in combat that the El Salvador Army required. "There are about 1,500 teachers in the country from Cuba. Others are technical and health professionals. Some, very few, are military advisers," Rafael Solis, secretary to the Nicaragua Council of State, told me. "Our arms are from the Soviet Union and we don't know how they work so the Cubans are mainly here to instruct Nicaraguans in how to handle the weapons. There are no Cuban tactical advisers and no Cuban assistance at the tactical level." I saw Cubans in Managua but never in the field.

The Contra, while it had some effective, if brutal, small unit leaders, never really became a cohesive army. Headed by former Somoza National Guardsmen such as Colonel Enrique Bermudez, whose chief allegiance was to their own bank accounts, it was corrupt and inept. It didn't confine its tortures to captured Sandinista soldiers and campesinos who got in its way. In-camp murders of its own men, most of them farm boys from the Nicaraguan hills, created scandals that even their CIA handlers had difficulty covering up. Bermudez' chief military aptitude was looking tough for photographers visiting Contra camps in southern Honduras. He spent most of his time in the fleshpots of Tegucigalpa and Miami, drinking and plotting against rivals.

Bermudez's usefulness was stamped paid in 1991 when someone shot him dead early one evening in the parking lot of the Hotel Intercontinental in Managua. That space is always busy at that time of day, with taxi drivers waiting for fares while limousines bring the Nicaraguan wealthy elite to dinner. But no one saw the Bermudez murder. Some former Contra leaders halfheartedly blamed the Sandinistas, but most Nicaraguans believe his killer or killers were former Contra he had mistreated. Some suspected the CIA but that is unlikely; those of its puppets who were no longer of any use or threat were allowed to take their loot and fade away, if they were quiet about it. Bermudez, however, was not a quiet man.

The Contra civilian leaders installed by the CIA stayed in Miami out of harm's way and were little involved aside from holding press conferences and posing for pictures, for which they were well compensated from United States' taxpayer dollars.

10

Camouflaged Proconsuls

IN THE 1850S, JUST PRIOR TO THE AMERICAN CIVIL WAR, William Walker, a "'grey-eyed man of destiny" from Tennessee, made himself a popular hero, especially in the American South, when he invaded first Mexico and then Nicaragua. Walker, sort of the Oliver North of his time, was a lawyer, a doctor and a newspaperman. Some historians believe he wanted to establish a slave state in Nicaragua where slavery had been abolished some years before.

After conquering Nicaragua with an army of fifty eight Americans, his "immortals," Walker had himself elected president. But his firing squad justice, combined with outrage that a foreigner held the keys to the national treasury rather than any love of *patria*, brought the Central American countries together. That rare alliance lasted just long enough to chase Walker out of the country. He hadn't learned his lesson, however, and was soon back. This time he was cornered on a Honduran beach. He surrendered to the captain of a British ship on station there who promptly turned him over to a detachment of Honduran soldiers who just as promptly shot him.

Walker was at first a partner of Cornelius Vanderbilt, who was making his fortune hauling "49ers" gold seekers to San Francisco across Nicaragua. Eventually Walker betrayed Vanderbilt, or maybe it was the other way around. Walker's significance to our time is that nothing has changed much. Karl Marx was then still a callow youth haunting the British

Museum in London, and England's exploitation of Nicaragua's Miskito Coast substituted for latter day commie bogeymen in American delusions. Walker's grim charisma gave a patina of glamor to manifest destiny and mercantile dreams.

Most Americans have forgotten, although most Mexicans haven't, that in 1914 President Woodrow Wilson, his Princeton sensibilities offended by gross Mexican misgovernment, decided that President Victoriano Huerta would have to go. Wilson ordered a United States fleet to anchor in Veracruz and Tampico harbors "to protect American lives and property," specifically oil wells and oil company employees, although there was no evidence that either were threatened. Americans had invaded Mexico at Veracruz before, in 1847 in a real estate deal for Texas and California. And by 1914 American Marines had already been in Nicaragua five years.

Wilson's invasion was the first time the United States joined morality with commerce in foreign policy to justify exporting American-style democracy with guns into someone else's country. When Mexicans refused to be baited, Admiral Frank F. Fletcher sent a small party of sailors ashore. They were arrested by Mexican police and held for several hours before they were released unharmed. Fletcher demanded a written apology for this "insult to the American flag" and a 21-gun salute. The Mexicans dithered and Fletcher landed troops and seized the city at a cost of 19 American and 300 Mexican lives.

If anything, Wilson's crusade only shored up Huerta's stock in the eyes of the Mexican people who went on to settle their revolutionary affairs in their own way. Huerta was soon chased out of the country by Mexicans fed up with killings excessive even in their long revolution. Veracruz now is a relatively prosperous seaport, adorned with heroic monuments with circumspect references to the "invaders" of 1847 and 1914 without mentioning who they were or where they came from.

In the 1980s American officials still smarting from Vietnam devised a way to carry out armed foreign policy and avoid public outcries at home. "Low intensity conflict" is a marketing device to bring lesser nations into line with United States trade policies and global goals of efficient government through the use of surrogate armies. It is cheap, especially in American lives. No less blood is spilled; it just comes from local bodies and thus has great attraction for certain theorists, usually those whose military experience and whose knowledge of the way people die in violent conflicts has been vicarious.

But even low intensity conflict must follow certain restraints, else taxpayers at home will get queasy. The Reagan and Bush Administrations were so accommodating to El Salvador, so quick to accept excuses, that their influence on the military was muted when troops slaughtered civilians in "conflictive" zones, or their off-duty death squads killed people in batches too large even for American newspapers to ignore.

In Guatemala the Army had not even that slender restraint. When President Jimmy Carter weaned them from United States arms suppliers they turned to Argentina and Israel. They could ignore liberal United States protests to their thuggery. American weapons suppliers soon broke the Israeli competition, via an eager president and a compliant Congress, and in the years after 1986 the United States contributed some $28 million in "non-lethal" military aid to Guatemala. Non-lethal is aid that supposedly doesn't kill. Trucks that haul soldiers to a targeted peasant village are non-lethal; what the soldiers do there, with their machine guns from Israel, is lethal, but not of congressional concern. That charade was played for years in Congress in debates over help for the terrorist Contra raiding into Nicaragua from Honduras. Boots are non-lethal; bullets are lethal. Such little distinctions make lawmakers feel good and the recipients are tolerant of such hypocrisy as long as they get what they want.

Like their counterparts in the diplomatic service, American military men ran career risks if they failed to heed the administration line on Central America. General Fred Woerner was fired as head of the United States Southern Command in mid-1989 for suggesting nonmilitary options to bring down Manuel Noriega, Panama's thuggish dictator. Woerner had previously run afoul of hard liners in the Reagan and Bush Administrations for his skepticism of their assumptions about military matters in Central America.

In spite of insistence in the United States embassies that the war in El Salvador was always "just turning the corner," the guerrillas continued to grow, in strength and in war skills, all during the 1980s. There could be only one answer, the Pentagon and the State Department, reasoned: the Sandinistas in Nicaragua had to be supplying them with weapons and ammunition and other military materiel.

There was enough truth to the charge to alibi all sorts of attacks on Nicaragua, military and propaganda. Certainly the Nicaraguans gave sanctuary to the Salvadoran guerrillas; I talked to them in Nicaragua.

But if massive amounts of supplies were getting into El Salvador from Nicaragua via Honduras it had to be the world's slickest clandestine haul route, rivaling North Vietnam's Ho Chi Minh Trail. It would also be in sharp contrast with the Sandinista's failure to give civilian Nicaragua an efficient distribution system. And, not least, if that was the route along which weapons were moving, failure to interdict them made fools of some smart American soldiers. United States claims of evidence, produced only reluctantly and rarely, were flimsy. "We can't show it to you," United States Ambassador to Nicaragua Anthony Quainton told me in 1984, "because we would compromise our sources."

Quainton, who later ran afoul of Reagan's Administration because his reports to the State Department tried to impart truths about Nicaragua, said the weapons were being shipped in dugout canoes across the Gulf of Fonseca between Nicaragua and El Salvador. I could find no evidence of such shipments when I visited that region, but the State Department did eventually produce two pieces of "evidence," duplicate copies of a news story by a *Miami Herald*

Central American correspondent. Dillon, a careful reporter who later wrote a devastating book about the Contra, was told by local residents that Nicaraguan Army trucks did bring loads of some kind of materiel to the gulf and put it onto small boats.

A "news briefing" in 1984 in Washington by Ambassador to El Salvador Thomas Pickering and General Paul Gorman, the new chief of the United States Southern Command, was supposed to prove once and for all that the Salvadoran guerrillas were obtaining their weapons and munitions from Nicaragua. The briefing included a video film as well as still photos taken from C-130 aircraft, crewed by Americans, of "mother ships," supply canoes, small fast boats, and mule trains, all carrying Soviet block weapons to the guerrillas on El Salvador's southwest coast. The pictures looked more like bread mold than military movements but General Gorman assured reporters that the visual quality was much better in the aircraft cabins.

Other exhibits included Bulgarian ammunition manufactured to NATO standards, a mortar sight made in Vietnam and maps and combat orders captured in fights with the guerrillas. Gorman bore down hard on the number of weapons captured from the guerrillas which were of Soviet-block manufacture or American in origin and proven by their serial numbers to have been used in our war in Vietnam.

If those shipments were being made across the Gulf of Fonseca what were the Salvadoran military and the CIA doing? American warships were stationed off that coast and often came into the gulf. The CIA's gunboats, which during that same time were shelling the Port of Corinto and other coastal towns, were certainly capable of shooting up dugout canoes even though Ambassador Pickering and General Gorman complained that Congress had not given the Salvadoran Navy sufficient funds.

CIA boats had recently shelled and sunk two small ferries. Air traffic was almost constant over the region, Colonel Edward King noted in 1984, only several months before General Gorman's news briefing. King, who had combat experience in World War II and Korea, was skeptical of the reports of shipments, noting that he "found no evidence of any of the normal residue that would be left at an unloading and loading site."

American officials had at first claimed the Contra were created to interdict weapons going to El Salvador which, were their reports of arms shipments true, would have been one of the greatest United States surrogate failures yet. Later they said it was to prevent a Nicaraguan invasion of its neighbors, specifically Honduras. A Contra spokesman assured me, in all the sincerity he could muster, that the purpose of mining the Port of Corinto was not to cripple the country's economy, which I had assumed was the ostensible reason. No, he said, it was to prevent imports, oil and weapons coming into the country to fight the war. If that was so, they were as inept at that as at everything else since the only shipping they damaged seriously was a Japanese freighter arriving to pick up a load of Nicaraguan cotton. All the time, of course, the purpose was really to bring down the Sandinista government.

King examined the country around Somotillo, which was supposed to be the tank route of the Nicaraguan invasion of Honduras and found the ancient Soviet tanks barely able to function. "On the basis of observable tank and troop deployments, the nature of the terrain and road network, and the nonappearance of logistic facilities for offensive operations, it appears that there is very little evidence to support the frequently voiced possibility of any type of offensive operation against Honduras by the Sandinista Army," King said. "The Sandinista armed forces are just not positioned, equipped or supplied in a sufficient manner to undertake an attack against Honduras." To counter that illusory invasion threat United States Army engineer units dug an eight-mile long tank trap, a ditch, on the Honduran side of the border. I was also an infantry soldier for many years and I was in the same area in the years before and after King was there and my observations were the same.

Other embassy people later claimed that weapons and ammunition were being hauled across Honduras from Nicaragua to El Salvador, and Gorman and Pickering repeated the charge. Anything is possible but it is extremely unlikely that many trucks crossing Honduras could evade searches by customs officers or the thieving Honduran Army. Gorman's evidence was more substantial but the conclusions only slightly less ludicrous than the claim made to me that same year by Brooklyn Rivera, the charismatic leader of the Miskito Indians allied with the Contra and based in Costa Rica, the farcical "southern front."

Rivera told me, in what seemed to be total sincerity when I talked to him in a suburb of San Jose, the Costa Rican capitol, that the explosives that damaged several foreign ships and destroyed Nicaraguan oil storage tanks and other dock side facilities at Corinto had been hauled across Nicaragua in trucks from Costa Rica. Contra swimmers had placed the explosives, he said. Actually, as Rivera knew and I knew from studying the wreckage, CIA gunboats shot up those oil tanks and medicine and food warehouses at Corinto.

The harbor at Corinto was actually mined by CIA boats. Like many clandestine activities during the Reagan Administration, the intelligence committees in Congress, supposedly the ultimate insurance against wild, unsupervised capers, were not informed. In 1984 CIA Director William Casey admitted to the Senate Select Intelligence Committee that he had neglected to inform it of the mining of the Port of Corinto.

Prior to the 1984 elections United States reconnaissance planes were routinely supplying intelligence to Salvadoran units on the ground chasing guerrillas and no one, in the press or Congress, asked whether they were above the limit of fifty five advisers established by Congress in El Salvador. Neither did anyone ask if Americans were actually in combat. Reconnaissance work is indeed combat but if any of those fliers were ever hit by ground fire that information was never made public.

One weakness of the intelligence effort revealed inadvertently at the Pickering-Gorman press conference but not picked up by reporters was the weighty reliance on defectors. Deserters from enemy units can be good sources of information, but interrogators must always be wary of possible plants. The fact that the Salvadorans, and their United States handlers, were relying so heavily on defectors emphasized the overall weakness of the Army's intelligence gathering effort. That seemed to be all the intelligence they had. Even more suspect is intelligence squeezed out of captives. The United States Embassy and the Reagan Administration were ready at any time, apparently, to believe confessions extracted under torture.

In May of 1986 a member of the FMLN was arrested in San Salvador and three weeks later was produced by the Treasury Police at a press conference. Luz Yaneth Alfaro Pena told reporters that international donations to Salvadoran human rights groups, including the Mothers of the Disappeared, were mostly diverted to the guerrillas. "Ninety-five percent of this aid goes to the FMLN. Only five percent goes to the people it was intended for," Alfaro said.[38]

She named three senior church officials she said were aware of the diversions, including Archbishop Arturo Rivera y Damas, who had replaced the martyred Archbishop Oscar Romero. A church spokesman denied the charges and noted that "the police have many ways of pressuring people in captivity and we don't know what her psychological resistance is to this." Alfaro denied that she had been pressured into confessing, as they all do, whether it is true or not. A United States Embassy spokesman was quick to say that the embassy believed Alfaro's confession was not extracted by torture.

The Salvadoran Army had long excused its failure to cope with the guerrillas by saying they melted into the countryside when the tide of battle turned against them. But in southwest El Salvador the guerrillas would have had their backs to the sea and should have been fair game for a de-

---

[38] Reuters, June 1, 1986.

termined army exercising classic "hammer and anvil" counter-guerilla tactics. Pickering said the mangrove swamps made sweeps by the Army impossible. Perhaps, but a disciplined army would have tried harder to flush out the guerrillas than that one did. Reporters might have asked what the Army had been doing for the three years prior to the C-130 surveillance in that area. All the action reported at the press conference had taken place within the previous month.

Four years after that press conference, where Gorman gave the familiar litany that the Salvadorans had at last begun to act like fighters and even operated at night, the guerrillas fought their way into the capital, stayed there a week and bloodied the Army which was caught napping as usual. The most telling failure, as Gorman conceded, was that the Army had never yet intercepted any of the cargo canoes. "We know the stuff is coming," he said. "We have yet to get our hands on it (a slip of the tongue, there), or they have yet to get their hands on it. They are as frustrated as we are." Gorman wound up by blaming Congress for not adequately supporting the war effort.

Skeptics of the arms shipping charges included the CIA's own analysts. David McMichael, a Marine officer for ten years, wounded in Vietnam, was not a typical anti-war type. Yet in 1984 not long after he quit the CIA in disgust he was marching in the Thursday morning vigils in front of the United States Embassy in Managua protesting the war. McMichael's job in the CIA was analyzing political and military developments in Central America.

"There has not been any proof, no interception of a shipment, or even any verified reports of shipments from Nicaragua to El Salvador," McMichael told me. "The whole picture that the (Reagan) Administration has presented of Salvadoran insurgent operations being planned, directed and supplied from Nicaragua is simply not true," he told *The New York Times* about the same time.[39] "The Administration and the CIA have systematically misrepresented Nicara-

---

[39] Philip Taubman, The New York Times, June 11, 1984.

guan involvement in the supply of arms to Salvadoran guerrillas to justify its efforts to overthrow the Nicaraguan government."

How many other CIA analysts as well as intelligent, knowledgeable people in the State Department, the Pentagon and other United States agencies dealing with Central America shared McMichael's opinions but were reluctant to risk their careers to say that the emperor had no clothes? Certainly there were many. McMichael was directed by the CIA to write a paper on his findings on political conditions in Nicaragua. He reviewed intelligence reports over the years since 1979. "I could not accept the conclusion, held widely within the Administration, that this was a well-established Marxist-Leninist state." Despite a "surprising degree of support" for his conclusion among his colleagues, the paper was never published. "It made them too uncomfortable."

McMichael said he had done a great deal of soul-searching before going public with his dismay at the CIA and Administration. But he concluded that, as a patriot, he could do nothing else. "I think Congress and the public should know that within the CIA there is pressure to bend information to fit policy." Anyone who followed the wars in Central America should not have been surprised by the revelations in the 1990s that the CIA had doctored reports on the Soviet Union for decades to support administration claims of communist capabilities.

Both the Reagan and Bush Administrations were always nervous when public talk likened the wars in Central America to Vietnam. People in the State Department and the Pentagon knew that the war in El Salvador was much like Vietnam and they went to great lengths to deny the parallels. In both cases a local government indifferent to the majority of its people was propped up by American money and weapons. In each case, the United States supported a military fighting, and generally poorly, only for the gain to itself. Add a corrupt power elite unwilling to concede any role in government to the majority of the population and the similarities are striking.

Among the American proconsuls attempting to distance the Central American wars from Vietnam was Colonel John Waghelstein, the United States Military Group commander in El Salvador in early 1982 through mid 1983. He rejected the Vietnam analogy, "having served in both places."[40] I talked to Waghelstein in 1983 and he understood the necessity of giving the Salvadoran public a stake in a better government. He also seemed to recognize that the army he was advising was made of straw. Supporting his analysis of the dissimilarities of the two wars was the fact that the United States fought the war in Vietnam with its own troops while in El Salvador proxies were the human ingredients of "low intensity conflict." Otherwise, the two conflicts were as similar as any wars in the 20th Century.

The Salvadoran Army's uselessness made it a liability to the United States. A 1992 Rand Corporation study, in concluding that United States policy in El Salvador was a failure, said the military "had the United States trapped...They knew the Americans were implicated in their war for their own national security interests...so threats to withdraw aid had no effect." The study's author, Benjamin Schwarz, said the cost to American taxpayers was more than $6 billion rather than the $4.5 billion usually cited. The big difference, he said, was in some $1 billion "in covert expenses."[41]

A number of Americans, some of them civilians in military roles, died in both El Salvador and Nicaragua, mostly in aircraft crashes. Among them were two pilots killed in 1986 when the Nicaraguan Army, using a Russian surface-to-air missile, shot down their cargo plane as it was dropping supplies to the Contra "Southern Front" in southeastern Nicaragua. Cargo handler Eugene Hasenfus, described to me by a pilot who knew him as a "human forklift," parachuted out of the plane. He was captured, tried, jailed and eventually freed by the Nicaraguans in a goodwill gesture and propaganda ploy.

[40] Col. John Waghelstein, The New York Times op ed page, August 9, 1984.
[41] Report from El Salvador, El Rescate Human Rights Department, Jan. 20-27, 1992.

Nicaraguan investigators said documents retrieved from the plane showed the crew were members of the United States Military Advisory Group (Milgroup) stationed in El Salvador. But Secretary of State George Schultz said the plane had been "hired by private people" and had "no connection" with the government. The Hasenfus fuss should have been embarrassing to the Reagan Administration but it weathered the criticism that followed it, thanks largely to a cowardly Congress and press. The CIA denied any ties to Hasenfus or his mission and again the incident was allowed to die, even in Nicaragua, as new threats and activities took its place in news accounts.

In spite of the accords of 1992, hailed by both the government and the guerrillas as bringing an end to the killing war, although not to the issues that caused it, the United States continued to maintain that El Salvador needed a strong Army. Ambassador William Walker said United States help should continue "to professionalize the Army."[42]

The spirit of the 1850s William Walker lives on in Central America. During all the 1980s various American adventurers, all waving rhetorical anti-communist banners and inspired by Ronald Reagan's hype about "freedom fighters," injected themselves into the action. You could find them at bars in Tegucigalpa admiring each other's knives and sidearms and talking nostalgically of other wars and looking for a little safe action that would give them bragging rights in other such places around the world. They perfected the art of hinting at bad exploits and speaking in fragmented sentences while implying that if their work weren't so secret they could *really* tell some stories. Some were surprisingly knowledgeable, others barely knew what country they were in.

Some were deputy sheriffs from the southern states where "getting your man" is not so easy for a lawman these days when civil rights laws discourage the shooting of blacks. Many of these anti-communist zealots can only be described as peculiar or weird. Some found more excitement

---

[42] Ibid.

than they anticipated and a few at least wound up victims of the people they thought they were going to help. One of these was an expendable drifter named Steven Carr who was twenty six when an American reporter solicited his story in a Costa Rican prison where he was being held for gun running after apparently being betrayed by the CIA.[43]

Certainly Carr talked too much. He told the reporter he hadn't been old enough to fight in the Vietnam war and came to Central America "to raise hell. I grew up with John Wayne movies, I was in ROTC, the Civil Air Patrol, and I was weaned on that stuff." He said he had been accepted by the Contra and described a raid he had accompanied on the "Southern Front" out of Costa Rica into Nicaragua during which, he said, some thirty Sandinista soldiers may have been killed.

Carr said he made contact with the Contra through an American citrus farmer in Costa Rica named Bruce Jones who was later expelled from Costa Rica after *Life* Magazine fingered him as a CIA agent. Carr told FBI agents he had helped ship weapons from Fort Lauderdale, Florida, to Ilopongo, the Salvadoran air base outside San Salvador from where Hasenfus's and many other Contra arms shipments were dispatched.

Carr became "very paranoid and frightened" because of his role as a federal witness, his sister told news reporters. He had reason to be. One night he went outside his home in Van Nuys, California, to retrieve something from his car and didn't come back. A police officer said he "apparently convulsed and died." A coroner's spokesman blamed a drug overdose. Carr wasn't the first, or the last, person with vague ties to the CIA who died under strange circumstances, usually of overdoses.

Almost as lost in fantasy as the unfortunate Carr, but far more deadly, were a bunch of good old boys, mostly Vietnam veterans given to "gun talk" in their southern hunting and fishing camps who decided to take on the job they scorned Congress for fearing to tackle. Their contradicto-

---

[43] Jacqueline Sharkey, Common Cause Magazine, Oct. 1985.

rily named Civilian Military Assistance group supposedly gathered only non-lethal equipment for the Contra. But some members decided that wasn't enough. At least two of them, Dana Parker, a Huntsville, Alabama, police detective, and James Powell, a Memphis flying instructor, were killed when the Sandinistas shot down their helicopter in September of 1984. Parker was reportedly a moonlighting member of the Alabama National Guard's 20th Special Forces Group.

The Nicaraguans said the helicopter had attacked a military training camp at Santa Clara near the Honduran border, killing three children and a camp cook. Thomas V. Posey, a leader of the group, and United States Embassy officials said four senior Cuban military advisers had been killed in the raid. They said, however, that the helicopter, which had been given to the Contra by the CIA, was not involved in the attack on the camp. One account said it had flown to the scene on an "emergency rescue mission."[44] Posey, who said members of his group did not engage in combat but were in Central America only to help the Contra and the Salvadorans with supplies, told reporters that he had been put in touch with Honduran General Gustavo Alvarez Martinez by United States Embassy officials. Earlier they had also helped him make contact with officers of the El Salvador Army.

The State Department in Washington at first said it had no knowledge of the men or their mission. Later, however, American officials admitted knowing of the group but said any help given the mercenaries was no more than embassies give to Americans abroad anywhere. No one ever charged any of these men with violating American neutrality laws even though the FBI made a perfunctory investigation. One CMA member, Jack Terrell, told reporters that FBI agents were asking about reports that the Americans were running drugs on their return flights from Central America. Terrell also mentioned a reported attempt to assassinate the United States ambassador to Costa Rica, Lewis A. Tambs. I heard

---

[44] Associated Press, Los Angeles, Dec. 14, 1986.

that one a number of times but I don't think there was any substance to it although it probably helped justify moving the embassy from its fusty old quarters in downtown San Jose to an enormous new fortress in a suburb.

One of the busiest people roaming around Central America was Rob Owen, an aide and gofer for Lt. Col. Oliver North, the Marine who ran his own foreign policy out of the White House basement, frightening congressmen just with his uniform. Owen, a one-time aide to Vice President Dan Quayle, constantly shows up in accounts of Contra leaders' skullduggery, some of which skirts drug dealing and murder.

The man who called himself Joe Kelso (see Chapter Eleven) kept running into Owen as he tried to follow stories of drug dealing by United States Drug Enforcement Agency agents in Costa Rica. Owen has been accused of being in on meetings where the assassination of on-again-off-again Contra Leader Eden Pastora was being planned.[45] No one asked Owen about that or most of his other alleged activities when he appeared before the Senate Intelligence Committee.

Operating outside North's bureaucracy of death, but with parallel goals and even less restraint, were such people as Major General John Singlaub, who headed the World Anti-Communist League, one of those secret gangs that overgrown adolescents love as backgrounds for their rituals of guns and war. Relieved as commander in Korea by President Carter for overstepping his role as the proconsul there, he was a busy fund-raiser for the Contra effort and other mischief any place in the world where the poor and downtrodden fought back against their oppressors and earned the label communist for their pains. Singlaub's name comes up again and again, in Central America, in Washington, D. C. and in southern bastions of super Americanism such as Dallas and Miami as a hustler for money for the cause. One of his dupes was Ellen Garwood, of a prominent Texas family, who gave him $65,000 as down payment on a helicopter "to take these brave men to the hospital," she said, meaning

[45] Philip Taubman, The New York Times, Sept. 7, 1984.
[46] Jimmy Breslin, Universal Press Syndicate, Dec. 19, 1986.

wounded Contra. Garwood said Singlaub told her the chopper was to be named "Lady Ellen."[46] In such manner do these knights of under-the-table delude themselves and their victims.

Soldier of Fortune magazine, a publication heavy on pictures and macho stories and advertising for badges, weapons and clownish clothing, bought stories from these voyeurs of misery or assigned writers to do pieces on military encounters. The best of the articles were a strange combination, mixing insight into the despair that caused insurrections with tough guy bravado about eliminating "subversives" whose leaders are mostly depicted as outsiders, usually Cubans.

One piece on the "pacification" of the highland Indians of Guatemala included a comment that Lake Atitlan "has become so polluted that many native fish species have disappeared and the indigenous people who until recently used it for both drinking water and a sewer have suffered from gastrointestinal illnesses. Development of a potable water supply is a major project."[47] You could find that comment, wholly true, in *Friends of the Earth* or *Audubon* Magazines. The article went on to say that "It is dissatisfied people, more than weapons, that make a war." Did the weapons hustlers who advertise in the magazine read that? Mostly, however, SOF was filled with adjectives about "commie rats."

Even the article on Guatemala, the most moderate and balanced of any I saw in those magazines, failed to mention the casual massacres by the Guatemalan Army in its war against the people. Another issue of the magazine after George Bush's invasion of Panama carried so many jazzy war stories that it seemed unnecessary for the United States Army to have been involved at all. Again, there was no recognition of the United States provocation of Panamanians, of the American support for money laundering banks or that the villain in all the pieces, Manuel Noriega, was a creature of the United States all along and that his support for drug runners paled in comparison to others.

---

[47] Morgan Tanner, Under the Volcano, Soldier of Fortune, August, 1990, p. 78

Legitimate United States soldiers became instruments of imperialism in a twisted version of defense under the doctrine of Low Intensity Conflict. In places like El Salvador they were usually called advisers, especially when assigned to guide their local "counterparts" in how to carry out their missions. Sometimes they were called trainers, usually when their numbers exceeded the limits Congress had insisted on for advisers for a particular country. Often these were highly skilled Special Forces (Green Berets) soldiers, trained in a wide variety of weapons, American as well as foreign, proficient in Spanish, as expert at stalking and garroting a sentry as at stitching up a stomach wound. The Special Forces soldiers were carefully screened for psychological stability as well as intelligence. They lived with the people they were advising or training. Their Salvadoran counterparts realized that good relations with their advisers were essential to continued materiel support from the United States as well as keeping Congress off their backs.

Many foreigners wondered why, after twelve years of fighting, the El Salvador Army needed tactical advice, especially from soldiers who may not have had nearly the same amount of combat experience. In part, at least, the advisers were there to stiffen the backs of their counterparts, to hold down their thievery and to moderate the behavior of their troops.

Advisers are supposed to work closely with their counterparts but at the same time keep a detached distance from them. One who failed to do that was Major Eric Buckland, who was advising the Salvadoran Army in its psychological operations center during the 1989 guerrilla offensive that caught the high command by complete surprise. The guerillas, so the Army command reasoned in its rage, were being supported if not directed by traitors inside San Salvador, the capitol. The Army had long hated the Catholic priests who preached to the poor of El Salvador that they had rights. Particularly annoying were the Jesuit priests of the University of Central America, UCA, mostly Spanish intellectuals who frequently denounced the Army and its auxiliary death squads.

The assassination in the early morning of November 16, 1989 of six Jesuits priests and their housekeeper and her daughter is told in Chapter 12. For here the story is of Buckland and the State Department and other United States entities that rallied to defend the killers. The first response of the Salvadoran Government and the American Embassy to news of the killings was to accuse the FMLN guerrillas of committing the murders in disguise as Army soldiers to rouse the world against the government. That was obviously the intent of the assassins who left a sign on the door of the Jesuit residence: "The FMLN executes government spies. Victory or death! FMLN." The State Department continued to push that line until President Alfredo Christiani announced that soldiers had been arrested for questioning.

Even before the murders Buckland had been told by a Salvadoran colonel to whom he had become very close, Carlos Armando Aviles, that the Army was going into UCA and "clean out" the Jesuit priests there.[48] Two months after the murders Buckland reported that information to the head of the United States Military Group advising the Salvadorans. That officer went to Salvadoran Army headquarters and confronted the high command. His indiscretion not only put Aviles in extreme danger but it also meant that never again was a Salvadoran officer likely to confide in his American adviser.

Aviles was jailed, not for blowing the whistle on his comrades, the embassy said, but because he lied to his superiors when he denied he was Buckland's informant. He flunked a lie detector test but was released after reporters began asking questions. "Nobody got on television and announced that Aviles did something," an administration source was quoted as saying.[49] Meanwhile, the Bush Administration, alarmed at its client's latest atrocity and aware that killing priests en masse is more damaging in the public's eyes than other slaughter, ordered FBI agents to El Salva-

---

[48] Associated Press, Austin, Texas

[49] Transcript of FBI interrogation of Maj. Eric Warren Buckland, Jan. 12, 1990, p. 5.

dor to question Buckland.

His responses deserve special attention by all Americans concerned about their country's growing militarization.

"Everything just kept eating and eating and eating at me because I knew I had an obligation as a U.S. Army officer and as an American to pass this on and I sat on it. And I failed to do my duty," Buckland told FBI Agent Paul Cully in a long interview in San Salvador.

Buckland described the Salvadoran officer corps as a Mafia-like organization ready to do anything including murder to protect itself.

When the State Department saw Buckland's testimony he was declared "mentally unstable." His wandering answers to the FBI might seem proof, or perhaps they reveal a soul in torment. "I really care for this country (El Salvador)," he said. "What I didn't want to happen was to watch these guys cover it up and try to get away with it. Which I didn't want them to. And then have the press get in such a way that the Congress reacts and the guys had lied and they screwed themselves.

"I did not feel disloyal to the United States, but I felt for a long time that I loved the ideals of my country, but I don't much like the people there. And I really loved the Salvadorans and I like their military...I realize I had a struggle. You know, he (Aviles) talked about them (the Jesuits) being killed..."but I really had the impression that we cleared this up...I can honestly say that if I had known, I probably wouldn't have been too upset that they were going to do it..." (Ellipses are in the transcript).

Aviles, Buckland said, went out of his way to have him go along to a meeting at which some secret project was being planned. Buckland wasn't in on the meeting, but Aviles wanted him nearby, to know that it happened, Buckland later surmised. There was apparently another reason also, as Buckland was to find out. Aviles told Buckland that Army Chief of Staff Emilio Ponce had sent him to see Colonel Guillermo Benavides Moreno. "I said who's Colonel Benavides? And he said something to the effect that Colonel Benavides was a hard charger, being of the old school…"

"I said, 'what's the problem?' And then he said that Benavides wanted to do something stupid. And to the best of my knowledge it involved getting into the UCA.

"Benavides had been making noises about going in after Father (Ignacio) Ellacuria, a Jesuit priest and instructor, basically well respected (and the rector, or head of UCA). He was the most outspoken about the government. At that time he was an enemy figure, if you will. That goes back to the old school that the enemy is not necessarily the guy carrying a weapon, it's the mouthpiece too." Ellacuria was "dirty," Buckland said. "An action was going to be taken."

"To kill him?" the FBI man asked.

"Yeah," Buckland said. "To go in at Ellacuria. I can honestly say I had no love for any of the leftist people. Okay. I loved El Salvador and I can honestly say I knew the ramifications of any of those kinds of murders to the country, but I didn't think a whole lot about somebody getting killed."

The guerrilla offensive, Buckland said, was "almost a disaster in the city. And I can remember different days feeling doom and gloom…I just felt like this was the end. Yeah. I felt like, oh my God, we're going to fall. I can remember talking to somebody in the Embassy and the last thing I said was 'I'll see you on the roof of the embassy, a la Saigon.' It was bad."

Aviles told him, Buckland said, that "the military was going in and clean out the UCA." What did that mean? the interrogator asked.

"To find out, you know, to get the dirty people in there."

"To do what?"

"Kill people, you know, to take stuff, whatever it was. I don't remember at the time thinking they were going to kill the priests."

The FBI man asked why Buckland hadn't told American officials earlier.

"I had several feelings," Buckland said. "One, whenever Aviles told me anything, I felt an intense loyalty to him." He went on to say "I guess I was really trying to pro-

203

tect El Salvador because I had knowledge...I didn't trust the American government. I thought they'd pull the rug out from under the country. I mean, I was kind of lost. I wanted to kill everybody too. You know, I wanted to go out and fight, but we couldn't go out and fight. I got caught between the right thing to do and the loyalty. You know, down here loyalty is number one, here integrity's number one. And I switched." He did, after the murders, tell what he knew and what he thought.

The Pentagon and the State Department released only small details of the Buckland interrogation and even that reluctantly. But it was cited in the trial of Benavides and his subordinates and then someone leaked to a Mexican newspaper a full transcript of the summary given here of his questioning by the FBI. Some of it was printed in Mexico, and eventually the transcript was passed to me by Central American Mission Partners of Oakland, California. The State Department's early version, until the full truth came into the light, was that Buckland had not reported what he knew because he "understood that information was already known by the Salvadoran investigators, so he didn't bring it to the attention of United States authorities immediately."[50]

Shortly after his initial report Buckland and his immediate superiors went to the office of Colonel Ponce, the chief of staff. Aviles was there too and Buckland began to realize he'd been betrayed. "Colonel Aviles said that we had spoken about the Jesuits in general terms, but the basic feeling still was that the FMLN (the guerillas), the Army or some extreme right-wing group had done it, but that's all anybody knew. You know, even that was way off from what we talked about.

"I knew I'd just been called a liar. I did everything in the world I could to cover Colonel Aviles...I sat there like there were some thousand buffalos sitting on me. I just felt like shit...His (Aviles') eyes were bulging, he was agitated, he was jumping around in his chair. I couldn't even look at him. I'm still feeling bad."

[50] Lindey Gruson, The New York Times, Washington, D. C. Jan., 19, 1990, p. A3.

Buckland told the FBI agent of his three small sons and how they were growing up back home without him but that he "thought I could save the world."

"You thought you could save El Salvador?"

"Sure, I was going to be Lawrence of Arabia, you know, Eric of El Salvador. I thought I could go down and by saving, by helping El Salvador I could keep this stuff from ever getting to our country.

The FBI man was sympathetic: "It really bothered you that you were betrayed by them after you were trying to help them?"

"It breaks my heart," Buckland replied, "because I realize that I don't know how deep or how wide this thing goes, but somebody's dirty.

"I knew they hinted, at a minimum to me, I had knowledge that they were going to go in...They did it. He told me. You know, like I said. And then denied it. Something else was going on. I knew it was a political thing, too. They're playing games, they not only had to go kill people, then they have to do something with it. Then they just had to throw me in the middle. You know, to tell me, I don't know what he wanted me to do, I don't know what he expected me to do. I don't know why he was jerking me around.

"You know, like I said, he threw me little things. But I was used. I don't know how. There was a plot in there somewhere and I was in there somewhere. I was somebody's card. I was Aviles' card, I think. He had an alibi that night because we (Buckland and another American adviser in their quarters) saw him. And he also told me I was there on Benavides. I had doubt about Benavides. And I think had I not spoken it would have broken another way and I somehow would have been in there doing the same stuff again as I'm doing now which he could probably give a shit less about. They would've opened up some doors for Aviles and his boys. That's all that I can think that it was.

"And in the end, they killed six priests. You know, I don't even care what their political preferences were, but they killed them, they were tools." It wasn't vengeance,

Buckland said. "I can understand somebody going nuts, but I can't understand just killing them to do something with them."

The FBI man then asked Buckland "Do you feel that it was because of your loyalty to El Salvador that made you overlook those killings or to accept those killings? Do you feel your loyalty got in the way and that's why you accepted them when you normally would not?"

"I got caught up in the country, you know," Buckland said. "We're at war. Who understands better than us, we're here, we're at the front, you know, at the cutting edge. So I know I can see, I can look into their hearts. That's bullshit.

"I probably would've kept my mouth shut if I thought it was reasonable and apparently from what I knew about this and didn't go running to tell anybody either before, when it was innuendos at the worst, and after what I was told, I didn't say squat. And it's because I guess I thought I knew, you know, I knew better."

Then, after all that agonized squirming over the truth, Buckland disavowed his own testimony.

11

Prologue to a Farce

*"A popular government without popular information,
or the means of acquiring it, is but a prologue to a farce
or a tragedy; or perhaps both."*
—James Madison,
1822, former United States president

EUPHEMISMS WERE WEAPONS IN THE PROPAGANDA WAR
the United States waged in Central America as it crafted new
covers for old approaches to imperialism. "Structural adjust-
ments" disguised economic offensives; "Low Intensity Conflict" soothed American guilt over bullying smaller nations
and hid the human cost of bloody conflicts.

"Communism" needed no disguise; its overthrow as a
world wide menace had long justified violations of constitu-
tional or statute law, no matter who got in the way and
would be hurt. Marketing Communism as even more a
threat than it legitimately was provided profitable employment for thousands and kept many congressmen in office
long past their shelf lives. The battle against Communism
shielded commercial interests that used their vast wealth to
gain the ear of officials whose thumbs were on the right but-
tons. And if those officials failed to recognize their duties
they were expendable. In mercantilist America the number
of recruits eager and willing to do the corporate bidding
was inexhaustible.

Guatemala affords an example of the misery caused

by United States policy, or the absence of a policy to which the American public has access. The civilian death toll at the hands of death squads and the Army in Guatemala since 1954 is more than one hundred thousand, higher than in either of the better known conflicts in Nicaragua or El Salvador. Another forty thousand have "disappeared" and are likely dead. The military concedes that its civil affairs program entails killing thirty percent of the population of an area to convince the other seventy percent to behave as the Army wishes. Actually, the Army welcomes guerrilla resistance, which has been rather ineffectual, as justification for keeping a presence in the Indian-populated mountains.

Even well publicized killings go unpunished; Myrna Mack, an internationally recognized anthropologist was stabbed to death in September of 1990 while she was investigating the plight of Guatemala's one million internal refugees. Her sister, Helen Mack, accused the former chief of staff of the Guatemalan Army of responsibility. A National Police investigator, Jose Merida Escobar, who identified her murderer as a former employee of Army Chief of Staff Edgar Augusto Godoy, was himself slain. Merida, who had received numerous death threats and was told by the Interior Ministry to defend himself with his own weapon, was also investigating the murder of Michael Devine, an American who operated a jungle restaurant in Guatemala. With Merida's murder there is little likelihood Mack's killers will ever come to trial although the soldiers who killed Devine were sentenced to prison. Killings of peasants continue, under whatever government, and few arrests are ever made.

Political instability is the conventional reason for the country's desperation, and it is largely correct. But the facts behind that turmoil are seldom recognized. Guatemala is ruled by an oligarchy that glories in the excesses of the conquistadores, unlike the cultural rejection of those freebooters found in Mexico and the countries to the south. When Hernan Cortes and European disease shattered the Aztec empire in 1521, he rid himself of one of his most quarrelsome lieutenants, Pedro de Alvarado, by sending him south to subdue the Indians in "new lands," which meant present day Guatemala. Alvarado was efficient; he slaughtered two thirds of Guatemala's Indians and enslaved the survivors.

Spanish oppression of its colonies led to revolution and independence for Guatemala in 1821. In 1827 Guatemala abolished slavery although not until 1944 was forced labor for Indians ended. German and American commercial interests, primarily agricultural with emphasis on banana production, really ruled the country for the next hundred years. In 1944 with the United States busy at war in Europe and Asia, a reform coalition succeeded in holding Guatemala's first real election, choosing a lawyer named Juan Jose Arevalo as president. He and the next president, Jacobo Arbenz, instituted many reforms, including a social security system, the right to organize in unions and to strike. A state bank to free small businessmen and farmers from the clutches of loan sharks was established and an effort begun to distribute idle farm land to families willing to work it.

"But we found that our government was really ruled by a supranational government, through the United States State Department," said Guillermo Toriello Garrido, when I met him in 1981 in his exile in Cuernavaca, Mexico. Toriello's tale encapsulates as well as any I know how American actions in the absence of a public policy led to further oppression of people who had been mistreated by outsiders for centuries. As we sat in the spring-like early morning at an outdoor restaurant I noticed a bulge in the outline of a pistol in the burnished leather of the briefcase he always carried. That was his protection, he said, for the day when the military government of Guatemala sent the killers after him.

Toriello was probably seen as a traitor to his class; from a landed family, he was a student leader at the University of Guatemala in protests against outside exploitation. In 1945 Toriello left his law practice—he had represented some German, Japanese and Italians whose lands in Guatemala had been taken from them at United States urging during the war—and became minister of foreign affairs. Later that year he was the Guatemalan delegate to the United Nations

209

founding convention in San Francisco.

The United Fruit Company had for fifty years been acquiring lands and at that time held some 500,000 acres, 85 percent of which was idle.[51] "When President Arbenz asked me to join the government I at first refused but when he told me we would make an agrarian reform, I agreed," Toriello told me.

"A big campaign was started in the United States by the United Fruit Company and the State Department to convince the American people that we were a communist government," he said. Toriello was sent to Washington, as ambassador, to tell Guatemala's side of the story.

"President Arbenz told me to tell President Eisenhower that we will pay United Fruit the declared value of their lands," Toriello said. That may have been good for the satisfaction it gave, but everyone knew that the company set its own valuations, for tax purposes, and those land values were low, totaling $1.8 million.

Toriello was up against a powerful cabal. Secretary of State John Foster Dulles's law firm represented United Fruit; his brother, Allen Dulles, director of the Central Intelligence Agency, had also been a lawyer for the company. General Walter Bedell Smith, an Eisenhower advisor and former director of the CIA, joined the board of United Fruit after helping to overthrow the Arbenz government. John Moors Cabot, undersecretary of state for Inter-American Affairs, and his cousin, Henry Cabot Lodge, United Nations Ambassador, were both large stockholders in the company.[52] After months of being blocked by Cabot, Toriello got a chance at a diplomatic reception to talk about golf with Eisenhower, an avid golfer, and he was able to set up an appointment with the president.

It didn't go well. Cabot was there in the Oval Office and when Toriello tried to explain Guatemala's long oppression and the plans for agrarian reform, Cabot, Toriello

---

[51] Tom Barry, Beth Wood, Deb Preuch, Dollars and Dictators, A Guide to Central America, Grove Press, New York, p. 119.
[52] Martin Tolchein, The New York Times, Washington, D. C. Jan. 15, 1990.

told me, interrupted and said "don't listen to him Mr. President. These people are communists."

"I told Ike that we were trying to make Guatemala a country of, by and for the people after enduring so many tyrants," Toriello said. He showed Eisenhower a map of the country with the United Fruit holdings marked. "They even owned the lighthouses.

"I couldn't convince him that we were moving toward a new capitalistic system patterned on that of the United States," Toriello said. Eisenhower told him to talk to John Foster Dulles, he said.

Dulles, he said, described the Arbenz government as a "beach head for communism in Central America." Not long afterward the CIA, working with the dictator Anastasio Somoza in nearby Nicaragua, gathered an army on a United Fruit plantation in Honduras and with bombers mysteriously appearing overhead, smashed the Arbenz government and ended its experiment in independence.[53]

Toriello, then Guatemala's representative at the United Nations in New York, protested the affair, labeling it "an aggression, making it clear that we thought the United States government was behind it.

"John Foster Dulles said I had 'insulted the United States'," Toriello said sadly.

Colonel Castillo Armas became president and immediately gave the land back to United Fruit, cracked down on the unions and turned back most of the reforms. Vice President Richard Nixon gave the United States stamp of approval in Guatemala City: "This is the first instance in history when a Communist government has been replaced by a free one."[54] Guatemala since then has been ruled by a series of brutal, even crazy, dictators, usually with figurehead presidents.Toriello had hopes for John Kennedy's Alliance for Progress, which was supposed to include the United States' Latin neighbors in deliberations about their future.

---

[53] The full depressing story has been told in *Bitter Fruit*, by Stephen Kinzer and Stephen Schlesinger, Doubleday, 1982.
[54] Richard Nixon, What I Learned in Latin America, This Week, Aug. 7, 1955.

"Within only a few years, the Alliance demonstrated itself to be an instrument exclusively at the service of the great United States monopolies and their allies, the dominant privileged classes of our countries," Toriello wrote.

None of this was a secret in the United States. Books were published about it and the subject was resurrected in magazines and specialized publications periodically. When Guatemala's official criminality became too much during President Jimmy Carter's term, 1976 to 1980, he cut off the flow of weapons to its Army. Israel filled the void with guns and ammunition and training in their use. Shortly after Ronald Reagan was elected he heeded the cry that communism was a threat and reopened the spigot of military toys.

Guatemala's genocide against its Indians continued after the wars in Nicaragua and El Salvador abated in the early 1990s. Even as international groups were protesting in mid 1993 the failure to bring Myrna Mack's murderers to justice, the chief of staff of the United States Army, General Gordon Sullivan, was in Guatemala City reassuring the government that American weapons would continue to come their way. During the 1990s revelations of CIA alliances with the official killers surfaced again and again. But each time the screams of outrage died as the United States news media turned to new excitments, sports and televison stars, British royalty or other sinners.

The propaganda war in Central America went on all through the armed conflicts and continues today. It was fought on many fronts, from the jungle homes of peasants who knew only the hurt that came their way, through the editorial boards and newsrooms of American newspapers and television stations. In Nicaragua, in the field, techniques for winning the hearts and minds of the Nicaraguan campesinos were laid out in a pamphlet titled Psychological Operations in Guerrilla Warfare. The pseudonymous author is listed only as "Tayacan" but it has the ideological fingerprints of the CIA all over it.

Because it was propaganda doesn't mean the manual's every word is sinister. Most of it is perfectly rational, the sort of guide anyone, in any field, should be expected to follow.

"The essence of armed propaganda," it said, should include "freedom of thought, freedom of expression and concentration of thoughts on the objectives of democratic struggle." The goal, said the manual, was a "guerrilla who in a persuasive manner can justify all of his acts whenever he is in contact with any member of the town/people..."

Good guerrillas, the manual said, have "respect for human rights and others' property, help the people in community work and protect the people from Communist aggressions."

But there was a dark side. Guerrillas, the manual said, "always involve implicit terror because the population, without saying it aloud, feels terror that the weapons may be used against them...If the government police cannot put an end to the guerrilla activities, the population will lose confidence in the government, which has the inherent mission of guaranteeing the safety of citizens. However, the guerrillas should be careful not to become an explicit terror, because this would result in a loss of popular support."

Kidnap all officials, establish a public tribunal where local officials will be shamed, ridiculed and humiliated and take them out of town "without damaging them publicly," the manual said. When a local citizen is shot it should be explained to the rest that he was attempting to inform to the Sandinistas that the "freedom commandos" were in their town, apparently whether that was true or not.

"Selective use of violence for propagandistic effects" will be conducted in front of the assembled populace of an occupied town "so they will be present, take part in the act and formulate accusations against the oppressor." Mao Zedung never said it better.

In development of agitators against the government, the manual says, "if possible professional criminals will be hired to carry out selective 'jobs'." Instructions were given for creating "martyrs" by demonstrations and "apparent spontaneous protests" and confrontations with the authorities "to bring about uprisings or shootings."

Opponents of the Sandinistas were apparently following this line when they stoned Sandinista police, inviting retaliation, at Nandaime before the 1990 election when United States Ambassador Richard Melton happened to be present to watch martyrs being created. Just what an American ambassador was doing at a political rally in a small rural town miles from Managua was never explained, but the Sandinistas ordered him and some of his staff out of the country. Following dictates of the manual paid off; the incident made the Sandinistas look bad before the world.

Some of that manual's more commonsensical elements could have been instructive in the Reagan National Security Council. Four years after Reagan stepped down from his throne new evidence was turning up that his operatives broke laws, lied to Congress, wasted taxpayers' money and ran their own foreign policy in the name of anti-communism. The American people learned at a special White House press conference that American missiles had been traded to Iran for American hostages. "Residual" money from the deal bought arms for the Contra in their camps in Honduras after a disillusioned Congress had cut them off. Many people in Central America, and not just the Sandinistas, had wondered for some time where that money was coming from. Eventually Reagan was to testify, in a confused and embarrassing videotaped cross-examination, that he had known nothing of it all. Among the keys to the sorry tale were the notebooks kept by Oliver North, a Marine lieutenant colonel on detail to the National Security Council, the body charged with keeping the president informed of matters affecting the security of the nation.

How career military officers noted more for their eccentricities than their intellects were chosen for these jobs has never been clear. North probably would have been a good battalion commander for a beach assault. But he was not what a person of a civilized country, or probably any other, would want carrying out, not to mention making, secret policy at the very highest level. Yet he was managing a war in Central America based on the vague maunderings of

President Reagan. And he was dealing with some of the world's sleaziest con men for hostages all the while his boss, the president, was righteously telling the public he would never bargain with terrorist hostage takers.

The White House told the public that only those directly involved, North and a few others, knew what was going on. The press was frightened off by a stock response to any inquiry about George Bush and the scandal: "The vice president's role in the Iran-Contra affair was completely examined in the congressional inquiry, and we have nothing to add." The public seemed fatigued by the barrage of information that continued to keep the scandal alive without resolving it.

The propaganda offensive of the 1980s spilled over to the home front too. The campaign was an attempt to counter the witness of many citizens who were going to Central America to see for themselves what was happening there. Otto Reich, who held ambassador rank as head of The Office of Public Diplomacy in the State Department, toured the country touting the Reagan Administration line, that an American attempt to bring democracy to the people of Central America was jeopardized by an "the external factor...an armed minority gaining and holding power by force."

A commission headed by former Secretary of State Henry Kissinger found, Reich said blandly, that "the Reagan Administration has not exaggerated the outside role." Other Central American countries were threatened, he said, including Costa Rica which "is suffering tremendous pressures." He didn't mention that the heaviest pressure on Costa Rica was coming from the United States, which wanted that country to abandon its neutral stance and establish an army.

The Reagan Administration was attempting to shore up respect for human rights, Reich said, rejecting my contentions that the militaries and the death squads had taken heart and resumed their depredations when Reagan succeeded Carter in office. "We have to build democratic institutions," Reich said, "elections to let the people decide who will govern them, where (political) candidates can articulate their positions. They need an independent judiciary and we are sending teams to help where justice has broken down."

One "little sign of progress," Reich said, was the conviction of the Salvadoran soldiers who had killed four American churchwomen. Not long after that I saw those men in their posh, special section of Mariona Prison. Reich said American maneuvers in Honduras near the border with Nicaragua "were requested by the Hondurans because they are concerned at the buildup in Nicaragua." General Gustavo Alvarez, Honduran chief of staff, certainly requested whatever American military aid he could wheedle with his tales of communist dangers (see Chapter Fourteen). But most Hondurans resented the increasingly arrogant American presence in their country.

Reich's denunciations included Robert White, the ambassador to El Salvador when the churchwomen were killed. White, Reich said, "has ignored the fact that El Salvador is a totally different country now than it was when he was there" but was continuing to hammer at the country's human rights record. Reich's was the skilled pitch of a salesman, with each question a twist on fact, the whole show financed illegally by the American taxpayers it was designed to influence.

As late as 1984 a Contra spokesman in Honduras was insisting that "the CIA has no involvement in our operations." He was Edgar Chamorro, who not long after that admitted that he had passed CIA money to journalists in Costa Rica to slant their stories against the Sandinistas. (See Chapter Six)

"Our commanders are Nicaraguans, our drill sergeants, our mortar trainers, our pilots are all Nicaraguans," Chamorro told me as we drank beer at the Honduran Mayan Hotel, the hangout of Contra commanders as well as the staging area for American troops arriving in Honduras. Not long after I talked to Chamorro he defected from the Contra and denounced their terror tactics, the same incidents he had denied to me had even happened. He later testified to Contra atrocities at the World Court trial of the United States by Nicaragua. Nicaragua won the case but the Reagan Administration ignored the verdict.

Among the weird North Americans who performed on the Central American stage during the Reagan reign was the man who called himself Joe Kelso. I don't necessarily buy his story. But it fits with the kinds of things that did happen in the shifting scenes of war and duplicity in Central America in the 1980s. His tale includes enough background truths that I think it deserves at least a mention, if for no other reason than that it has been ignored, so far as I know, by both the general press and the specialized and alternative media. It highlights the dangers to even peaceful Costa Rica, that desperately neutral country, in the paranoia that racked all of Central America for so long. Kelso's deposition in a long and involved lawsuit arising out of one of the many side-shows of the war against Nicaragua shines a light from a different direction on the unsavory characters involved in what became known as the Iran/Contra scandal.

This story starts with Eden Pastora, a vain man dubbed "Commandante Kodak" by United States reporters based in Costa Rica where he postured through the war. Earlier in the Nicaraguan revolution, before the final triumph, when Pastora was known as "Commandante Zero," he led a daring commando raid on the National Palace, seizing diplomatic hostages whom he exchanged for political prisoners held by the dictator Somoza.

After the 1979 victory, however, Pastora broke with the Sandinistas when they would not give him the high rank in the new government he thought his heroic stature called for. He became a leader of the Contra southern front, operating out of Costa Rica. Despite his vanity he retained some principles and he would not cooperate with former Somoza National Guardsmen, such as Colonel Enrique Bermudez, the chief Contra in the field. Pastora also refused to take orders from the CIA and in the summer of 1984 he called a cease-fire, saying he had run out of funds. He was lousing up the CIA's low intensity conflict.

One day at the end of May in 1984 Pastora was holding a press conference at a shabby place called La Penca just inside Nicaragua. A Libyan terrorist named Amac Galil, recruited in Chile and calling himself Per Anker Hansen, a Danish freelance photographer, placed a large camera case under the table at which Pastora stood, and ducked out the door. Explosives in the suitcase were detonated by a timing device and most of those present were hit by metal fragments.

Pastora was only slightly injured. Linda Frazier of the English language *Tico Times* lost both legs and bled to death while Galil fled in a boat downstream to Costa Rica and disappeared. Two other reporters were killed and a dozen wounded. One of the wounded was another American, Tony Avirgan, who with his wife, Martha Honey, makes up a freelance news team based in Costa Rica. Avirgan and Honey say American officials in the region planted accusations that the Sandinistas had attempted to kill Pastora[55] whom they considered a traitor to their cause. Avirgan and Honey accused John Hull, an American with large land holdings in Northern Costa Rica, of being an agent of the Central Intelligence Agency and of complicity in setting up the bombing. Hull sued them for libel, in a Costa Rican court, and they won.

Avirgan suspected a "renegade faction" within the Sandinista Party may have pulled off the La Penca bombing. On the other hand, he said, the Sandinistas believed Pastora was worth more to them alive, mucking up the Southern Front, than he would have been dead. Or it may have been the work of infiltrators within the party. Daniel Ortega brushed off the bombing as a "small incident" in a long war.

Hull was accused by Costa Rica of allowing drugs to be shipped out on "back hauls" from his farm airstrip after they delivered weapons from the United States to the Contra. Hull was eventually charged in a Costa Rican court with murder (the La Penca deaths) and drug and arms trafficking. A millionaire with a visceral fear of the communists he thought were everywhere, he made his fortune farming in Indiana. He skipped bail in Costa Rica and returned to the United States where he was always just getting ready to un-

---

[55] Martha Honey, and Tony Avirgan, The Nation, Oct. 5, 1985, p. 311.

dergo heart surgery when American officials were asked why this country refused to honor Costa Rica's requests for his extradition. He had, for some reason, taken out Costa Rican citizenship.

Joe Kelso, which may be his real name, had no direct connection with the La Penca bombing. But he says he was ordered to standby in a San Jose hotel room at about the same time as the bombing, to be available to make someone "negative." The order never came but he assumes the someone was Pastora. Kelso's story comes from conversation with him and from a legal deposition for Avirgan and Honey when they sued Hull and a number of other characters whose names became familiar in the Iran/Contra hearings.

Kelso, who hinted at being a former CIA agent, said he was then an investigator for the United States Customs Service, looking for evidence of complicity in drug dealing by American officials stationed in Costa Rica. He was also, he said, looking for a ring of counterfeiters working in the United States Embassy in San Jose, the nation's capital, who were producing forged American passports. These people were apparently Costa Ricans, but it is doubtful they could have been doing what Kelso says they were doing without some American in the embassy knowing about it. In his deposition Kelso said he was communicating with his bosses in their offices in the United States through couriers because the embassy was "dirty," or "not secure." After he made his report, he said, the embassy was closed 45 days to clean it up. Certainly the embassy in that little country is one of our most unusual, and large ones, in all the world.

Kelso discovered "numerous discrepancies" in Drug Enforcement Administration totals of cocaine seized, he said, and he suspected the DEA officials were "skimming" drugs from seizures. "We would have two witnesses, both of them extremely credible people; counted the kilos (weights) coming off the airplanes (after drug arrests). It was directly half the amount by the time it got back to San Jose."

Kelso in his deposition mentioned a right wing group called Costa Rica Libre which was apparently working with some Americans in training a paramilitary organization for the day when Latin machismo would once more assert itself in their country. Costa Rica Libre, said Kelso, who is no liberal, was also dealing with the Colombia Medellin drug cartel, and its training camps were sites of big drug laboratories. At one point in his deposition he casually mentioned that he had Vice President George Bush's private telephone number for use when absolutely needed. Much of this may not be the truth, although some of it obviously is, and Kelso's talk would be of no real value in assessing the history of American foreign policy in Central America in the 1980s if it weren't for his report of finding a cache of weapons.

He stumbled on the weapons, mostly automatic "assault" rifles, in a warehouse in northern Costa Rica. They were supposedly destined originally for use by Pastora's southern front Contra. Kelso was beaten up by guards and rescued by John Hull, he said, in a tale as disjointed and dramatic as any airport newsstand paperback. Pastora's resistance to doing the CIA's bidding had rendered the weapons surplus, apparently, and by the time Kelso found them they were available for sale for $50,000 "per unit" although Kelso never spelled out the number of weapons.

When Kelso told of the discovery to his "control," the man to whom he reported and whom he identifies as "A" in Washington State, he was told to forget ever seeing them and to keep his mouth shut. Kelso dropped the subject, he said, but a short while later, he said, he inadvertently discovered that these weapons were also available, for free, to a group called M19.

M19 was a Colombian left wing guerilla organization. Why would the CIA, and right wing Americans working against Nicaragua's Sandinistas, give valuable weapons to leftist guerrillas? Good question. Kelso's answer is that someone (he doesn't specifically say it was the CIA although that is the impression he seems to want to leave) offered the weapons to M19 if it would assassinate President Oscar Arias of Costa Rica. Why again? Well, first, Costa Rica had long angered the United States by refusing to have an army.

And specifically at that time President Ronald Reagan was very upset with Arias for his prattling about a Central American peace plan, for which the Costa Rican president was awarded the Nobel Peace Prize in 1987.

Arias's overture threatened to frustrate Reagan's wars in the region. His plan required that all foreign troops be withdrawn from all Central American countries which, if Reagan had chosen to abide by it, would have meant pulling the terrorist Contra out of Honduras as well as the increasing number of Americans stationed there. Arias was highly critical of the Sandinistas in neighboring Nicaragua but not enough for Reagan.

But was anyone sufficiently angry at Arias to want to kill him and run the risk of being implicated in his death? The peace plan had already been adopted by the other countries of the region and the United States didn't intend to abide by it anyway.

Kelso spins a wider scenario: M19's murder of Arias would provoke the United States, out of duty to its wards in the hemisphere, to go into Central America with guns blazing to "clean up" not only Nicaragua and its alleged communist government but also Noriega in Panama and any stray left wing types who might be hanging around Costa Rica too. He said the CIA was calling it the "48-hour sweep"—it would all be over in all three countries in 48 hours which, insofar as Nicaragua might be concerned was a dangerous hallucination. When Kelso reported this new intelligence to his control, "A" became even more upset. Kelso was told to shut up and to stop snooping around or he would be shut up.

That may be partly why Kelso was willing to give testimony in the Avirgan-Honey lawsuit against Hull, Richard Secord, John Singlaub and other members of what the couple call "the enterprise." It was hardly out of any contrition on the part of Kelso, who insisted that he had seen some kind of executive decree, which he could not further identify, which authorized him, under certain orders, to make "negative" anyone needing that final treatment.

221

Talking to Kelso reveals an intelligent but unschooled man of no nerves whose conversation can be coldly chilling but not because of any false bravado. He talks tough and he is. But under that tough exterior may have lurked a deep resentment against the CIA.

Early in his career as a spook, when Kelso was proving himself, he said, he took part in a "sting" operation in the United States against a German Nazi war criminal who was selling stolen American missiles to Iraq. The sting was sufficiently real or security was so bad that Kelso and another man were arrested and jailed by Customs agents and he was ordered by the CIA to plead guilty in a Denver federal court rather than have too much of the truth come out in the open during a trial. But his then CIA control did not, or could not, keep a promise that he would be freed quickly and Kelso spent time in prison, at first a dangerous maximum security place but later in a California country club jail. He says little of that incident in his deposition or in private conversation, mentioning it only to prove his bona fides. But although the tone is moderate one need not be a psychologist to suspect that Kelso harbored some resentment for that jail time and what he obviously sees as a betrayal.

M19 was just one of a number of guerrilla groups plaguing Colombia, some of them collaborating with the country's vicious drug cartels whenever it suited both parties or at least one of them and the other could pull a betrayal for a profit. Mostly the drug traffickers joined forces with right wing death squads in their common fight with the leftist guerrillas. But not always." During past crackdowns, (in Colombia's battle against drug kingpins), the traffickers have turned to Colombia's guerrilla groups to rent extra firepower," Avirgan and Honey say.

In 1985 the traffickers are believed to have hired M19 to take the country's Supreme Court hostage. Eleven Supreme Court justices died, along with some thirty hostages and all the guerrillas themselves when the Colombian Army refused to even attempt to negotiate but blasted into the court building with tanks. In 1991 M19 gave up its weapons and became a legitimate political party. For its civic pains a number of its leaders, including a presidential candidate, were assassinated by drug hoodlums. "Colombia's largest group, the Revolutionary Armed Forces of Colombia, is feuding with the traffickers. In the last four years, paramilitary squads organized by the traffickers are believed to have murdered 750 members of this guerrilla group's left wing."[56]

Kelso's tale may be all fantasy, but he named names of some of the plotters and CIA hangers on in the deposition before they ever appeared in public print. At one time, he said, his assignment was to kidnap Robert Vesco, a United States fugitive financier who had been given safe haven, for a price, in Costa Rica. Other tales as bizarre as Kelso's emerged from Costa Rica in those years. One was a supposed attempt to bomb the United States embassy and blame it on the Sandinistas. An alleged effort to kill United States Ambassador Lewis Tambs, a swashbuckling political appointee, was also laid at the doorstep of the Sandinistas. Neither of those incidents ever came off, if indeed either was ever contemplated.

Another Kelso story had the CIA planning to airlift a platoon of Contra soldiers from Honduras in Sandinista Army uniforms, to near Pastora's headquarters. They were to kidnap Pastora and hustle him to a small town in southern Nicaragua and there, after assembling all the local people to watch, hang him. The purpose: to generate worldwide outrage at Sandinista barbarism. That incident, if it ever was planned, also didn't come off but because the CIA had long proven itself capable of such stunts the tale had a surface credibility.

Kelso's account of how he thwarted the Arias assassination so nearly borders on the ludicrous that it has a paradoxical sound of truth to it. Kelso said he had details of the plot from five different sources, including at least one from inside M19. According to Kelso, Arias was to fly to a regional meeting in Bogota, Colombia's capital. The plane was apparently to be blown up in flight although there was an-

---

[56] Ibid.

other scenario. It had the M19 guerillas gunning down Arias when he arrived. They, in turn, were to be killed on the spot. Kelso seemed to be most concerned about whether the assassination was sanctioned by some legitimate authority rather than out of any sympathy for Arias or distress at what his killing might lead to.

He tried to get someone to say it was approved, apparently by the "highest authorities" and when no one would speak up he took it on himself to prevent the assassination from happening. He did it, he said, by simply having officials at the national airport forbid Arias' plane from taking off until its overdue fuel bill was paid. Kelso is a cryptic talker and his story at times is difficult to follow. He says Arias was furious at this interruption of his official visit and persuaded someone to send a jet from Texas which then took him to Bogota. Apparently the M19 hired assassins were not told to look for a foreign jet. The story is far-fetched, especially to those not accustomed to the twilight world in which Kelso moved. It doesn't sound so strange to others who have traveled in that world, however.

The propaganda war was not always so lethal, at least to the top echelon players although for those at the broad bottom levels of Central American society the eventual outcome was often just as deadly. Accounts of Nicaragua in United States newspapers never improved, coverage was still slanted, mostly still dependent on State Department briefings and handouts.

When President Daniel Ortega announced at a meeting of regional presidents in Costa Rica in 1989 that his government was going to lift its 18-month cease-fire with the Contra, the criticism was almost unanimous, and unquestioning. It was denounced in newspaper editorials, by congressmen who presumably had some knowledge of what was going on, and even by many supporters in the United States of Nicaragua's long fight for independence. Blunt-talking George Bush got good coverage on his "skunk at a garden party" characterization of Ortega. But it was days before any of the stories included the fact that the cease-fire was unilateral; the Contra hadn't agreed to it, nor abided by it. Eventually some reports did include Ortega's remark that "we ceased and they fired," more because it was a catchy, Reagan-type phrase rather than from any sense of fairness.

More characteristic was the failure of any news accounts, editorials or analyses to even speculate on the probability that a stepped up series of ambushes and attacks were a systematic provocation. The Contra had been terrorizing rural Nicaraguans during all the cease-fire. Ambushes of unarmed civilians, attacks on farm homes and killings of elected officials, teachers and health workers continued in spite of the Sandinista stand down. Later the attacks had increased and some had even been reported in United States newspapers, although never to the extent or in such detail as stories of lesser atrocities in the Middle East.

No writer on the scene, nor any pundits writing from this country, so far as I was able to determine, speculated on the likelihood that the atttacks were deliberate provocations designed to bait the Sandinistas into doing just what they did, lift the cease-fire and go on the offensive and take the public relations consequences. There was plenty of speculation that it might have been Sandinista soldiers, disguised as Contra, who had killed their own people to make the other side look bad, long a regular ploy of Contra spokesmen.

In that sense, Ortega and his government fell into the Contra trap by reacting after several ambushes, one of which resulted in the deaths of 18 reservists on their way to register to vote. Only the glee with which President George Bush and his administration greeted Ortega's announcement lent any credence to a small possibility that plans for the provocation were not shared by the Contra with their bosses in Washington, D. C.

In the official Bush Administration view, Ortega's decision was a desperate move to prepare an excuse to put off the February 25, 1990 election and blame the Contra and the United States. Well, it was a political war, after all, and Bush was as entitled to put forward that interpretation for rephrasing by editorial writers all across the country as he was to fight an undeclared proxy war in the first place. *The New York Times*, in its declaration of outrage—"Foolish and Thuggish"—said Ortega's '"ostensible" purpose was to "draw attention to cease-fire violations by the Honduras-based rebels." No recognition there of the responsibility of an elected head of government to respond to lethal attacks on his constituents. No outrage about the mother who lost two children, with another badly wounded, while she lost a leg and an eye in an ambush, or of scores like her.

"Ambushes have occurred," the *Times* editorial said without actually conceding that the Contra had conducted them, "although the casualty total is in dispute." Now that is objectivity. The same editorial stated without any explanation that Ortega "found few Latin American takers" for his action which it said was a violation of the Central American peace plan. *Times* editorial writers might read Latin American newspapers as well as State Department handouts some time.

Among those few newspapers which are truly independent, including Mexico's, Ortega's announcement was accepted with the gravity it deserved. The *Times* editorial glossed over the fact that a key element of the peace plan, the disarming and removal of foreign troops in the region—the Contra in Honduras—had never been seriously considered by the leading player in this game, the United States. Mexican newspapers explored the idea.

How did President Bush know Ortega's Sandinistas were so desperately afraid of losing the election that they were willing to thumb their noses at world opinion? Because polls told him so. It's not surprising that an administration that won office on the basis of how issues would play in polls rather than on principle would resort to polling for its foreign policy moves. How were the polls taken? By telephone, just as they are at home. I don't know how many telephones there are in Nicaragua, but I do know they're rare. One telephone book, about the size of the directory for Grand Island, Nebraska, includes every number in the country. Most Nicaraguans who can afford a telephone, it is safe to guess, were not strong supporters of the government.

One National Public Radio reporter who attempted to call the polling office for some explanation of methodology was bumped along to other phone numbers until he finally reached the ultimate source—the United States Embassy. What would a telephone poll, had such miracles existed in 1776, have shown in the American colonies? Especially if the polling was being paid for by George III?

Nicaraguans fully expected the United States to invade in the mid-1980s as Reagan tried to whip up an element in the population that saw communists coming across the southern horizon. For a time trenches were being dug in most Nicaraguan backyards for taking shelter from air raids the public was expecting, assumptions fueled by the sonic booms of United States Air Force reconnaissance planes that could be heard every day over the country for a time.

As distant as the White House and the State Department were from reality when it came to Nicaragua, the Pentagon was well aware that the Nicaraguan Army would be no pushover. An invading army could have won, probably rather quickly, although goof ups in Panama had made many senior United States soldiers wary. But even a relatively quick victory would have been costly. Nicaragua is not Panama and the Sandinista Army was not the Panama Defense Force. Nor was it anything like the corrupt and cynical army of El Salvador. The Nicaraguan soldiers had been fighting a real war, at least on their side, for years. Where in the 1920s a United States Marine platoon could go where it wished in Nicaragua and do as it pleased, it would have taken divisions, and weeks, if not months, to bring the country under control in the 1980s. Nicaragua would have fought, and hard.

12

Church vs Church

THE CHURCH IS SMALL BY LATIN AMERICAN STANDARDS AND modern in style, with more light than one usually finds in these Catholic edifices. Its exterior reflects the sleek architecture of the neighborhood, Managua's upper middle class suburbs. A cooling wind blows here in summer, shaking the coconut palms' metallic leaf shards, high above the muggy lake shore where shattered Managua sprawls in the ugliest urban setting in all of Latin America. This is Cardinal Miguel Obando y Bravo's church and his sermon reflects his modish parishoners, women in Miami outfits, men in conservative, lawyerly business suits. Children in crisp dresses and starched shirts sit demurely in the pews by their parents; there is none of the capering one sees in the big churches during Sunday mass in most of Central America. This is a serious place, the cardinal is a serious man. His heavy sermon reflects disappointment with those, such as his martyred colleague Archbishop Oscar Romero in neighboring El Salvador and others, who believe themselves capable of bringing the Kingdom here on earth rather than waiting their turn in heaven.

Among the anomalies in the Central American wars of the 1980s were the clashes, for directly opposite reasons, of two governments and two Catholic Church hierarchies. In Nicaragua a revolutionary leftist regime clashed with this right wing cardinal of peasant stock who sided with an ousted oligarchy that had lost some of its privileges and perquisites, including its immunity from taxes. In sermons and radio broadcasts as well as interviews with foreign questioners, the cardinal denounced the government's failings, of which there are many, but never acknowledged its unmistakable achievements.

In El Salvador, on the other hand, the church was headed by a member of that country's ruling oligarchy, an aristocrat who instead of placidly blessing the country's owners, surprised and outraged them by challenging the brutality by which they ruled. Archbishop Oscar Arnulfo Romero paid for his pious impudence with his life, shot down in his pulpit as he was saying mass.

Romero probably sealed his doom when he wrote a letter to President Jimmy Carter a month before his death in 1980 imploring the United States to cease supplying military aid to the Salvadoran Army which he accused of "the use of repressive violence, producing wholesale deaths and injuries."

Romero embodied the radical "Liberation Theology" that boomed out from pulpits all over Latin America on the tides of the Conference of Bishops held in Medellin, Columbia in 1968. In simpler language than the intellectuals who espouse it would explain it, Liberation Theology means simply that "it is well to be humble in this world as Christ taught, in order to win a better life in the hereafter, *but you deserve something in this life also.*"

This split over liberation theology may not rank with the great religious schisms of the past, but it is tearing the fabric of the Catholic Church in its most populous region of the world. Like most inter-family fights, it is creating new openings for others. Protestantism, particularly the "born again" brand, is making large gains in Latin America. Fundamentalists seeking souls don't waste their time on lofty ideals of human rights and equality of all women and men; rather they talk in simple phrases, often through bullhorns in city squares, of salvation certain and soon and, when they deal with earthly matters they shriek of hellfire and Communism, all in the simplistic terms of the American Bible Belt.

There are Catholics, and others, who believe that Obando, who was beloved of Reagan, got his red cardinal's hat as part of a deal with Pope John Paul II. The scam, as the cynics see it, went this way: Pope John is Polish and very conservative. Not for him and not for Obando such distractions as women's rights. The deal, so the skeptics surmise, was that Reagan would grant trade credits to brave Poland, then defying the Soviet Union. In return the Pope would name a cardinal willing to harass the Sandinistas that Reagan was convinced were trying to subvert the western world. Whether such an agreement was ever discussed or not, that is what happened. Poland got the credits it desperately needed and the Pope chose the man the late dictator Anastasio Somoza called "my little Indian," to be the church's chief officer for Central America.

If Obando saw a spiritual threat in the Sandinistas, he had a secular motive also. The CIA was secretly supplying him with money, according to testimony at the trial of Clair George, former CIA deputy for operations (covert activities). George was on trial in 1992 for lying to Congress about his knowledge of the Iran/Contra scandal. Alan Fiers, Jr., a George subordinate, testified that he had been directing clandestine money to Obando. When Congress learned of this, CIA Director William Casey told Fiers to find a new way of supporting Obando's opposition to the Sandinistas.[57]

Fiers "arranged for (Oliver) North to funnel to the church private donations, some of which were laundered through the Heritage Foundation, according to a staff member of the House Iran/Contra committee. (During the 1987 hearings, the Iran/Contra committees steered clear of this subject for fear of embarrassing the Cardinal.)"[58]

The paradox of church aristocrats defending the poor while those from peasant backgrounds side with the oligarchs is reflected also in the United States attitude toward the church in Central America. When the Sandinistas roughed up Obando's bishops the State Department loudly de-

---

[57] David Corn, The Nation, Aug. 31/Sept. 7, 1992, p.201.
[58] Ibid.

plored. But when the Army of El Salvador murdered six Jesuit priests, their housekeeper and her daughter in 1989, the State Department at first tried to divert the blame onto the guerrillas and then, when a cover up became too much even for some members of the military, browbeat and intimidated a witness.

The Jesuits, headed by Father Ignacio Ellacuria, the rector of the University of Central America, epitomized "Liberation Theology" in Army eyes. They sympathized with the peasants, whom the Army considered "subversives" when they protested their chronic mistreatment. But Ellacuria was a voice of reconciliation. He had been talking with Salvadoran President Alfredo Christiani, praising Christiani's "political will to bring an early conclusion to the war through political means."

That may have been the reason for killing him and his colleagues. Elements in the Army were scornful of Christiani's peace overtures and may have seen the mild Ellacuria gaining too much influence. Ellacuria had been called a Marxist who supported "the objectives of the communist revolution" two years before he was killed. Such public accusations are often a kill signal to death squads.

Pope John Paul denounced the killing but his comments, many Catholics felt, were milder than might have been expected if priests opposing the Sandinistas of Nicaragua had been the victims. The Pope said the killings were "barbarous" but rather than call for the government to crack down on its Army, he hoped "the assassination of these priests encourages a rejection of violence and respect for the life of our brothers and sisters so that we may achieve the fruits of peace and reconciliation in this suffering country."

The United States Embassy's response was even more shameful. When Lucia Barrera de Cerna, the priests' cleaning woman, told church officials she had heard voices, protests and then shots at the priests' building and then had seen men in uniforms leaving the place, Ambassador William Walker's staff put in motion a strategy of denial and threat. Fearing for her life, church officials took her to the Spanish

Embassy. There she told Salvadoran Judge Ricardo A. Zamorra of what she had seen and was then escorted by Spanish and French diplomats to the airport to be flown to the United States.[59]

None of the press accounts I saw of the Barrera case expressed surprise or examined the reasons for her taking refuge in the Spanish Embassy. Neither did anyone wince at the spectacle of Spaniards and French officials seeing her safely out of a country controlled by the United States.

The United States Embassy was not to be denied access to Barrera, however. Legal Officer Richard Chidester and an FBI agent insisted on accompanying Barrera and her husband on the flight to Miami, to help her get into the United States, they said. Once in Miami she was whisked away by the FBI for a week of interrogation during which a Salvadoran, Lieutenant Colonel Manuel Antonio Rivas Meija, joined the questioners.

At the end of the week of isolation and grilling, without a lawyer present, this simple peasant woman told her interrogators, as she later put it, "what they wanted to hear"— that she had seen nothing that night. State Department officials leaked that comment to the press, and the Salvadoran government announced that Tutela Legal, the Catholic archdiocesan human rights office, had coached Mrs. Barrera to implicate the Army. The answer to that came from Maria Hernandez, director of the office and one of the few Salvadorans to talk back to the Army and get away with it.

"He's a liar," said Mrs. Hernandez of the embassy official who passed the charge on to the press. Archbishop Arturo Rivera y Damas was equally indignant. "Instead of being protected, as people in the United States Embassy in El Salvador had promised," he said, "she was subjected to authentic brainwashing and the blackmail that she would be deported (back to El Salvador) if she didn't tell the truth…" The State Department's final comment: The archbishop was "poorly informed." Later, however, her testimony was repeated in court at the trial of soldiers for the priests' murders.

---

[59] Ibid.

Probably the most outraged official voice over the killings came from a mild-mannered machine politician and Catholic, Representative Joe Moakley, a Massachusetts Democrat. Moakley, who had made few waves in his time in the House of Representatives, was chairing a special House task force when he incurred the not-to-be-ignored anger of the Salvadoran Army in a speech at UCA:

"Colonel (Rene Emilio) Ponce (Army chief of staff) has said over and over that these murders should be considered the acts of individuals and not the responsibility of the Armed Forces as an institution. Colonel Ponce is just plain wrong."

Moakley said he had followed events in El Salvador for ten years and had always been told "not to expect very much from El Salvador. I have been told over and over again by the people in my own government that violence is just part of the culture. Killing and corruption, I am told, have always been common in El Salvador.

"Well, I love my country, but I think it's pretty arrogant for anyone from a nation with a $300 billion defense budget, $25 billion in arms sales, a huge military foreign aid program and the highest murder rate in the western world to criticize another society for its tendency towards violence."

In Nicaragua, one of the most controversial incidents in the Sandinistas' ten years in office was the Pope's 1983 visit. According to most press accounts, the Sandinistas made every effort to harass and insult the Pope, staged a protest rally and tried to block access by the people to His Holiness. Most Nicaraguans I spoke to when I was there two months after the papal visit had a different version. I talked to many Catholics, lay and clergy and all of them said the government had gone out of its way to make Pope John Paul welcome. "The Pope made a big error when he came to Nicaragua," said an American nun who had then been in Nicaragua eleven years.

"He had evidently been primed before he came to believe that Nicaragua had become a Communist country," said another nun. Who misled him? "I hesitate to say. But somehow he was misinformed and so he came here with a prejudiced attitude. He came with a prepared speech and he gave it. He didn't listen.

"When the seventeen mothers of sons killed by the Contra asked him to say a prayer for them, he ignored them," she said. When they set up a shout, insisting that he say something, he thundered "silencio" at them over the public address system. Critics said the mothers were incited to heckle the Pope. The nuns, priests and laymen I talked to didn't believe the charges.

"As I watched the Pope I realized he had missed the whole point of the Revolution, of what the people of Nicaragua have done," one of the nuns said. "He didn't hear the people, he missed an opportunity to be their pastor. A pastor is one who watches over his flock, with love and attention.

"We only saw him scolding, saying 'be quiet'." She shook her head. "To say 'silence' to people who have suffered as much as the Nicaraguan people have..."

"The man missed an opportunity to get closer to the common people, the ordinary people," said another nun.

Some seven hundred thousand people, more than a quarter of the country's population are supposed to have shown up in the Plaza of the Revolution to see the Pope. Although such figures should be accepted with skepticism in Central America, pictures taken of the event show a vast multitude.

In one remote area an American nun helped her flock hold bake sales for weeks to raise money to buy gas for the trucks they would ride for a day to Managua. Raffles were held, people donated rice and beans, and a song fest energized the community the night before the journey. Women cooked quantities of tortillas and beans for food on the eight-hour trip. The government released two months of gasoline rations to drivers of forty five trucks from that community. In another area, the Army loaded worshippers onto military trucks and hauled them to Managua for the occasion "so anybody who wanted to go could go."

"And he didn't listen" she said.

234

There were different assessments, she concedes. When the Mothers of the Martyred set up a chant after the Pope refused to say a prayer for their sons, some people in the crowd were shocked. "'They said people should respect the Pope,'" she said. "But he ignored them and their pleas.

"As I watched the Pope I wondered if he realized that he was in a country where people's eyes were poked out if they were on the wrong side, and here he was telling people to 'be faithful to your bishops'."

The Catholics I talked to took the side of Father Ernesto Cardenal, minister of culture, in his encounter with the Pope. Cardenal, one of Nicaragua's leading poets, met John Paul at the airport and knelt and attempted to kiss the Pope's ring. The Pope, told that Cardenal was one of the four priests in the government who had defied his order to give up their secular posts, pulled his hand away, shook his finger at Cardenal and lectured him on his duties as a priest.

The Reagan Administration soon found a different view of what happened during John Paul's brief visit. Two months after the incident a Nicaraguan defector, Miguel Bolanos Hunter, was produced for reporters in Washington by the State Department, at a conference room at the Heritage Foundation, a right wing think tank, to tell how he and other members of Nicaraguan security had organized and instructed the mothers to embarrass the pope.[60] Bolanos, who said he had been an officer in the Nicaraguan intelligence service, said Sandinista agents organized Managua block leaders to pack the plaza with trusted accomplices who turned away faithful Catholics who wanted to see and hear the pope.

According to Bolanos one of the mothers grabbed the microphone from the pope's hand as he began to pray on another subject and asked him to pray for her martyred son, an act that was "practically a sacrilege, an act of total disrespect." The pope then left the plaza without finishing his prayer which, Bolanos told reporters, meant the disrup-

---

[60] A study in U.S. Human Rights Policy Toward El Salvador, CAMPESINO, Winter 1992.

tion "was a success because many people thought the lack of respect was spontaneous and the pope was simply against the revolution." That's not the way many people who were there remembered the incident. Certainly vast numbers of people managed to get into the plaza, and if the Sandinistas tried to prevent them they failed badly.

The Sandinistas described Bolanos' story as more CIA distortion. "Why would the Sandinistas go to those extremes to get the whole world mad at them for insulting the pope?" one nun who was there asked.

Nicaraguans love a scandal and if it involves sex they are doubly entertained. So when one of Obando's chief aides was photographed running naked down a Managua street from a jealous husband whose wife he was supposedly romancing, the public howled with glee. Obando said the Reverend Bismarck Carballo was set up by the Sandinistas who suborned a prostitute named Maritsa Castillo to ask him for counseling. While they were meeting at her home, according to Carballo, a man who said he was Maritsa's husband suddenly appeared, waving a pistol and shouting with rage. He ripped the priest's clothing off and chased him into the street.

Nicaraguans might have accepted Carballo's guilt as a fornicator except that a television crew just happened to be stationed across the street when the pudgy priest burst out of the house covered with nothing but his own skin. It was likely a set-up, although Carballo's ponderous arrogance led many Nicaraguans to want to believe he was violating his vows of celibacy with another man's wife.

Miguel d'Escoto, foreign minister for the Sandinistas, was one of the priests who defied Pope John Paul II and stayed in the government. A Contra spokesman told me that d'Escoto "was a CIA agent in Chile" when the Agency was masterminding the overthrow of the elected leftist government of Salvador Allende in 1973. "He helped overthrow Allende. He's wearing the same hassock but now he's working with the KGB."

d'Escoto denied the story. The spokesman, Edgar Chamorro, told me in Honduras, before he broke with the Contra, that the church in Nicaragua had been "penetrated by the Communists" and Obando was rooting them out. Chamorro's was the voice of the Catholic heirarchy (he had been ordained a Jesuit priest but later went into secular public relations) and of the ruling old family, social-commercial establishment in Nicaragua. After his defection from the Contra Chamorro recanted most of what he said while he was their spokesman.

Many Nicaraguans were outraged by the response of one of Obando's bishops to the rape and killing by a Contra raiding party of seven teenage girls picking coffee in the northern hills. Bishop Pablo Vega, in an exchange with some American college professors visiting Nicaragua, was asked why there had been no comment from the church hierarchy about the incident. "There are worse deaths than the physical death," the government newspaper *Barricada* quoted Vega as saying. More than anything else I heard about the church from priests and nuns in Nicaragua that comment caused the most despair.

No one in the church ever denied that Vega had said it and it was consistent with the church's silence on many other atrocities committed by the Contra. Bishop Vega was physically booted over the border into Honduras in 1986 for allegedly lobbying Congress, in Washington, D. C. for more money for the Contra. When I asked a Sandinista official why they risked condemnation from outside the country for kicking out Vega the answer was that "we couldn't put him in prison or the whole world would have been against us. But we couldn't allow him to continue to support an enemy sworn to destroy our government."

The pope's scorn of the liberation theologists, and his active opposition to them in the service of Reagan, is nothing new in Church, or Latin American, history. The great Mexican priests Hidalgo and Morelos, who put out the flag of revolution against Spain in 1810 and were executed for their impertinence, were first excommunicated. They challenged the social order, of which the church was an integral element.

The Church Inquisition of 1810 said their pronouncements of the sovereignty of the people was "manifest heresy." It called Morelos "a heretic, a propagator of heresy, pursuer and disturber of the ecclesiastical hierarchy, profaner of the holy sacraments, schismatic, lascivious, a hypocrite, irreconcilable enemy of Christianity, traitor to God, King and Pope."

The CIA's propaganda manual for the Contra in their battle against the government of Nicaragua urged, as part of its doctrine of "armed propaganda," that the Contra capitalize on citizen "indignation over the lack of freedom of worship and persecution (sic), of which priests are victims." The Sandinistas certainly clashed with the traditional, hierarchical church, but no one, so far as I know, not even the obfuscators in the State Department, ever accused the Sandinistas of forbidding "freedom of worship."

That didn't stop rightist zealots in Catholic lay organizations such as Opus Dei and the Knights of Malta, who threw in their lot with Reagan and others who saw communism behind every cry for justice in Central America.

More than one observer has noted the similarities between Catholic rightwingers and Protestant fundamentalists. They share a penchant for authority and a loud anti-communism.[61] They also share a secrecy fetish that generates conspiracy theories, and a lust for intrigue. Both attempt to cultivate ties to the CIA and other intelligence agencies.

On one of my trips into the Nicaraguan countryside, in the north in Contra country, I hitched a ride with Henri Nouwen, the renowned Dutch theologian and writer. "I am overwhelmed at how much the United States is motivated by fear," Nouwen said in one of our discussions. I had never considered it that way before, but I thought then and think now that he was right. "The fearful person always says there is not enough for everyone," he said. "They say `I'll protect mine' and attempt to hoard goods. But the more you hoard, the more enemies you have. Then you build walls around yourself and soon you've built your own prison."

---

[61] Joanne Omang and Don Oberdorfer, The Washington Post, June 19, 1983.

I went with Father Nouwen to a mass in a small Managua parish where the neighborhood was celebrating the return of a local reserve battalion from six months in the north fighting the Contra. "As I embraced these boys in their army fatigues and hugged these mothers, mourning their sons killed with American weapons, I experienced again something of the distinctive spirit of this revolution," Nouwen wrote a short time later.[62]

"This is not a violent people struggling for power," he said. "This is a people who have struggled against poverty, exploitation, hunger and illness, and who now are determined to resist any effort to destroy the freedom they have won. Of all the Latin American countries I have lived in, only Nicaragua offers such a deep sign of hope. It is the hope of a new society in which the people themselves are the main architects. It is the hope, in a continent long dominated by foreign powers, of a new society free to chart an independent course."

It is true that the Sandinistas exploited the "popular church" in their battle against Obando. It was a church that urged, to capsulize its own words, "question authority." Its foundation was the base community, often headed by lay persons, in areas where there were no priests or nuns. The emphasis was on pragmatic Christianity, local help to local folks. Such a focus, so far as the hierarchical church was concerned, diverted attention and effort away from the worship of God.

This tear in the religious fabric wasn't confined to the Catholic Church. Mainstream Protestant churches produced their share of religious leaders who dared to challenge the combination of privilege and naked power that ruled in El Salvador and Guatemala and attempted to reverse the course of history in Nicaragua. For many fundamentalists the Sandinistas' programs were dangerous to Christian souls. Preachers counseled their flocks not to cooperate with the government, the Sandinistas, in any way. "The faithful were told not to vaccinate their children; after all,

---

[62] Henri J.M. Nouwen, Forum Page, National Catholic Reporter, Aug. 26, 1983

God would care for the health of true believers. Participation in the literacy campaign and public schooling was prohibited; the dangers of atheist-communist brain-washing were advertised. And parishioners were discouraged from helping to raise (farm) production; with Jesus' return so imminent, why worry about what we're to eat and drink?"[63]

The Sandinistas probably compounded the problem, or fell into the trap, by their immoderate response. They seized buildings belonging to the Mormons, Seventh Day Adventists and Jehovah's Witnesses whom they accused of actively aiding the Contra. Although the buildings were soon returned, their seizure gave ammunition to the Sandinistas' critics. The United States Embassy established a liaison with these churches with probably the only full-time staffer assigned to religious duties in the whole State Department. A particular target of the embassy and its right wing Christian allies was the Evangelical (Protestant) Committee for Aid to Development (CEPAD) which despite its name is a moderate, primarily social service agency that cooperated with the government on such issues as agricultural training, public health and education. Soon after Bob Fretz of the embassy began attending regular Sunday morning bible classes conducted by Dr. Gustavo Parajon, president of CEPAD, the Christian right began a smear campaign against Parajon and CEPAD. Among the attackers was the Institute on Religion and Democracy (IRD), a rabidly right wing United States organization that parroted the Reagan Administration's accusations of communist infiltration in all the Central American liberation movements, secular as well as religious.

Press releases from such organizations about dissident Nicaraguans who claimed preachers were being arrested and tortured, got almost completely uncritical acceptance among many church publications and even the general press in the United States. They were effective propagandists, especially since they had funds to funnel to pastors who took the proper line and who otherwise would have been as im-

---

[63] Penny Lernoux, People of God, Viking, 1989, p. 283..

pecunious as their parishioners. American fundamentalist church aid supported or helped support some 500 pastors in Nicaragua.

Among American evangelicals who brought their campaigns to Central America, and to Nicaragua, were Pat Robertson of the Christian Coalition and a one-time Republican candidate for president, and Jimmy Swaggart, who was in Nicaragua just before he was discovered buying kinky favors from a prostitute. Swaggart was especially entertaining. He would prance about the stage in a white suit with a microphone in his hand repeatedly shouting "He will return!" or some other phrase. His translator, in an all-black suit and also holding a microphone, mimicked Swaggart's every move right behind him, almost in spoon fashion. No Catholic priest could match him for comedy.

CEPAD, supported by 35 Protestant churches, was an early target of the right wing churches and the embassy as was Parajon, who graduated from Dennison University in Ohio, got his medical degree from Western Reserve University, and has a public health degree from Harvard. Under his guidance the organization attempts to educate Nicaraguans in everything from using latrines "instead of going behind the nearest bush," to composting vegetable scraps to improve their gardens, and crop rotation and terracing for farmers. It puts a heavy emphasis on schools and all aspects of health care, economic development and other prosaic ends beyond just saving souls.

CEPAD tried to be neutral in the political gamesmanship between the fundamentalists and the Sandinistas, but there was no middle ground. CEPAD has been closely allied with the National Council of Churches in the United States, a generally liberal mainstream alliance. The council in 1983 directly challenged the Reagan Administration's war against Nicaragua after CIA gunboats shelled the Port of Corinto. Medical supplies from the council destined for the beleaguered country's hospitals and clinics were among the goods destroyed.

Not all Protestant evangelical churches supported the

Reagan Administration's continuing disinformation campaigns. After defeat of the Sandinistas, moderate protestants objected when the Chamorro government's new education minister, Humberto Belli, introduced school text books with a decided religious flavor. CEPAD's Protestant member churches, Lutherans, Nazarenes, Baptists and others, objected that the texts violated Nicaragua's constitution, adopted under the Sandinistas but which the Chamorro government has not dared to try to change. The Protestants, in a letter signed by Parajon and other church leaders, pointed out that the constitution says Nicaragua has no official religion and that public education will be secular. But Belli did not respond to their entreaties.[64]

His emphasis on "Christian values," the Protestants fear, will bring conflicts between them and Catholics which had been almost non existent since the 1979 revolution guaranteed freedom of religion. Prior to the revolution Protestants were often discriminated against, even stoned in public.

Sex education was also a touchy issue, just as it is in the United States and for the same reason, and with the same division of philosophies and ideologies. More than fifty percent of Nicaragua's children are born out of wedlock. When the Sandinistas attempted to teach sex education in the schools Cardinal Obando, with the support of Belli, objected. And once the new government was in office, sex education was out of those schools that continued to function.

In this mix of conflicting religious philosophies, the most dangerous of all to Nicaragua, and the other countries of Latin America, eventually may be the Pentecostals who sought their converts among Catholics and Protestants in both the mainstream and the fundamentalist churches. For poor people with little entertainment or hope of a future in their lives on earth, the Pentecostal preachers' tirades about hell fire and promises of eternal bliss in the next world were powerful messages. Watching people jumping in their

---

[64] CEPAD (Council of Evangelical Churche of Nicaragua) Report, July-August, 1989, p.2.

seats to Swaggart's repetitive wails of the imminent return of Jesus was to be impressed at the ability of people to share in their own deceiving.

Although Pentecostal preachings contain almost no religious nutrient, they condition people to acceptance of the status quo and to opposition to any secular attempts to help them better their lives. The Pentecostal's simple message attracted more than just the poor. According to one report the Full Gospel Businessmen's Fellowship International, an American group, "has grown into one of the most powerful evangelical organizations in Latin America.[65] "Its influence reaches all the way into the cabinet of El Salvador's President Alfredo Christiani. His deputy minister of the interior has been reborn, as have the police chief and numerous members of the general staff of El Salvador's armed forces." Lutheran Bishop Medardo Gomez expressed another aspect of that shift: "The middle and upper classes think the Catholic Church has betrayed them, because it serves mostly the poor and often criticizes the military." That is the secret that alarms the likes of Cardinal Obando.

Another view of the same trend came from an American priest deeply involved with the Sandinista movement. Peter Marchetti is a Jesuit and land reform expert who had worked with many Latin countries before he became an adviser to the Sandinistas. "There are instances where big cattle raisers who stand a chance of (their land) being expropriated because their lands lie idle will begin to try to take control of the local parish. First, they try to co-opt the pastor, and, if the pastor resists, then it becomes a 'religious' conflict between these cattle raisers and the priest.

"It's extraordinary. These people, who have always been Catholics, as soon as they begin to lose their traditional place in society, shift from a traditional Catholic faith to a sort of evangelical theology along the lines of protestant fundamentalism. Their political conflict with the priest turns into a dispute over which group controls the keys to the church—those who attend mass and support the revolution

[65] CEPAD Report, Dec., 1991, p.7.

or those conservative cattle raisers who all of a sudden are advocating lay-controlled prayer groups to reduce the influence of the populist priest."[66]

I spent a few days with a devout Catholic family in Esteli which illustrated another aspect of the religious split in Nicaragua. All the family were staunch Sandinistas. The parents were traditional Catholics although they were critical of Pope John Paul for refusing to bless the martyred young men when he was in Nicaragua. But an eighteen-year-old daughter in the family had gone over to the fundamentalists. "It is wrong," she told me, "to make images of the Virgin Mary or of Jesus." She had been, at age thirteen, one of the "brigadistas" who took the literacy campaign to the countryside.

Religious uncertainties have been used by the United States and the CIA as well as elements of the churches themselves in the political wars of the region. But the Catholic Church has mostly itself to blame for the inroads into its memberships by the Protestant sects. That schism is itself a matter of churchly dispute, with some traditional Catholics seeing a North American conspiracy as the cause of their decline. Others, however, recognize that fundamentalist churches offer more emotional stimulation than the Catholic "supermarkets for the sacraments." A 1986 Vatican document, according to Latinamerica Press, says the church "gives too much importance to structures and not enough to drawing people to God in Christ."

One need only look at the cathedrals and churches, even in small towns, to recognize a preoccupation with grandeur. The Christian base communities often ignore such worldly magnificence while appealing to the direct and current needs of the people.

The Sandinistas were also accused of anti-Semitism by the United States, a campaign aided and abetted by the Anti-Defamation League of B'nai B'rith, a Jewish defense group. As proof, B'nai B'rith cited attacks on Managua's synagogue a year before the revolution of 1979 by a group of men who it said claimed to be Sandinistas. The synagogue

---

[66] Der Spiegel, Hamburg, Germany, March, 1991.

was later taken over by the government because, Sandinista officials said, the country's small Jewish population, about 50, had left the country. Jewish groups said the people had fled. The Sandinistas claimed that some of Somoza's cronies who were Jewish had indeed had reason to flee but that other Jews were welcome in Nicaragua. Some Jews served in the government and I encountered a Jewish Witness for Peace group in a vigil in front of the United States Embassy in Managua in 1984 as it expressed its backing for the Sandinistas and its opposition to American support for the Contra.

I questioned members about the reports I had heard of persecution of Jews by the Sandinistas. They had heard them too, they said, and that was one of the reasons for their two-week tour in Nicaragua; they wanted to see for themselves. While some Nicaraguans were no doubt anti-Semitic, they said, they were convinced that the government frowned on it and certainly did not foment it. Reagan Administration charges of anti-Semitism by the Sandinistas were refuted in 1983 by United States Ambassador Anthony Quainton in a confidential cable to Secretary of State George Schultz. "The evidence fails to demonstrate that the Sandinistas have followed a policy of anti-Semitism," Quainton wrote. "Although most members of Nicaragua's tiny Jewish community have left the country and some have had their properties confiscated there is no correlation between their Jewish religion and the treatment they received."[67]

The Nicaraguan government routinely seized property from those Nicaraguans of all creeds who left the country and did not return for six months or more. Quainton's report, like many others, was ignored. Another organization, the New Jewish Agenda, regularly deplored American interference in Nicaragua's affairs, and in 1983 the Union of American Hebrew Congregations adopted a resolution opposing "any direct foreign military intervention in any country in Central America."

I was accused in a right wing Seattle hate sheet of being

---

[67] Interview with Peter Marchetti, Working Papers, March-April 1982.

anti-Semitic when in one of my columns I made a passing reference to Israeli support for the Contra. I had talked with a Sandinista lieutenant near the Honduran border which had suffered a Contra bombardment that the Sandinistas said included seven thousand artillery and mortar shells. The lieutenant and I were standing in the shattered doorway of a small house where an almost direct hit from a mortar shell had killed an eight-year-old girl three days before. Her blood was still spattered on the door frame.

The lieutenant, a belligerent young man resentful of North Americans, unhooked from his web shoulder harness a grenade he had taken from a dead Contra. "From the United States," he said, handing it to me. I returned it to him and said it was not made in the United States. "You misunderstand," he said. "It was made in Israel but you paid for it." That single reference to Israel in my column led to the accusation that I was anti-Semitic. Israel's support, not just for the Contra through agreements with the United States but also for its help to Colombian drug cartels, to the Guatemalan Army and to Manuel Noriega in Panama, has indeed created resentment against Israel among some Central Americans. Most Nicaraguans, however, treat Jews as they do anyone else who comes in peace.

The Christian faith of many Central Americans would almost melt the hearts of the meanest death squad member. Almost. One of the saddest tales from El Salvador, a country with at least seventy thousand brutal stories, was the history of a gentle couple, Alejandro and Exaltacion Ortiz, who lost five sons in the war. The oldest was a priest, Father Octavio, who was the first to die in 1979 when a National Guard tank opened fire into the church building in San Antonio Abad where he was instructing thirty youngsters in the catechism. Four of the children died too. Those deaths, the first of tens of thousands, were never investigated.[68]

The Ortiz's other sons were killed over the next eleven years either by death squads or in combat with the guerillas against the Army. For eight years the senior Ortiz

[68] Maryknoll Revista, March 1994, p. 15

were refugees in camps in Honduras. They returned to become delegates of the word and to tell their stories to foreigners who came to El Salvador to learn from the victims what the war was all about and what American tax dollars were buying.

The Catholic Church must share the blame for much of the misery of Latin America, as many modern church people acknowledge. Theirs is a hard road and martyrdom is easily available and always close at hand. The Church knows from bitter experience, in El Salvador and Nicaragua as well as other countries, that it can lose the support of its wealthy parishioners if it becomes too concerned for the plight of its poor. Priests can be killed, but worse, for the church hierarchy, economic support can be withheld. That way lies oblivion.

13

The Internationalists

A WINDMILL'S BRIGHT-TIPPED VANES SPIN LIKE A PRAYER-wheel in the sunshine against the blue sky in the middle distance. Beyond it stands the perfect cone of Momotomobo, the wonderfully named volcano that marks the northern shore of Lake Managua. All around us sorghum, nearly three feet high, tossed in the soft breeze that made digging in the vegetable garden tolerable. This was the Hans Gutierrez Cooperative, an experiment in hope and faith where retarded teenagers learned to write their names, if they were able, and to live on their own, some of them. For the more pro-foundly retarded, it was a blessed somewhere else, away from the dark back rooms where they were kept hidden from neighbors in Managua's shanties before Frances Romero came along. Romero, a Seattle psychologist, mother of two, was no missionary; she probably is not even religious.

But if anyone was doing the Lord's work in Nicaragua, it was Romero. She was what became known in Nicaragua and El Salvador and the other countries of Central America as an "internationalist," a scornful term used both by natives who resented outsiders and by anti-communists in the United States who saw help for Nicaraguans, even handicapped children, as attempts to thwart efforts to bring a United States Main Street democracy to the heathens. When Romero came to Nicaragua in 1983 with her husband Marco, who had recently retired from an engineering job at the Boeing Company and was going to work for Aeronica the national airline, she saw a need and moved to fill it.

At first she worked with disturbed youngsters in the educational system the Sandinista government launched after its triumph over the Somoza dictatorship in 1979. Gradually she turned her attention to the retarded sons and daughters of the poor who were now, after the revolution, beginning to receive attention from the government. The system tried hard to train the children in the basics, tying their shoes, feeding themselves, maybe learning to read and write.

But Romero noticed that as they neared puberty, the financially strained system was unable to care for them. Their parents were told to take them home where they were difficult, often impossible, to handle. Girls were vulnerable to sexual predators, boys were the butts of practical jokers with vicious streaks. One fourteen-year-old offered neighborhood entertainment when idlers gave him rum and tequila and then laughed and applauded as he staggered through the streets, accosting women and talking to the dogs and attempting to sing ribald songs.

Romero began organizing the parents, urging them to contribute what they could to hire special teachers with the patience to cope with these often disruptive children. She honed her skills of persuasion to wheedle materials, books and desks, kitchen equipment. She hired cooks. Eventually she talked the government into giving the co-op a 120-acre piece of land, carving it out of a much larger state farm near Ciudad Sandino, not far from Managua.

She begged the Army to lend trucks to haul the children to the co-op each morning and return. When the Army needed the trucks, which was often, the Romeros used their own cars, which soon began to suffer for it. Romero dreamed of a dormitory where the children could live. She got donations from church groups and eventually a Norwegian charity supplied enough money for a water well and buildings for several classrooms and a kitchen.

Gently, with subtle hints and a hidden but sure hand, Romero guided the parents toward a democratic organization, with a board of directors and elected officers. She tried to create a microcosm of democracy, prodding the mothers and fathers to function in a democratic give and take. She was slowly inculcating the idea of collective decision making, of involving every parent of the children before voting on changes. Exaggerated expectations, an authoritarian tradition of passing orders down from the top and delusions of power, however, all combined to create a precarious management balance.

Crops were planted, and harvested, and some of the least retarded of the children learned to market their produce to the shops in Ciudad Sandino. All the children but the most handicapped worked half of each day in the rows of vegetables, under close supervision so they wouldn't pull valuable plants with the weeds. Half of each day they spent in classrooms, learning the alphabet, numbers and, for some, how to read. Nearly every child was a success story. Carlos, who was fifteen when I saw him on my first visit to the center but looked ten and had the mental capacity of three, was learning to speak his name. A speech therapist repeated the name time after time, urging Carlos to hold his head up and say it after her. Eventually he would tell everyone who came to the place that he was Carlos, looking into another's eyes for the first time in his life.

When Marco Romero drove me to the center at a later year a gleeful, chattering Carlos almost literally climbed up his body. A large, boisterous and mildly retarded girl was into everything, a pain in the neck to everyone at the co-op, until Camilo, a refugee teacher from El Salvador helping out at the co-op, hit on the idea of giving her a job. She was assigned to care for a smaller, fragile and profoundly retarded girl who couldn't cope for herself. Responsibility worked wonders in dampening down the behavior of the larger girl and both were happier.

At last the Hans Gutierrez Co-Op was functioning and Romero began backing away from active participation after having spent some $30,000 of the family's own money getting it going. Change came slowly and then swiftly, and with responsibility, recklessly. The president of the board, without telling or consulting anyone else, one day fired all the teachers, one of whom had worked months teaching another autistic child to speak his name. Frances had to spend weeks at the Labor Ministry resolving that problem while searching for other teachers.

A bookkeeper, hired by the director, her boyfriend who had been instrumental in winning approval from the government for the co-op's land, decided the children needed a skill; she thought they could learn typing even though the least handicapped could barely write their names. She ordered ten typewriters but Romero heard about it and canceled the order.

Next the bookkeeper decided that the co-op needed a guard post at its entrance and before anyone knew what was happening a contractor was constructing a small square relatively expensive cement building where the watchman could lounge during the daytime although he slept in the kitchen at night. These seemingly irrational acts were not the work necessarily of corruption although that may have been involved. But they illustrate the problem attendant on giving authority to people who have never exercised any or even seen it used judiciously close up.

And then came the election of 1990. The Sandinistas were voted out of office, the free enterprise government of Violeta Chamorro, groomed and sponsored by the Bush Administration, took over the reins of a shattered nation. Privatization became the watchword of the new government. Disputes arose immediately over the rights of property. The news reached the center quickly; someone told the parents that now that they controlled the co-op they could sell the land. Marco Romero calculated that on the basis of comparable land sales the parents could sell out and each family be paid about $4,000. That is an enormous sum of money in a country where salaries of professionals are often less than $100 a month.

Apparently not all the parents were convinced, so a vilification campaign was launched against the Romeros, accusing them of embezzling co-op funds and of high-handed treatment of the staff. When representatives of the Norwegian foundation said they were coming to visit, the staff arranged a party and some of the less handicapped children were coached with songs for the visitors. But when the Norwegians arrived leaders of the anti-Romero group began denouncing them and the party disintegrated into a series of shouting matches. Frances Romero spent the next month bringing together all the co-op's books and other pertinent papers which she turned over to a parents committee. Then the Romeros sold their house and left Nicaragua, where they had planned to spend the rest of their lives, and returned to the United States. Most of the children went back to the dark back rooms of their parents' homes.

The Romeros, whose home was always open house for a varied collection of foreign visitors, most of them do-gooders spending a little time in Nicaragua trying to alleviate some of its miseries, were among the most prominent of the internationalists in the country. But there were many others, of all kinds of backgrounds and skills and understanding. One estimate said more than 60,000 Americans had visited Nicaragua between the 1979 revolution and 1987. Some were drifters in whatever were the current fad areas of the world, from Nepal to Poland, but most came to learn and many to help.

In 1987 I accompanied a young Seattle doctor, Drew Hittenberger, a specialist in prosthetics, on an inspection of a factory carving wooden legs for soldiers maimed by Contra mines. Carpenters using draw knives, hand drills and scrap steel turned out legs that Hittenberger said seemed to be as efficient as the technologically advanced prosthetics he worked with at home. The place also fitted the legs and cared for the veterans while they learned to use the contraptions. Hittenberger had some suggestions for the staff for care of a five-year-old boy who had lost a leg when a car ran over him. They would spend the next decade and more "growing" new legs as his body grew.

Another Seattle doctor, Richard Kovar, a family practitioner who had worked in other backward countries, found in Nicaragua's medical efforts "a truly awesome accomplishment that I haven't seen attempted anywhere else in the Third World." Infant deaths from had been cut by one third, he told me, largely through emphasizing rehydration of afflicted children, a relatively simple cure but one often neglected. But Kovar was outraged "that the health sector has been targeted (by the Contra) in all violation of medical neutrality." I met North American medical technicians, social workers, farmers, small business people, teachers, school board members, and a judge in addition to religious ministers and missionaries visiting Nicaragua to see for themselves what was really happening.

Many came to Nicaragua neutral, even disposed to defend their country against charges of fomenting violence and bringing hardship to the people there. All, at least those I met, were appalled at what was being done by their government in their name and with their tax dollars. Jean Eberhardt, daughter of a State Department official who speaks excellent Spanish, is a contractor in Washington State; she supervised a construction "brigade" that built a school house and then a two-story building for a women's sewing co-operative at Santo Tomas, in Chontales Department in Central Nicaragua. Local women learned to make clothing for sale using donated sewing machines. Eberhardt continues to lead a sister-county relationship with Chontales that has paid for the education of one doctor. It also contributes a stipend to some rural teachers.

Those Americans who went in droves to Nicaragua during the 1980s to see for themselves what was going on were continually sneered at as dupes of the "Marxist Sandinistas." They had, said one columnist always eager to tout the Reagan Administration's side of the story, "taken foreign policy into their hands to an extent never seen in American history." There was a perverse truth to that complaint, one the visitors would have gloried in.

The columnist was raving against church people in the Sanctuary movement that was giving shelter to refugees from Central America who had come to the United States illegally. The column's nonsense included the statement that "The Sandinistas have persecuted the Catholic Church so relentlessly that an estimated ninety five percent of the church members are now strongly against the government. But does this move the many North American church people who go there? Not much." As far as El Salvador was concerned, she said, "That tormented country does happen to have an exemplary government in place." This at a time when the Army and clandestine death squads were terrorizing the populace. Finally, the writer said, the deluded church people "see Salvadoran refugees in the United States as 'political refugees'. Every bit of evidence shows this to be false—the great mass of the approximately 500,000 Salvadorans in this country are seeking a better economic life."[69] Columns like that allowed the Reagan Administration to get away with its lies and deceits and its terrorist campaigns.

Some of the visitors to both El Salvador and Nicaragua were no doubt dilettantes and many were more a burden than they were a help. But even those who were shepherded by local groups were able to see at least a little something of what was happening.

Probably the most determined group standing up for Central America's persecuted and dispossessed was Witness for Peace, which between 1983 and 1993 sent more than four thousand people into the five Central American countries to lend their support to the people. Some Witnesses were held for a time by Contra operating on Nicaragua's southern front when their boat was captured on the San Juan River, but they were not harmed. Many volunteers worked in Guatemala where they visited villages attacked by the Army. Others accompanied refugees back to their homes, in Guatemala and El Salvador, in the face of military opposition. Often it was only the presence of these literal witnesses that forced the military to permit the refugees to return.

Among the most interesting of the many foreigners who came to El Salvador to try to rectify what he felt were his own government's murderous mistakes was Charles Clements.

---

[69] Georgie Ann Geyer, Univeral Press Syndicate, Jan. 1985.

Certainly he was among the most resolute. A graduate of the United States Air Force Academy, he had flown transport planes in Vietnam and had been detained in a psychiatric ward for his anti-war views (at a time when the United States government was protesting Soviet use of such wards to shut up its dissidents). After he was kicked out of the Air Force Clements went to the University of Washington Medical School and followed that up with some medical missionary work.

He went to Central America with a pack full of medical supplies and crossed the border from Honduras into El Salvador where for a year he practiced medicine on the run on the slopes of the Guazapa Volcano within sight of the bright lights of San Salvador. Dr. Clements and most of his patients survived only because of the El Salvadoran Army's ineptitude and failure to follow up air strikes in its scorched earth efforts to deny the guerrillas food and other support. Clements' account of his tribulations in his book, *Witness to War*, is one of the more powerful indictments of heedless American intervention in the lives of small nations.

For a time a regular shuttle seemed to be running between congressional office buildings in Washington, D.C. and Managua. Congress people were attempting to find out for themselves, they said, what was happening in Central America. Many more of them came to Nicaragua than to El Salvador or the other countries, partly because it was the center of activity as they saw it, with the Contra given a patina of glamor by rightwing public relations types, while the war in El Salvador seemed a quagmire with no end in sight and, worse, no rational reason for continuing.

Partly they came to Nicaragua because, in spite of what the State Department might say about dangers or human rights abuses, Nicaragua was safer than El Salvador as a place to be poking about. Few went to Guatemala, the most dangerous place of all, probably for that reason. Most of the official visitors to Nicaragua, such as former Secretary of State Henry Kissinger, came and went so fast they barely had time to see the earthquake ruins on their trips into Managua from the airport. Some of their visits lasted only hours, after which the publicity mills ground out lofty assessments of what either the United States or Nicaragua should be doing, usually colored by views fixed long before the trip began. It wasn't all just people from Congress. New York Mayor Ed Koch made a whirlwind trip that took, in series, all sides of every controversy and made many Nicaraguans realize they weren't by comparison so badly served by their own politicians.

The murder of Americans by the Nicaragua Contra or the Salvadoran Army or death squads usually drew denunciations back home, in newspaper stories and some times in Congress, or at least in the Congressional Record. But little ever happened and the incidents were quickly forgotten except by the victims' families. In 1981 two Americans working in El Salvador's land reform program were shot dead in the restaurant of the Sheraton Hotel in San Salvador, later the Hotel El Salvador, one of the favorite hangouts of the Salvadorn oligarchical elite and American officials. The two, Mark Pearlman, Seattle, and Michael Hammer of Potomac, Maryland, worked for the AFL-CIO American Institute for Free Labor Development. Killed with them that evening, as they were relaxing after a day trying to unravel land ownerships, was Jose Rodolfo Viera, director of El Salvador's land reform program.

Many witnesses saw two enlisted soldiers walk up to the table where the three were sitting and shoot them point blank. Eventually the gunmen were convicted and given light sentences. The man they said ordered the murder and who drove their getaway car, Lieutenant Isidro Lopez Sibrian, was released by a judge who ruled there was "insufficient evidence" to try him. Lopez Sibrian, who was related to a member of the Salvadoran Supreme Court and was a former aide to Roberto d'Aubuisson, godfather of the death squads, went back to active duty with the Army. That brief biography not only explains why Lopez went free, it also tells everything the world needs to know about the political-government situation in El Salvador. Lopez was later implicated in a plot with other Army officers to kidnap Salvadoran businessmen for ransom.

Another officer accused in the Sheraton case, Capt. Eduardo Avila, was to be prosecuted for ordering the murders four years later but a Salvadoran court dismissed the charges. The United States Embassy was "somewhat disappointed" by the ruling.

Even at the height of the Contra war Nicaragua was essentially a law-abiding country where public murders were rare. I tried to check out a number of stories of harassment of Americans by the Sandinista government but could never find any evidence to substantiate them. In my wanderings in Nicaragua I often talked to soldiers and policemen and always, without exception, found them more civil than those of the neighboring countries. I never met any of those people who allegedly were beaten up by Sandinista police or soldiers. At their worst those tales paled in comparison to the savagery some Americans met in El Salvador at the hands of the government or its representatives.

The Reagan Administration could not blame the death of Ben Linder, a young mechanical engineer from Portland, Oregon, on the Sandinistas, so American propagandists tried to vilify Linder himself. Linder, who went to Nicaragua just two months after graduating from the University of Washington engineering school, was slain with several Nicaraguans while supervising construction of a small, 250-watt hydroelectric "appropriate technology" power dam on a stream in northern Nicaragua. An accomplished amateur clown, Linder entertained children in rural towns by suiting up in his clown costume and riding a unicycle down their bumpy streets.

Linder was working for the Nicaraguan Ministry of Electricity through the Nicaragua Appropriate Technology Project, of Bellingham, Washington. His murder, by a Contra raiding party, probably after being tortured, did not elicit much outrage from officials in the Reagan Administration and drew one of the nastiest responses by a politician in the long Contra war. When his parents met with a congressional committee they were badgered, rather than comforted, and one congressman suggested that Linder "had asked for it," by going to Nicaragua and working against his own government.

Linder probably made a mistake in carrying a rifle. He was not trained as a soldier and was ill prepared to cope with the type of warfare engaged in by the Contra. The presence of a weapon was excuse enough for the Contra to kill him, for the same reason they justified killing armed coffee pickers.

Linder's parents and many people who knew him and others who sympathized with his efforts to better the lives of poor Nicaraguans believe his killing was premeditated, planned by the Contra as a warning to other foreigners to get out of Nicaragua. They called Linder's death an "assassination," aided if not abetted by United States policy. "The Contras know who the North Americans are and where they're working," said Carol Wells, of a California group called the Nicaragua Task Force, which coordinated visits to the country by volunteers working on energy projects and water and sewage systems. "They would not kill a North American without clearing it first" with United States officials, she said.[70] The Contra were undisciplined, but I doubt if they had orders, from the CIA or their own bosses, to shoot Linder, beyond a general suggestion that they harrass foreign supporters of the Sandinistas.

Americans who rejected the Reagan Administration's anti-communist view of Central America could expect little help from their own government when they got into trouble with local authorities. Jennifer Casolo found that out when she was arrested shortly after the Salvadoran Army killed six Jesuit priests in 1989 in its frustration at not being able to drive guerrillas out of the nation's capitol in the toughest offensive of the war.

Casolo's arrest, on charges of hiding weapons for the guerrillas in her backyard garden, was almost certainly trumped up to divert North American public attention

---

[70] Laurence McQuillan, San Francico Examiner, Jan. 9, 1983.

away from the killing of the priests. The Army went to great lengths to show that she was hiding weapons for the guerrillas, producing a video tape of the rifles being unearthed. Pictures she had taken were allegedly included in the weapons containers which seems a poor way to conceal incriminating evidence. I met Casolo, who was employed by Christian Education Seminars, an ecumenical group from Texas, in 1989 when she helped a group I was with meet Salvadoran Army Chief of Staff Colonel Emilio Ponce, with whom she was on speaking terms.

What made Casolo's arrest so outrageous was the United States Embassy's participation. First, an embassy official happened to be along on the raid that uncovered the weapons under Casolo's patio. "It's a good bust,"[71] said the official who, like all subordinate State Department officials, would speak only for "background." Perhaps the official meant the arrest was carried out in a professional manner, meaning Casolo wasn't beaten up as a Salvadoran would have been. Or it could have meant that the arrest was deserved. The embassy made it very clear to the Salvadoran government that it believed Casolo was helping the guerrillas. An investigation was inconclusive, but Casolo was kicked out of the country anyway.

President Bush's press secretary, Marlin Fitzwater, added to the charade when he said "There are implications (sic) of her involvement, that's for sure..." Such comments drew the wrath of many Americans at home. Forty congressional aides had an angry meeting with State Department officials, and Massachusetts Attorney General James Shannon, who had met Casolo on a trip to El Salvador, called the Administration's handling of her case "reprehensible. They're supposed to look out for the interests of Americans abroad. In this case, they've thrown the presumption of innocence out the window. They've tried and convicted Casolo in the press. They've given a green light to the Salvadoran government to do what they will with her. The Salvadoran government is clearly trying to get

---

[71] Patt Morrison, the Los Angeles Times,

human rights and church workers out of the country so they can do what they want to do without witnesses."[72]

Casolo was typical of many young Americans who worked in Central America, and particularly El Salvador, to counter what they believed was the outrageous, even criminal, conduct of their own government. A majority were women, college graduates, non-religious "counter culture" types and very bright. They were also skilled negotiators, usually fluent in Spanish, and fearless. Casolo scared the wits out me as she engaged in "auto chicken" with El Salvador's suicidal drivers when I rode with her. Normally, I hitched rides or rode buses and this was a new hazard I hadn't considered before in my travels in Central America.

Actually, Casolo and other Americans were lucky. During the guerrilla assault in the city that culminated in the slaying of the Jesuit priests, the Salvadoran Air Force, the meanest of the country's armed forces, dropped leaflets on San Salvador with this message:

"With God, reason and might, we shall conquer. Salvadoran patriot: You have every right to defend your life and your property. If in order to do this you have to kill FMLN terrorists and their internationalist allies, do it."[73]

It wasn't just in El Salvador or Guatemala that the internationalists were harassed or murdered. Their activities at home were monitored and some went to jail. Both the CIA and the FBI continually snooped around the Committee in Solidarity with the People of El Salvador in the middle 1980s. CISPES published a newsletter that attempted to focus on policy miscues of the Reagan Administration although it was never a very influential organization. But any pinprick usually produced loud bellows from the State Department or the White House.

The State Department's Bureau of Diplomatic Security told its field agents in a memo in 1988 that the information they were collecting "should be shared with appropriate law-enforcement contacts as well as official government of El Salvador

---

[72] New York Times, Nov. 27, 1989.
[73] Boston Globe, Dec. 6, 1989

representatives."[74] Nothing could have alarmed Salvadoran refugees more. Such information, they were sure, was going immediately to the death squads. The same information, circulating within the United States, was being used to try to intimidate activists. Salvadoran refugees in Los Angeles were continually harassed by someone, apparently Salvadoran agents, although none were ever identified. An activist church minister in Louisville, Kentucky, received a photograph of the six Catholic priests killed in El Salvador. Along with it was a note: "You're next."

In the early 1980s President Reagan ordered all the Nicaraguan consulates in the United States closed although its embassy in Washington continued to function. It was an attempt to curb the travels of Americans to Nicaragua by making it more difficult to obtain visas. Nicaragua simply dropped the visa requirement altogether and travel was easier than before. El Salvador went the other way. On my earlier trips there no visa was required. Then the country began demanding that Americans jump through the same hoops Salvadorans had to put up with when they asked for visas to visit the United States. Statements of good conduct from local chiefs of police and proof of property ownership were requirements to obtain visas to visit El Savador.

Americans weren't the only foreigners the Salvadorans found to be pests in their war against their own people.

Among the internationalists were many Scandinavians, chiefly Norwegians, and West Germans, Mexicans and some Britons and French. Americans, however, were the most numerous even though many of them were voyeurs or thrill seekers and some were more bother than they were worth.

Bulgaria seemed to have been assigned by Moscow to represent the Communist world in Nicaragua. Bulgaria had a technological display in Managua and when the Soviet Empire collapsed, the Bulgarians were building a new port on the Atlantic Coast. Nicaragua's new telephone equipment being installed in 1983 came from Bulgaria. But the Soviet presence was noticeable too. In addition to enormous helicopters

[74] Central American Report, Washington, D.C. Dec. 1989.

and obsolete tanks and heavy artillery, the Soviets built and staffed a large hospital after the devastating floods of 1982. A Cuban presence was mainly devoted to teaching and health care. Cubans built some houses in Managua's earthquake zone that understandably were slow to entice many Nicaraguans.

All these people were fair game for the Contra terror campaign. In 1983 a German doctor riding in an Army truck to a remote village was killed in an ambush, along with twelve Nicaraguans. When the Army caught the assassins, one nineteen-year-old Contra boasted to his captors that he had "killed the communist doctor" by shooting him five times in the head and five times in the chest. In such manner did the ideological tone from the United States infect Nicaragua.

A Swiss theologian, forty-two-year-old Jurg Dieter Weis, was killed by the National Police in El Salvador's Cabanas Department in 1988 as he was trying to assess the psychological effects of bombing on civilians. After Weis was shot, or perhaps before, his face was slashed in an attempt to hide his identity. An Army press officer said Weis was a doctor and he was carrying medicine and firearms for the guerrillas. The Army also said Weis and two guerrillas were killed in a fire fight, although no battles had been reported in the area for several months.[75]

A group of eight German women and men building houses for poor Nicaraguans was luckier. They were on the job only five days when they were kidnapped by a Contra unit in Southern Nicaragua and forced to go along as it tramped through the countryside twenty to thirty kilometers a day for more than three weeks even though some of them were ill.

The Germans were told that if the Nicaraguan Army tried to rescue them they would be killed and their deaths blamed on the Sandinistas.[76] About half the Contra weapons were from West Germany, the Germans noted.

They were amazed at the computerized "coder-de-

[75] Dave Lindorff, In These Times, Jan. 9, 1989.
[76] John Lindsay-Poland, The Progressive, May, 1989. p.32

coder" complete with printer the Contra used to communicate with their base in Honduras. The Germans believe the order to free them came over that gadget from the State Department when their plight became an issue in an election in the West German state of Saxony. German Chancellor Helmut Kohl was already under fire for supporting Reagan's Contra war.

Each of the Central American countries had its peculiar attraction for internationalists, of whatever political hue. El Salvador's and Guatemala's agonies were more complex and their dynamics more difficult to sort out than Nicaragua's. Those two countries were also more physically dangerous for unwanted strangers poking around. Guatemala especially nourished an oligarchy less dependent on United States goodwill than the others. Fewer Americans died there but that was because most were sightseeing tourists, not activists upset by the brutalities. Nicaragua was safer; I hitchhiked all over Nicaragua during the war years and I never felt threatened. By contrast I was always nervous in El Salvador whenever I met its soldiers, National Guardsmen, National Police, Treasury Police or one of the obvious members of the death squads.

Thus Nicaragua was the country of choice for many United States citizens seeking to right the wrongs they saw their tax dollars financing. Some Americans living and working in Nicaragua who were shamed and embarrassed by their country's policies began in the early 1980s to walk vigils at seven o'clock every Thursday morning in front of the fortress-like American Embassy on a busy Managua street. Some twenty to thirty United States citizens would parade in a small circle in front of the gate topped with razor sharp wire while chanting some peace litany.

I found those vigils to be rather corny and even embarrassing, but their participants defended them as the only way they could show the State Department and, as important, the Nicaraguan people, that not all Americans agreed with what their government was doing there. Often statements would be read and frequently there would be a celebrity, a Hollywood or television actor whose knowledge of the country or the Contra war was not matched by their fervent denunciations of American "imperialism." My knowledge of American celebrities is scanty and so I had to be told at one vigil that the man speaking was a well known movie actor, Martin Sheen. Another, whose name was familiar to me, was Daniel Ellsberg. It seemed to me those vigils degenerated into squealing sessions for brat-like junkies who barely knew where they were or what they were saying. Many of them came there following a rather well worn trail of America haters to rub shoulders with the celebrities.

The Sandinistas were never the saints many Americans, particularly the "*sandalistas*," made them out to be. Those revolutionary groupies, with their wild exaggerations and attacks on United States policies, probably did as much damage, in building suspicion back home, as the Sandinistas' enemies did. With their American 1960s counter culture life styles, so out of synch with conservative Nicaragua, they blindly defended every action of the Sandinistas, no matter how egregious or plain foolish, and would concede no faults. But their chief damage was in their strident denunciations, not just of United States policies but also of motives; America, and Americans who had doubts about the Sandinistas were pictured as unrelieved evil rather than misguided, poorly informed or, in the case of Congress and the press, the tired cowards they really were. In the days immediately following the election of Violeta Chamorro the exaggerated public groveling of the *sandalistas* disgusted not just moderate Americans who felt badly about the defeat but they put off the beaten Sandinistas too. Some of them, I am sure, were CIA hirelings.

Not often was the United States as bold or as forthright as when Ambassador Deane Hinton in 1986 told the American Chamber of Commerce in San Salvador that "common criminals are having a field day" in the country. "El Salvador must make substantial progress in bringing the murderers of our citizens, including those who ordered the murders, to justice, in advancing human rights, and in controlling the abuses of some elements of the security forces,"[77] Hinton said.

His speech, which had obviously been cleared in Washington in one of its more militant days, outraged his audience. A business group took out a full page ad in a San Salvador newspaper to denounce "this insult to the Salvadoran people, which does not admit or tolerate these 'proconsular' attitudes...appropriate for a delegate of ancient imperial Rome to peoples vanquished, put down and subjugated."

In spite of some unpleasant encounters with United States foreign service officers, I came away with a great deal of respect for most of them. They too were internationalists and their jobs were often impossible.

The night before the 1984 El Salvador I infiltrated a party hosted by Ambassador Thomas Pickering (who later became United States ambassador to the United Nations) for official United States election observers. His comments about the next day's election reflected the Reagan Administration's line but there was a humane side to it that made me sympathize with the man. I didn't know it until long afterward but his life had been threatened just days before that meeting, and in El Salvador that is a serious matter. General Vernon Walters, a White House no-nonsense trouble shooter had been sent to El Salvador especially to inform Roberto d'Aubuisson, the rightist leader of the country's semi-clandestine death squads, that he would be held personally responsible if anything happened to Pickering and that United States assistance would be "terminated."

It is too bad the Reagan Administration didn't issue a blanket instruction to d'Aubuisson and his thugs not to kill their own countrymen and women.

Most of the observers at the embassy party seemed suspicious of United States involvement in the election and Pickering took their hectoring with good grace. One member of a lawyers' group told the ambassador of a man he had seen that day in the notorious Mariona Prison who had been "tortured

---

[77] CUSCLIN, Bulletin of US Citizens Living in Nicaragua, July, 1986.

to confess to something he knew nothing about" and had never yet been charged or seen a lawyer. Pickering asked the lawyer to give his staff the prisoner's name and the circumstances and "we'll look into it."

"This man's been locked up four months without charge and you say you'll 'look into it'," the lawyer snapped. Some of Pickering's staff lost their diplomatic cool as a woman identifying herself as a Texas Quaker asked the ambassador "doesn't your conscience bother you?" about stories others told of people who had been tortured and lost family members to the death squads. "The violence doesn't come from just one source," Pickering replied. "It comes from many sources." That didn't satisfy the white-faced Quaker. "We're talking about who our government is supporting," she shouted.

Another shouter was William Doherty, of the AFL-CIO who had just visited Salvadoran labor leaders locked up in Mariona. "They're still being accused of terrorism," Doherty said.

Of union leaders not in prison, Doherty said, "they're endorsing Duarte for president and trying to get out the vote. If they don't, this dog on the right (d'Aubuisson) will win." But Doherty, whom many internationalists thought worked for the CIA, added that "the overwhelming number of our (labor) people don't support the guerrillas because they're Marxist-Leninists." That repetition of the Reagan line didn't reduce the suspicion of Doherty among that crowd of observers.

I got into the party as an official "observer" to the elections on the recommendation of a friend, Donovan Cook of Seattle's University Baptist Church, who was a genuine observer. Cook had been told by an embarrassed embassy staffer that many of the invited official observers hadn't shown up. Did Cook know anyone willing to watch at a polling place? He did, and I got an invitation to the party. I don't know what people recruited in the United States to be observers were told, but if they got the same alarming report on El Salvador that we received that night beside the pool in the flower garden of the ambassador's residence, I can understand why many of them chickened out.

"We ask you not to jog in the streets. Our people don't," said an embassy security officer after our observer duties had been spelled out for us. I ran in the streets early each morning. "Don't ride the buses," he said. "Take a taxi." I rode the buses to try to find out what people were thinking. "If you're in a restaurant and you hearing shooting, call the embassy," he said. Some of the observers around me were exchanging worried looks. I couldn't tell whether that ferocious litany was meant as bravado, bureaucratic overkill to impress the observers with how hard life was in El Salvador or as cover if something should happen. In any case it represented a total misunderstanding of what was likely to occur.

I went to a number of polling places the next day and the only frightening things I saw were soldiers standing beside the polling tables. Many people stood all day in the hot sun in their Sunday clothing, shuffling forward in long lines, to drop their ballots in large clear plastic boxes supplied by the United States. Voting was secret if the voter folded his or her ballot properly, but many did not even try to fold them under the watchful eye of the soldier on guard. They just wanted to vote and get a stamp on their *cedulas*, the internal passports which all Salvadorans are required always to have with them. Without a stamp to prove they had voted they were likely to end up headless in a ditch the next time they met an Army or police patrol.

On election night I watched votes being counted at a precinct in a San Salvadoran slum called *Mexicanos*, and it looked honest and fair to me although not nearly as tightly run as the 1990 election in Nicaragua when I also watched voters and vote counters.

Later that night I went to election headquarters in the El Presidente Hotel to watch vote totals being tabulated. The place was full of well dressed Salvadorans and foreign observers. I asked a number of the latter what they thought of the election. They all expressed admiration for its honesty and all remarked on the dedication of the Salva-

267

doran people spending their Sunday in the broiling sun to show their faith in democracy. Did they suspect that the stamps in the *cedulas* might have something to do with that? Most hadn't noticed the stamps or had not given them any thought, as I wouldn't have had I not been there two weeks and made an effort to understand the voting system. One man I asked was Michael Novak, whom I had never heard of but who introduced himself as a "well known Catholic writer." Novak was indignant that I would impugn the Salvadoran people's love for democracy by such an inference. "Nonsense," he said. Others bristled too. When my stories of why the people voted were published in Seattle I was denounced in letters to the editor.

14

An End to War?

AURORA BAEZ PERSONIFIES THE TRIUMPHS OF THE LITERACY
campaign launched by the Sandinista Party shortly after the
1979 Nicaraguan revolution. "I learned much more than to
read and write," she told me as we sat in the twilight on
her front porch. She was on the city council in rural Santo
Tomas in Chontales Department a hundred miles east of
Managua, deep in Contra country. "It fulfilled me as a person. I was re-born with the revolution."

The street in front of Doña Aurora's house is a four-
block-long speed bump, a dry river bed except in the rainy
season when it *is* a river. You can break an axle or an ankle
there and as we talked a rooster, arrogant in burnished
bronze, found the boulders unbecoming to his dignity and
sought a more level field to strut. Like most of Nicaragua,
Santo Tomas after voters threw out the Sandinistas and installed a free enterprise government acceptable to George
Bush and the United States, was gray with poverty, hungry
and fearful of a precarious future. Now, Doña Aurora told
me, crime was up; hope was down. The dollars that anti-
Sandinistas boasted would shower down on the country if
the people voted for Violeta Chamorro had not appeared.
And they weren't likely to. Uncle Sam, victorious over an
alleged communist threat to the hemisphere, has washed his
hands of Central America.

"Life for the poor gets harder every day while the rich
get richer every day," Doña Aurora said. I had seen her last

in 1990 when I hitchhiked to Santo Tomas trying to gauge how the election was likely to go and she was the undisputed first citizen of this town. Its most outspoken Sandinista in the face of a determined opposition (Santo Tomas voted for Chamorro in the election), Doña Aurora organized and managed the *comedor infantil*, the children's kitchen where more than three hundred hungry youngsters were fed one good meal a day.

Stocky, in her early fifties, with a smooth square face out of which a gold tooth smiles, DõnaAurora was unable to go to school as a child. The literacy program made her a new woman, although it was not everywhere the miracle the Sandinistas claimed. It was a success generally, however. And now its positive gains and other efforts by the Sandinistas to improve the lot of Nicaragua's poor are being lost as the country's revolution and its destruction become a Cold War footnote. An education is once again more difficult to attain as the new government, heeding the economic mandates of the International Monetary Fund and the United States Agency for International Development, attempts to privatize everything, including the schools.

In 1991, as a freshman medical student at the University of Nicaragua, Maria Salvadora Gonzales Solis could barely scrape up the $20 annual tuition and the $15 each for the three books she had to buy. The next year tuition went up and Maria, the top scorer at the Santo Tomas high school for admission to the medical school, needed more books. Without aid promised by a Washington State sister-county program Maria, then 18, wouldn't be able to fulfill the family dream that she become a doctor, said her mother, a worn woman who went through six grades of school. Her husband, a saddle maker, attended school three years as a child.

Maria faced five years of schooling and one as an intern at a hospital in Managua or Leon and then two years of "social service" in a rural area. She will return to Santo Tomas to practice, "to give something back to my people." That dream depended on outside help.

Even in the lower schools education is no longer free. If a student can't afford to buy his or her books "the teacher asks what are you doing here?" said Alejandra Martinez, the mother of three daughters in school in Ciudad Sandino, a Managua suburb. Senora Martinez commuted daily by bus to Managua and then walked a mile to her job as a maid to supplement her husband's $160 a month salary as an employee of the Managua city government. As prices rose steadily their combined lower middle class paychecks barely fed the family of five. And Josue Martinez's job was one of thousands the IMF said should be eliminated to help pay the country's debts.

Alejandra, who never attended school, also learned to read and write in the *alfabetization* and improves her reading with her employer's newspaper each day. Josue was one of the lucky ones in pre-revolution Nicaragua; he managed to go through the first grade before he had to go to work. The Martinez' goal in life is to educate their daughters but even with their two jobs they worry. Four books for Magda, the oldest girl, cost 22 cordobas, more than $4, notebooks $1 to $1.50. Actually, the books are only rented and if a book is lost or damaged the student must pay its full cost or there will be no grades, which means not passing to the next year's higher level. Students must pay also to take tests, for the costs of the paper. Again, if they don't have money they don't get the grades that allow them to continue in school.

Children in three families on her block were not going to school, Alejandra said, "because they have no money for clothing, books or other school supplies such as pencils. They also do not have enough to eat," she said.

"There is no help from the government for education," Alejandra said.

Even the United States Department of State, early in Ronald Reagan's Contra war, conceded that while the Sandinistas might be communists, they had improved the country. In 1983 I was told by a staff member of the embassy in Managua that "they have brought literacy to the people. My maid has learned to read and write and now she is learning math. It's a great source of pride to her. But I look at her books and there is a high political content." Even that grudging credit, however, was further than State Department people would go later on if they wanted to keep their jobs.

The new government, under education minister Humberto Belli, was charging tuition under a sort of supply side theory that if everyone pays for education more people will be able to attend school because teachers will be paid more and therefore there will be more teachers. The idea infuriates those who say many poor Nicaraguans can't pay anything for education which is guaranteed in the country's constitution. Belli, a Catholic intellectual and long time critic of the Sandinistas and an admirer of Ronald Reagan, supervised the burning of four million textbooks, on history, geography and language because of their "political content."[78]

They had been furnished to the country by the Norwegian government. With $12 million in United States Agency for International Development funds Belli bought seven million new books to "depoliticize" the curriculum. But two years later many schools still did not have the new books and many students wouldn't have been able to afford them anyway.

"Education is going backward 20 years since the (1990) election," Doña Aurora told me. "Health care is worse, thanks to a government mentality that wants to privatize everything. Unemployment is up and there is no possibility of finding work. There are no medicines." Tuberculosis is on the increase, doctors report.

Her assessment is echoed by Carlos Tunnerman, who was education minister in the Sandinista government. "The main accomplishment during ten years of Sandinista rule was to establish education as a fundamental right for every Nicaraguan," he said. Now illiteracy is rising again and many children no longer go to school.

Tunnerman conceded that the Sandinista textbooks car-

---

[78] Boles, National Catholic Reporter, Sept. 15, 1989.

ried ideological messages and that some of them should have been removed over time. "In 1979 (after the revolution) we found a series of texts that didn't seem appropriate because they talked of Somoza as a peacemaker, etc., but it never occurred to us to burn them. We sent them to the school libraries for whoever wanted to consult them."

A cynic could argue that it doesn't matter that education is being strangled. Many educated Nicaraguans can't find decent jobs, and college graduates are hawking chewing gum, car parts, newspapers, television antennas and almost anything else that is portable on Managua street corners and at traffic lights.

All of Dõna Aurora's five children have received college educations. She was a leader with the parish priest, Father Ignacio, of a group of 30 women who started the *comedor infantil*, a cafeteria for children. A Swiss organization helped finance its construction and the Sandinista government supplied some food as long as it could in the face of the war and economic embargo. But "the new government is not interested," Aurora says. She conceded, however, that the new government did contribute money for three salaried positions for the kitchen, including hers, at 700 cordobas or $140 a month.

A staple of the *comedor's* donated foods is soya, a gruel made of soy beans, which is boiled, strained and made into a drink called soymilk. The residue is dried, mixed with seasonings and formed into cakes and fried, like potatoes. I found a lunch of soy patties, soy cookies, soy milk and some other hard to identify soy products bland and not very tasty although adequate to satisfy hunger. Children, coming to soya early, like it, Aurora said, but adults don't. That comment expressed her philosophy; she is ready to accept change, if it is beneficial. Too many Nicaraguans accept the status quo with an unquestioning fatalism, Aurora says.

"The Nicaraguan poor are afraid of authority, a holdover from the Somoza years when they didn't dare complain," said an American nun who had been in Nicaragua for more than 20 years but still asked not to be identified.

"*Dependencia*" was Elia Romero's expletive for those of her countrymen who learned to rely too greatly on the assistance that came from outside admirers of the Sandinista socialist experiment. She was still a Sandinista but in doing a graduate school study of foreign aid over ten years she concluded that it too often had a crippling effect. Romero, a biologist, cited a Finnish program that brought in technicians to teach Nicaraguan campesinos better farming methods. Bulgarians brought tractors, too. Results were good, while the Finns stayed. But when they left after four years and turned the land and the tractors and other tools over to the natives the project fell apart and the farmers returned to the old ways.

"They (the Finns) never forced the farmers to learn how to run a farm, to fix the tractors," she said. No one had emphasized maintenance, and the machinery was operated until it would no longer function. Actually, the machinery was inappropriate for Nicaraguan small farmers in the first place. Years later rows of huge Bulgarian tractors designed for vast communes on the steppes of Central Asia rusted in Nicaraguan fields too small and too fragile for their enormous tires. Foreign help, primarily from western Europe, was more appropriately scaled later but Romero and others still believe that it should be in the background, subtle, rather than out in front. Nicaraguans, no less than other people, learn best by doing.

The poor of Nicaraguan are not poor for lack of effort. At Chacaraseca, a few miles from Leon, Nicaragua's second city, the people know only hard work, with little reward. For a time there was an electric generator, owned by the government but operated by a local co-operative, which provided some homes in the community with lights, carried by wires strung in tree branches and tiny poles stuck in the ground. But the new government took the generator "and gave it to a rich man," said Juana Mendez, because the community had applied to an American foundation for a $45,000 grant to electrify twenty eight houses. "They said we wouldn't need the generator any more." But the foundation rejected the request because it makes grants only for water wells, not for electrical systems. "We couldn't pump water without the electricity," said a puzzled Juana.

So the community dug a well beside the church. With shovels. Two hundred and fifty feet deep. "A man could stay down there only half an hour and he would run out of air," said Domingo Mendez, who supervised the digging over three months. Once the well was completed the community encased the opening with a cement wall to keep kids, dogs and chickens from falling into it and built a cement tank to hold the water that is hauled up in a bucket by a weary horse. Rather than a pulley, the rope from the bucket to the horse's harness slides in a groove in a thick tree branch cemented into the ground beside the well.

When the tank must be filled the horse plods along a path between two rows of young papaya trees, pulling the bucket to the surface. Then he backs up along his path to let the bucket down again, then back up again, all day long in the blazing sun. Each morning before dawn Juana Mendez bails water out of the tank into a bucket and carries it to as many as she can of the young trees in the little orchard that spreads downhill from the church. She still hopes for electricity which would allow her to irrigate all the trees each day.

One of Nicaragua's dilemmas was that the Chamorro government, oriented toward the wealthy haves as it was, still hadn't moved fast enough to satisfy the United States. On a national level, the economy had improved in the years after the election that brought Chamorro to office. Some foreign investment had come in, the currency was stable, at five cordobas to the dollar. Inflation, which had reached a numbing 1,300 percent before the 1990 election, was nearly zero. Those Nicaraguans with money, preferably lots of it, were in good shape. New supermarkets had sprung up all over Managua and even in some of the other cities. But prices were high and many people in fertile Nicaragua went hungry.

One way of solving the country's back-breaking economic problems, according to IMF dictates, is to fire government workers, such as Josue Martinez. Raul Lacayo, president of the Central Bank of Nicaragua, said 150,000 people were on the government payroll when the Sandinistas were defeated. Two years later it was down to about 60,000, he said, and further reductions were planned. Keeping jobs for Josue Martinez and others like him was a major goal of the still vigorous Sandinista Party, the opposition to Chamorro's government.

The gap between the haves and the have-nots is as wide, or wider, than even before the revolution. Nicaraguans given land formerly owned by the Somoza family or its cronies or by big landowners who fled during the Sandinista years fiercely resisted giving it up. On the other side, peasants who joined the Contra because of Sandinista oppression or mismanagement insisted they had a right to land. Although the land question in relatively sparsely populated Nicaragua is not as volatile as it is in crowded El Salvador next door, it could still throw the country back into civil war.

Conflicts still flared years after the war's end in areas of Northern Nicaragua between some still armed Contras and the Army.

In some cases former Sandinista soldiers joined former Contras, their previous enemies, in their frustrations over land questions. One constant friction was the continued domination of the Army by the Sandinistas, in the person of Humberto Ortega, its chief of staff. The brother of Daniel Ortega, the president defeated by Chamorro, he was kept on untill 1995 in an effort toward conciliation. Humberto Ortega's position not only enraged the former Contra, it aggravated those North Americans such as Senator Jesse Helms, who wanted to root our every vestige of Sandinismo. Paradoxically, many Sandinistas and leftists also criticized Humberto Ortega's handling of the Army. "It is the Army of the rich now," one ardent Sandinista told me.

"Violeta's line is that since the Sandinistas got forty one percent of the vote (against her UNO coalition of fourteen widely differing parties), they can't be ignored," said Trevor Evans, an English economist working in Nicaragua. "But the rightwingers, such as Vice President Virgilio Godoy, say the government shouldn't deal with the Sandinistas. They say 'we should smash them'."

The Ortega brothers got along reasonably well with Antonio Lacayo, Chamorro's son-in-law, who was really running the country. Both sides had to constantly cool off their own hot heads who would have liked to re-ignite the flames of war.

Disillusionment, over the pace of undoing the land reform, with the lack of credit for farmers and the inability of most Nicaraguans to buy even the essentials has created a national cynicism expressed in crime. Where hitchhiking was easy and acceptable in the Sandinista years when getting on a bus was impossible, hitching rides now became dangerous. During the war I used to hitch rides wherever I went; but on trips to Santo Tomas and Chacaraseca two years after Chamorro's election victory friends cautioned me not to even think about it. "There are desperate people out there who will kill you for your shoes," one warned me.

Nicaragua has been "polarized and paralyzed," said Donna Vukelich, an American long in Nicaragua. "Public schools are not functioning, the government gave away public enterprises such as factories and airlines. Consumers have been hit hard by rising prices, even the wealthy. The thousands looking for jobs can't find them." Many Nicaraguans who fled the country during the war and returned after Chamorro's victory "want to get even" with those who got the land, Vukelich said. "There is a spirit of revenge in the country.

"People at the bottom are desperate and apathetic," she said. "Everything is for sale. Citizens formerly active in public life have withdrawn. In the 1980s people were poor, but they had a goal.

"Now seventy percent of the population can't meet their daily needs. Crime is high, there is no safety," she said. "Drugs and prostitution are growing problems. There is a wave of murders of the wealthy," Vukelich said.

Although some United States aid to Nicaragua in the

early 1990s was going into projects to improve roads and construct water systems and to feed some of the poorest, most of it was in credits to help the country repay its debts. The United States wrote off a $291.9 million debt of the Somoza regime that it would not forgive during the Sandinista years. United States loans helped the government pay off $360 million in debts incurred by the Sandinistas. Mexico forgave $1.1 billion of the $1.2 billion Nicaragua owed it for oil, and Venezuela wrote off another $270 million in oil debt. Nicaragua still sought international help to settle $1.6 billion in commercial bank debt, ie, debt not contracted through the government. Still owed two years after the election were some $3 billion to the former Soviet Union and another $3 billion to 12 other mostly Eastern European nations.

Even the presidents of neighboring countries, no admirers of the Sandinistas, were alarmed when Washington, at the insistence of Helms and other rightwingers, cut even the small aid it was planning to give Nicaragua because it wasn't privatizing the country fast enough.

During the 1990 election campaign that turned the Sandinistas out of office, members of the UNO coalition boasted that a flood of American dollars would follow an election with Chamorro triumphant. That flood hasn't come and Nicaraguans, although their currency was stabilized two years after the election, are poorer than ever. Whether some of the country's surface prosperity will trickle down to Santo Tomas and Chacaraseca and thousands of other rural communities is doubtful.

In El Salvador the situation in the early 1990s seemed better. North Americans and Europeans who worked with Salvadorans were unanimous in claiming that their Salvadoran friends work harder than Nicaraguans do. Salvadorans also cooperate more willingly with one another, they insisted. I put all that down to a kind of small town boosterism. To me those claims of Salvadorans' superior enterprise sounded similar to the slurs that the Ticos of Costa Rica hurl at Nicaraguans. But as I got to know both countries better I began to share the viewpoint that, at least, Salvadorans work better together than do Nicaraguans. That could be explained, at least in part, by differences in populations; citizens of El Salvador are forced by the country's very density to cooperate and share. Nicaraguans, with more wide open spaces and less crowding, are more individualistic.

Part of my changed perception was a result of a visit I made early in 1989 to Santa Marta, in El Salvador's Cabanas Department. The villagers of Santa Marta, about three thousand of them, had spent most of the war in the Mesa Grande refugee camp a few miles away and over the border in Honduras. Eventually they, like so many other Salvadoran refugees, returned to their dynamited village in spite of threats by the Army, and began to rebuild. When I visited the town women were washing clothing in the river and men and children were husking corn and building new homes. Even the rubble of the old homes was unusable. The first building, even before most homes were completed, was a school house. It was also the most imposing building in the community although that didn't mean much.

In spite of Santa Marta's misery I discerned a kind of civic pattern, a subtle community coherence new to villages such as this. The Army, in destroying the village and forcing its people out into a world foreign to them, had actually set the stage for something akin to what it had feared already existed but actually hadn't.

I talked with a village elder who said his name was Pedro Mendoza. He was addressed as "Don Pedro" by others but denied being the village leader although he was its most knowledgeable spokesman. It was not safe in Cabanas Department to be known as a leader but Don Pedro led me through a communal threshing yard. We passed a row of small tin granaries with conical roofs to the community's store house where jugs of cooking oil, sacks of rice and other foods waited to be dispersed to families. There was even a fairly new truck, not yet beaten to pieces on those miserable roads, to carry excess farm produce to market. All this represented organization which to the Army meant outside direction, which meant subversion. Which meant to the Army that these people were communists.

Don Pedro denied being a communist or even knowing any, but he freely admitted that the villagers had learned how to help themselves, to come together for their mutual benefit and protection, from *"internationalistas"* while they endured Mesa Grande. The villagers had been escorted over the Honduras frontier and back to Santa Marta by other internationalists, Europeans and American Witnesses for Peace. Otherwise, they probably would never have arrived in their old homes. But the Army wasn't through with them yet. The day before my visit Army helicopters had fired phosphorous rockets into the corn fields just outside the village, setting some of the still unharvested corn afire. And following the choppers soldiers came and threatened the people.

This was in January, and El Salvador was getting ready for a new national election in March. When ARENA, the right wing party of El Salvador's oligarchs, wins the election, Army officers told the silent villagers, they would be back. "Then there won't be a house standing here," they said. Don Pedro knew it was not just bombast; they had done it before. He brushed off my questions about the election as being irrelevant to the village. How, he asked, were the people of Santa Marta to get to Victoria to register to vote or to apply for a registration carnet? And how could they afford the twenty centavos registration cost?

Santa Marta, I learned several years later, after the peace accords had been signed and the country presumably was returning to a peaceful existence, had been selected as a pilot project for reconstruction,[79] something of a show piece for visiting North Americans. United States Ambassador William Walker, accompanying Congressman Joe Moakley, a Massachusetts Democrat, to Santa Marta was quoted as saying that American aid funds should go to the municipality rather than to non-governmental organizations focussing on employment for the community's residents. Certainly

---

[79] CEPAD (Council of Evangelical Churches) Report, December, 1991.

roads leading into Santa Marta needed improvements but even more important was help with agricultural production, crafts skills, and such things as bakeries and dairies.

Building roads, whether in the United States or El Salvador, funnels money into larger scale, usually outside enterprises rather than creating wealth for locals. By April of 1992 the promised road and electrical lines were behind schedule and trees that the locals had specifically insisted not be damaged had been cut down. "This inauspicious beginning may mean that Santa Marta is turning out to be a truer model of post-war reconstruction than anyone intended."[80]

Some of the heaviest fighting of the Salvadoran war, and some of the most frightful atrocities, occurred in Chalatenango Department, north of San Salvador, beyond Guazapa Volcano and bordering Honduras and Cabanas Department. It was here, at Nueva Trinidad, that the local Army commander selected an especially beautiful tree in the town center, eucalyptus, I think, from which to hang captured guerrillas, suspected subversives or anyone else he believed might be an enemy. More than a hundred villagers had died at the end of a rope tied to a sturdy horizontal branch. After the peace accords the townspeople cut the branch from the hanging tree.

Hitching rides through Chalatenango I could see for myself what I had read, that this is one of the most heavily populated countries in the world. Much of the area is hilly jungle, the roads little more than dry creeks at that time of year, filled with boulders, pocked with holes. Everywhere there were people, men grubbing in corn fields, women carrying loads of wood, children begging rides, my competitors for seats in the few vehicles crawling through the countryside. I was headed for Arcatao, one of the many villages in this otherwise agricultural area, where I had an introduction to Father Manolo, a Spanish priest, one of two who minister to half a dozen of these many villages. Manolo was a tough and soft-spoken forty-five-year-old Spaniard who smoked constantly and was soon to be off to the States for a heart pacemaker. He pre-

[80] Mimi Hurd, Report on the Americas, May, 1992. p.10.

viously ministered to some of these same people during nine years in Honduran refugee camps. He wore jeans, a short-sleeve shirt, a spade-shaped beard and black-rimmed glasses. The previous priest, Father Ignacio, was harassed constantly by the Army, and Arcatao had its share of terrorism. Every family can tell tales of murdered or disappeared relatives, often more than one per family. They were hoping, during my visit, that the United States, which had supported the Army that bullied them for years, would now help to rebuild. I had just come from Nicaragua where two years earlier, following the United States-approved election and the nominal end of a war, the people in towns like Arcatao thought the same. Little of the small United States aid to Nicaragua has trickled down to those villagers. I didn't tell Manolo and others in Arcatao about that.

My good Samaritan on this trip was Kathy Arata of New Jersey, a cool and skillful driver, of the School Sisters of Notre Dame. This region was under control of the guerrillas during most of the war except for occasional incursions by the Army, and both soldiers and guerrillas were still in the area although neither was any longer stopping vehicles for inspection of occupants' papers. We arrived at night and I was given a cell in the "convent" across the square from the village church. The convent houses priests and nuns, on opposite sides of a walled-in courtyard, as well as visitors. A kitchen and several latrines are built into one wall. One could wash from a concrete cistern filled from a pipe leading to a well whose pump was turned on for two hours each day. It was powered by electricity from one of two church-owned generators which also ran the community's one television set, which blared out a car chase drama as I tried to talk to Manolo.

Locked inside the convent perimeter was a $30,000 Mitsubishi van, contributed by St. Joseph's Church of Seattle. "It is not to be used for transportation," Manolo said, an acknowledgement that if he would allow it the vehicle would become the community taxi and bus, soon destroyed on those roads. "We use it to take people to medical appointments in San Salvador. It is also an ambulance for people in Guarjila and other towns in the region when they have medical problems." Seventy percent of the children in the region, which includes about 15 villages and hamlets with a total population of maybe 15,000, have no living father or mother and some have neither, Manolo said.

Manolo took me to a school dance that night, a fiesta prior to the opening of the school year the next Monday, put on by the "popular teachers" who are the only kind available. They were all in their late teens and seemed to be poised and confident despite the baby fat. The dance was on a concrete open floor in front of the school. Rock music boomed out, powered by the church's other generator. Few townspeople danced but much of the town was there to watch. The teachers danced, when they weren't entertaining with guitars and songs, and many of the small children. One adult solo dancer was a man of about 30 who Manolo said had been injured in the head by the Army and was now *loco*, unbalanced. Teachers were paid $25 a month, by a German charity. The government contributed nothing, neither money, books nor supplies.

I met Elizabeth, in her late 20s, at the dance. A native of San Salvador, she took part in some mild political activity as a student at the University of El Salvador in 1981. When the Army came to her dormitory twice looking for her she fled the country, first to Mexico and then to Toronto where she worked for a Canadian refugee group and, for awhile, for a computer firm. She had just returned to El Salvador and was now going to teach at a school in a little town two hours walk from Arcatao. There was no road to the town.

Father Manolo was supervising site preparation of a planned community center, although he admitted he had no idea where the money would come from to pay for the various buildings, which were to include classrooms for local seminars for community adults and farmers. An outdoor amphitheater for community plays and other affairs was planned. I was astonished, when I returned a year later, to find Manolo's dream almost fully realized. The buildings were completed although some finishing remained, but the entire complex was ready for use.

Everyone in Arcatao seemed to have enough to eat. But malnutrition exists even so, Sister Kathy told me. "These people do not eat balanced diets," she said. Beans are a good staple food, but corn, from which the ubiquitous tortilla is made, is not. Rice is another staple, but this is not rice country and it must be purchased by people who seldom see real money.

One problem, common to all of Central America, is that people eat too much sugar. As a result, kids are often hyper and teeth are bad. "But there is no other food to eat," Kathy said, beyond corn, beans and sugar cane. During the war the guerrillas stressed preventive medicine and "in spite of the war the people learned a lot," she said. Signs plastered on the walls of several "*comedors populars*," tiny restaurants usually part of someone's house, still offered messages on nutrition, sanitation and other health concerns, including warnings about AIDs.

A social bombshell was still ticking in Arcatao and rural villages like it all over El Salvador, I learned from Father Manolo and a Norwegian couple working with refugees who gave me a ride. During the war many people left their homes in the villages and abandoned their lands outside the towns. Other people moved in, some as long as 10 years ago. Many of the newcomers improved both the houses and the land. Some put in water systems and toilets. Now the original owners were coming back and claiming their property in these "*pueblos fantasmas*," or ghost villages as they were described in the newspaper *El Diario de Hoy*. One section of the peace accords requires the original owners to be given back their property.

In my earlier investigations of the country's land reform, I had learned of the disputes over farmlands, usually large tracts owned by the rich who had in many cases taken it from campesinos decades earlier, but I had never heard of this problem of the small holdings before. Neither have I seen any reference to it in news stories from El Salvador since the war. But it is another of the seemingly insoluble problems likely to keep El Salvador in turmoil for many years. There was confusion about where the people who took over the absentee owners' property came from. As best I could understand it they had lived in the vicinity but had no land and very primitive homes, although the homes they were occupying after the war were crude enough. Some have concrete floors although most are of packed dirt. This issue seems to have been overlooked in the concerns over the future of lands once held by the large landowners.

The peace accords required large holdings of land to be split up and sold by the government to the campesinos who have worked it. That still leaves the original owners with some 200 acres, a large holding in El Salvador. The government, in theory, was to pay the big landowners for the land sold or given to the peasants with bonds, the same way the land reform of the early 1980s was managed. But where was El Salvador to get that kind of money? The campesinos can't afford it and Uncle Sam, so generous with war toys, isn't going to continue funnelling the millions necessary into El Salvador now that the war has supposedly ended.

Down the road at Neuva Trinidad the Norwegians and I sat in on a community meeting at which the property issue was being discussed by about a hundred people. The former owners would be returning soon, a village leader said, and they were victims too and should be greeted politely. But the crucial question was never brought up, at least as far as I could tell—what happens when someone is ordered to leave the home they've occupied for years and has no place to go? There were questions about what role these returnees had played in the recent years. One man, to the plea that the old owners be welcomed, said "I lost two children in the war. I believe in forgiving, but I have a hard time forgetting."

At this place I received once again a lesson in a Central American dilemma and another in coping with adversity. For many Latins maintenance is an unknown. Vehicles are driven until they stop and then deficiencies are addressed. Once break-down occurs, however, the people are ingenious at finding solutions. When the Norwegians' driver couldn't get the van started he removed the battery, for some unknown reason. But rather than unbolting the positive cable fastener he tried to pull it off and tore out the post and a few inches of the battery top. Truly now the battery *"no funcionar."*

Not to worry, however. A local man who owned a pickup truck removed its battery and put it in the van. *Ole!*, the van started and while its engine was running these two intrepid mechanics risked shock and put the battery back in the pickup. I had my own experiences with car batteries earlier in my life and I never knew that was possible. As we visited other villages along the road back to Chalatenango this happened twice more until the Norwegians worried we might be stuck in some town without a friendly truck owner when darkness came. Without a battery we had no lights and El Salvador, even with the war ended, is no place to be traveling at night, especially without lights.

People were still being killed in El Salvador after peace supposedly had set in, in grudge fights, in casual mayhem stemming from attitudes fostered by the violence of war. One man was killed while I was there by a mine, of which there are many laid out over the years by both sides in the war. The Hotel Sheraton, where so many plots were cooked up had become the Hotel El Salvador. It was no longer the hangout only of United States advisors. On this trip Blue Berets, United Nations officers, mingled in its bars and restaurants. High school graduation parties were under way the day I was there and proud parents were posing for pictures with their gowned and capped graduates in front of the hotel pool. Many were peasant families with the first high school graduates in family history.

During my walks around San Salvador I always marvel at the action at *El Mundo Feliz*, the happy world, where children in clean and starched dresses and short pants shriek through a wide variety of rides and merry-go-rounds, on dragons, cars, ships, motorcycles, ducks and rockets. Clowns are selling balloons and cotton candy and pizzas to these children of the wealthy and privileged. They are oblivious of the ragged people peering through the fence at this gaiety.

A different scene meets a stroller in downtown San Salvador on a Saturday, market day. Sidewalks and streets have been taken over by small vendors. It is a massive bazaar, the most crowded market I've seen in all Latin America, a dirty and noisy place centered on the cathedral, a lump of a structure that has been building for centuries and is nowhere near completion. I can't even find the entrance behind all the scaffolding and tin sheeting.

Around it are market stalls and tables of wristwatches, nail clippers, earrings, jewelry and all sorts of cheap garments. Hawkers are yelling, boom boxes blaring. Motorcycles and buses are unmuffled. It is a chorus of free enterprise at its most elemental. I seldom see anyone buy this stuff but the crowds in the streets are laden with purchases. Construction bustle is everywhere and workers are carrying loads of excavated earth, mixed cement, bricks and everything else on their backs all day long in the hot sun. One sign of at least a temporary peace in El Salvador was that no longer was a man with an assault rifle lounging at every corner, in front of every store, every McDonalds and shop. Security at one time seemed to be the chief employment of El Salvador, as it still was in Panama. At a Pops fast food joint I buy a milk shake and ask for *fresca*. The order taker and shake maker, a neat trim girl in a starched yellow and brown uniform, gently corrects me, asking if I mean *fresa*—strawberry? I do, and we laugh.

I doubt if a worker in a similar place in Nicaragua would have been so perceptive, or would have cared. Nicaraguans seem indifferent to whether one buys their wares or not. Salvadorans are definitely a more persistent breed of hustler. Salvadorans have perhaps less reason to be cynical, in spite of a dozen years of war and killing. Defending a corrupt government, as the United States did in El Salvador, may not be as bad, on a scale of national indecency, as attempting to overthrow one elected and supported by a majority of its own people as we did in Nicaragua.

In spite of the land questions, the smoldering animosities built up over a dozen years, indeed several generations of hate, a majority of Salvadorans and most of the foreigners who have lived here for years believe peace will last. Why? "The oligarchy has agreed to the peace because it is the only way they can make any money," said a young American woman who had worked with poor campesinos for four years. "The Army knows that the U.S. wants to wash its hands of the country, which is true. There will be no more guns, no more helicopters to kill campesinos, no more money to steal. The war is ended."

What compassion, common sense and a sense of humanity have failed to do, exhaustion may, she thinks. Tight new laws were being written, to stiffen the spines of the country's judges, as well as to protect them from retribution when they render verdicts unpopular with the country's owners. These are not just words on paper, she and others insisted, since they are accompanied by requirements for training, for judges and the police.

The National Police was abolished and a new police agency set up, under the direct control of the country's president, not the army as in the past. New policemen were being carefully selected, after written examinations and psychological tests. They were then given six months training, with curricula heavily oriented to human rights. Former members of both the police and guerrillas were allowed to apply. I am skeptical; the oligarchy and the army have too much at stake, perhaps even their lives, and they will not give up their plush and privileged existences easily. We shall see.

Miserable towns like Santo Tomas, Arcatao and Neuva Trinidad and all the others in between don't have to be that way. Latin Americans don't have to live in fear and misery. Father Manolo's community center in Arcatao in El Salvador and Father Ignacio's combined church and community center in El Corral in Nicaragua illustrate clearly the ability of these people to conduct their own affairs and create satisfying lives for themselves. If their own governments would support them, or even just leave them alone to engage in cooperative ventures, they could be productive, peaceful and eventually prosperous people.

Honduras became the host not just of the Contra but also of the permanent and transient United States troop presence within the country, both ultimately unwelcome. Even the Honduran military finally had enough of our boy, General Gustavo Alvarez Martinez, the "godfather" of the Nicaraguan Contra in his country. Alvarez had supposedly dreamed up the scheme adopted by CIA Director William Casey to base the Contra in Honduras in return for gifts of guns and gear for Honduras' armed forces.

In 1984 a group of young officers handed Alvarez a packed suitcase and put him on an airliner to Costa Rica, not an ideal choice of exile, from his standpoint. An international court in Costa Rica was just then hearing testimony in a case brought against Honduras and Alvarez for the disappearance of three young Costa Rican nationals in Honduras. His enemies blamed Alvarez for the deaths of more than 100 people he said were part of an insurgent movement within the country.

Alvarez, who was accused of stealing $30 million in United States funds allocated to his country's development, escaped to Miami which once again lived up to its reputation as a refuge for thieves from the south. Several years later Alvarez returned to Honduras where one day in 1989 six gunmen waiting outside his house shot him full of holes.

I was having a beer with a Honduran acquaintance in the bar of the posh Honduran Maya Hotel, the staging area for United States service personnel, when a National Guard unit from Georgia in blue jeans and Hawaiian shirts, their civilian uniforms, came in and demanded water. When the bartender had difficulty understanding their request they began shouting and pounding on the bar.

"These Goddamn Mexicans," one young woman snapped.

My friend, although embarrassed for me, was indignant. "Anyone south of the Rio Grande is a Mexican to them," he said. "You are not here to liberate us."

Costa Rica is the ideal of what visitors think a Latin

American country should be. The people are pleasant, friendly and socially progressive. It is the only country south of the Rio Grande where one can step off a sidewalk curb without checking twice in both directions for a motorist determined to rack up another pedestrian score.

I arrived in Liberia in northern Costa Rica by bus from Nicaragua, not enthusiastic about a layover of a few hours before going on to San Jose. But I was so charmed by my stroll through town, listening to the banter in the shops and cantinas, that I decided to stay the night and go on to the capitol the next day. Although a Spanish heritage is evident in Liberia's big public square and unpretentious but solid buildings, it also imparts a Norman Rockwell serenity. In the square on that Friday night citizens promenaded under the street lights and then settled down in stone and wrought iron benches or on the grass to listen under the soft tropical sky to the town band play a concert. The scene might have been out of the United States middle west in the early part of this century.

How did Costa Rica become a rational democracy, with open elections, a free press (although licensed by the state), an independent judiciary and one of the world's most liberal social welfare programs, while all its neighbors were wallowing in corruption, terror and government-sanctioned selfishness? One Tico (as Costa Ricans are known by their envious neighbors) told me that it was "because we had nothing to steal. The Spaniards ignored us because we didn't have enough Indians to enslave and there was no gold. The Yanquis left us alone because we had no minerals or oil."

"The small number of Indians created a labor shortage that kept rural wages high," another observer said. "Families saw little profit in owning more land than they could farm themselves. Costa Rica evolved without large haciendas or the powerful agrarian elites found in other countries. Today it is the only true, stable democracy in Latin America."[81]

That doesn't mean Costa Rica is perfect. An elite would like to see a stronger government, for the poor, which would

---

[81] Ibid.

crack down on the alleged excesses of the welfare system and unions. Newsmen must be licensed if they want to work in the country and the leading newspaper, *La Nacion*, is as biased as Nicaragua's *La Prensa* although not as sloppily irresponsible.

But there is social peace, and workers share in the country's bounty. The contrast between conditions in Costa Rican banana plantations, complete with decent workers' housing, and the squalor in workers' living quarters in neighboring countries is stark. But Costa Rica is under siege. Its magnificent forests are being cut down, by farmers craving land and who do not share in the general welfare and by big timber companies, most tracing their roots back to corporate boardrooms in the United States. As the forests disappear, cattle ranches proliferate, mainly for hamburger for North American fast food joints.

Brilliantly colored parrots and macaws, easily caught by jungle poachers, are sold from small boats at night on the ocean to floating dealers from the United States. The parrots are endangered, but stiff fines in the United States barely deter dealers who can get thousands of dollars for good specimens.

Costa Rica's beauty was probably best observed from the "jungle train" which until the end of the 1980s ran from San Jose to Limon on the Atlantic coast, stopping at every village along the way to pick up a load of bananas. You could count the railroad ties through knotholes in the floors if you tired of taking sass from monkeys in the trees along the tracks.

In 1948 a cabal of Costa Rican generals, envious of the fancy uniforms and the impunity from laws of their colleagues in neighboring countries, launched a coup and took over the government. All in the interest of national security and peace and prosperity, of course. The Ticos didn't buy it. Under the leadership of a coffee farmer named Jose (Don Pepe) Figueres the people rose up and ran the coup leaders out and elected Figueres president. Then, looking around them, they asked the pertinent question: Why do we need an army? The next year a ban on a military establishment was written into the constitution.

"During the 41 years that have elapsed since Costa Rica abolished its army, our fundamental freedoms have never been threatened, nor do we know a shameful history of repression," said President Oscar Arias in 1990 in an appeal to the people of Panama to reject United States efforts to recreate its army after our invasion of that country and the capture of Manuel Noriega.[82]

"During these 41 years, when military barracks have been turned into schools, our symbol has been the teacher who extolls excellence," Arias said. "The youth of Latin America has the right to have new heroes."[83]

[82] Tina Rosenberg, Foreign Policy, Fall, 1991, p. 81.
[83] Oscar Arias Sanchez, New York Times Op-Ed Page, Jan. 13, 1990.

15

Tio Sam Turns Away

LEAVING HONDURAS, I FEEL BETTER. THE APPREHENSIONS of the last few days, of the thieving soldiers at the Honduran customs station, roll away at the shabby Nicaraguan frontier post at El Espino. Maybe it is the border agent, a smiling kid in outsize military fatigues who will stamp my passport only after I exchange sixty dollars for cordobas. Our transaction, my crisp travelers checks for his limply greasy bills in hundred cordoba denominations with "100,000" stamped over the numbers, makes me a millionaire with a few wads of bills left over.

I no longer had a sense of being watched, of menace, that I had in Honduras. The shy comment during the bus ride from Tegucigalpa of my seat companion, a Honduran college student going home for a holiday, that life in the pretty countryside was *"muy tranquilo"* hadn't lifted my spirits. Yes, the land was very pleasant, but not until I was safely in Nicaragua could I relax.

Over the border I waited for a bus to fill up with passengers, mostly cowboys and their families, worn and silent people, each carrying a small plastic sack of...what? Their belongings? produce for the market? I couldn't tell. No one spoke and I wondered if it was only me who felt relief on leaving Honduras. The ancient bus groaned as it carried us a mile down the road to the immigration station where I showed my passport, my new small fortune in cordobas and assured the young men, these unsmiling and grim, that I would not stay long and become a burden on Nicaragua. Another wait and another antique bus, its springs flat from carrying too many loads of triple the design specifications, took us into Somoto.

I had been in this town before and had met the mayor but I couldn't remember her name. At the bus station several hundred people were waiting even though the next bus to Managua wouldn't leave for twelve hours, at three the next morning. I must have been very conspicuous standing in the road wondering what to do although no one seemed to even see me until finally a burly man, a farmer by the looks of him, stopped his wheezing pickup truck beside me. Could he help me? he asked. I told him I was going to Managua but I didn't think I could get on tomorrow morning's bus. He agreed with that and then made me an offer I couldn't refuse. For eighty thousand cordobas he would take me as far as Esteli, about thirty miles in the right direction.

First, however, we needed gasoline. The pickup bounced from pothole to pothole down the street to a mud-brick house. Behind it was a large steel tank on a wooden platform. My benefactor climbed onto the stand and stuck a rubber hose in the top of the tank and siphoned five gallons of gasoline into a can. He also filled a gallon-sized plastic jug with gasoline and set it in a crude frame bolted to the rusty roof of his pickup cab. From the jug ran a thin plastic tubing down through the broken rear window, across the passenger-side seat and under the dashboard where it disappeared into the engine compartment. At my question he untwisted the wire holding down the hood and showed me where the tubing ran to the carburetor. The truck's gasoline tank had long ago rusted out and it was this fueling system that allowed the thing to run.

The country brightened as we drove south, fields were green and trees were in blossom. But signs of decay and neglect were everywhere. This was farming season, yet the fields were fallow and I saw no farmers working them. The war, my enterprising driver explained. Farmers are afraid to go into the fields, he said, or they don't care to raise crops that must be sold under state guidelines and prices. He was the first working class Nicaraguan I met who blamed the Sandinistas for everything wrong in the country, including his wreck of a truck.

This was 1987 and Ronald Reagan's war, combined with Sandinista mismanagement, was strangling the country. As we rode along, the driver pointed to wooded areas where he said Contra fighters were resting. They would be out at night, he said. I doubted that, and still do. They were never known for their enthusiasm for night fighting. But if what he said was correct, that might have accounted for the fact that there were none of the roadblocks and checkpoints I had encountered on other trips to this same area. Had I not known better I wouldn't have been aware a war was going on all around me.

In Esteli the driver let me out on the road to Managua where I joined a dozen Nicaraguans also hoping to catch a ride. It was getting dark and although I knew some people in Esteli I couldn't remember where they lived and getting that kind of information in a crowd is often impossible in Nicaragua, or anywhere else in Latin America. I knew I would never be able to fight my way onto a bus with my handbag and suitcase and I was by now experienced in hitchhiking, Nicaraguan style. Several trucks stopped but they would turn off far short of Managua and I prefered not to chance being stuck at a lonely intersection for the night although I had no fears about Nicaraguan crime.

Eventually I got a ride on an enormous Russian dump truck with about thirty other hitchers even though it was not going all the way to Managua. The tires of this thing were as high as the top of my head, and without the aid of a young man who climbed up ahead of me, scaling a tire and then the four-foot-high side of the truck box, and who then lifted my bags up, I wouldn't have been able to get aboard. We roared off into the dark, a suddenly jolly crew, glad at last to be moving. Everyone was talking and the young man said he was a student returning to the University of Nicaragua in Managua. Two of our hitchers were nursing mothers, and other passengers shielded them from the wind and insects as they bared their breasts and let their babies suckle. A couple of passengers were businessmen, on their way back to Managua from sales trips in the north. None seemed concerned about the war and there was some singing when one of the businessmen produced a harmonica and we left fragments of music and song behind us in the night. The dump floor of the truck was very dirty and at first no one wanted to sit but as time went by more and more did so, spreading shawls and baby blankets out on the dirt and hunkering down.

Then a man opened the door of the cab as the truck roared along and climbed back to the bed and dropped down with us. In the starlight I could see him going from passenger to passenger and I realized he was collecting money. My companions seemed to expect to pay but this was a new hitch hiking experience for me. As best I could tell in the dark the fare was a thousand cordobas so I peeled off my smallest bill and the conductor accepted it.

That jolting ride in a monstrous truck as my companions sang in the soft tropic night prompted reflections on what I was doing here, what they were doing here. From the 1950s through the 1980s, as the borders of the United States were allegedly endangered by Soviet guns or guile, the metaphor for threats from abroad was falling dominoes. Once Korea fell, presumably serious people believed, Japan would topple, followed by South Asia, down to Australia and, who knows, perhaps Antarctica.

To hold up the phantom dominoes in Vietnam and thwart the advance of a monolithic, totalitarian communism that seemed always just short of invincibility the United States fought a war that diverted attention and money from problems at home, deepened citizen cynicism, precipitated a crushing national debt and killed hundreds of thousands of mostly innocent bystanders, including more than 50,000 of our own. In Central America, as we grew more sophisticated, we hired others to win hearts and minds with our money and bullets and their blood. We wound up a nation polarized and militarized, probably unable ever to take off our world policeman's uniform until we are too poor to continue to be its banker as well.

From this we seem to have learned nothing; the dead are mourned by only a dwindling few, except when the bugles of political patriotism blow. The human residue of our failed adventures will long haunt us with threats more subtle, and certainly more real, than those collapsed fictions of the Cold War. Now as the dominoes fall the other way and the hollow insides of Stalinist-type communism have been revealed, the United States looks for new police roles in the world's rowdy back alleys.

In the meantime, as we coast along on that legacy of anti-communism, a new and perhaps as threatening invasion is headed our way. It is certainly more real. They come from South Asia, the Caribbean countries, and Latin America and, like water from a leaking pipe, they can't be stopped at this end. These foot soldiers of domino policies, perhaps as threatening in their way as any John Foster Dulles ever conjured, do not carry AK47s, nor are they grouped in disciplined military units. They are soft-eyed and frightened, they come with little children, and they barely speak their own language. But they are willing to work and they scare hell out of Americans. These new immigrants do bring a threat to the United States that may in the course of history be as devastating as the imagined communist hordes that populated the nightmares of the American right wing from World War II until the Gorbachev thaw.

These refugees are fleeing for their lives or just for a better life, across this country's porous borders. Whichever it is, for safety or consumer goodies, the cause directly or indirectly stems from United States foreign policy—or fragmented pieces of different, often clashing policies—that never jelled nor were even coordinated between the various branches of government. Our intervention in Indochina, propelled by the holy cause of anti-communism, let loose refugee floods still unchecked.

Nearly one million Indochinese were admitted to this country from 1975 through 1992, most of them as refugees of the war we fought against all good sense and the intelligence assessments of our State Department and other officials who knew how flawed the domino effect was and how foolish would be our efforts to turn back the tide of nationalism. That many of those refugees are proving to be exemplary citizens is beside the point. Their lives were disrupted and ours affected by a policy based on ignorance and fueled by fears of political retribution for any office holder who failed to join the pack baying against communism.

As the Soviet Union was collapsing, new assessments of world policy were required, rippling to every corner of the globe. And, as the nationalist idiocies of the Balkans in the early 1990s showed, no country was far enough away to be immune.

"Political struggles in faraway places can be contagious. The rise of Islamic consciousness in the Middle East has contributed to the unrest in the Muslim republics of the former Soviet Union. War and brutality in Indochina, the regional war(s) in Central America, and the deepening crisis in Mexico have triggered a huge migration, which has already transformed the demography of the United States and will have a steadily increasing impact on its politics and its culture."[84]

It would be difficult, combing through the history of the past hundred years, to find an instance where United States armed interference in the politics of small nations has been beneficial, for us or them. Modern history shows a pattern of United States support for Latin American oligarchies and military strong men who promise to bring order to their disorderly countries. Once in power they turn either to looting or to dabbling in the occult of off-beat religions, or both. Civilians who are allowed to win an occasional election soon discover that their role is to cut ribbons, placate United States vice presidents when they come to call with

---

[84] According to Princeton N. Lyman, director of The State Department's Bureau of Refugees, the United States accepted more than 930,000 people fleeing from Indochina from 1975 to 1989. Those people are continuing to bring relatives here.

complaints about outrages, and generally front for the military.

Protection and support for American and local commercial interests has been the central impetus for each intervention, whatever the stated reasons of the hour. Prior to World War II American interference was propelled by fears of German commercial inroads in Latin America. That alarm had considerable justification because, with the exception of a few companies like Singer Sewing Machine, German firms were beating the pants off Americans in the hustle for Latin trade. Even the Japanese, in that era still known for cheap junk, were making gains.

Soviet adventurism in Latin America after 1950 was primarily opportunistic, needling to spoil Uncle Sam's dinner. They were rarely taken seriously by anyone but a few Latin American leftists and ideologues in the United States Department of State, the Congress, the Pentagon and the Reagan and Bush Administrations as well as columnists of the right.

Cuba's feeble attempts to raise the yeasting ferment of discontent in other Latin countries was serious enough, so far as Cuba was concerned, but it was never significant outside Castro's fantasies. Except in the equally deluded nightmares of the American right wing, Castro's communism never sold well anywhere.

Nicaragua and the guerrillas of El Salvador accepted Castro's weapons but few in their ranks bought his maniacal diatribes. Neither did many Cubans and it was only Castro's sense of when to pull Uncle Sam's beard that kept him in power so long. The United States could have muted Castro's appeal to Cubans long before had cooler heads in the State Department prevailed.

The threat to the United States from Latin American leftists comes not from invasions; it is in their ideas. They were showing the poor a secular version of Liberation Theology—the belief that they're just as good as the people who oppress them and just as entitled to the services, the goods and the benefits their lands could provide and which only those members of the oligarchies enjoy. Peasant farmers aren't by nature radicals. Their lives and work are framed in a conservatism that would make a Rotarian seem a flaming liberal. It is desperation that makes them a threat to the owners of their countries and to North Americans more concerned with quick profits than honest two-way trade.

Trade is available. Despite the desperate poverty of many of its people, Latin America has enormous potential wealth. We're losing the initiative for that trade again to the Japanese and the Germans and, to some extent to the erratic Brazilians. Before the 1979 Nicaraguan revolution Julio Martinez was the biggest Ford dealer in Central America. Then, thanks to the Reagan trade embargo, he was forced to turn to Hondas from Japan and Ladas from Russia. American Fords couldn't be shipped to Nicaragua. Martinez now sells Mazdas, Fords in disguise perhaps, but the point is that he and the manufacturer lost business because of a foolish instrument of spite.

A fraction of the billions of dollars we wasted in El Salvador propping up a greedy and brutal oligarchy could have nurtured thousands of independent businessmen and women in that unhappy country. Instead, we financed an army which saw every cooperative effort as "subversion." In the aftermath of our wars United States aid is still being used to reward and punish. Nicaraguans of every economic level were complaining in 1993 that they could not get credit. The banks couldn't get money to lend from the World Bank because the United States was leaning on it. Yet the United States Agency for International Development was spending its funds on consultants and a large staff in spacious Managua quarters. Why? because the conservative government of Violeta Chamorro was not sufficiently conservative for a congressional faction led by Senator Jesse Helms.

By contrast, in neighboring El Salvador, where the rightist government refused to condemn death squads trying to provoke former guerrillas into again taking up arms, the government was acceptable to Helms and his ilk. Along the roads of El Salvador's Chalatenango Department, hard hit by the war, hundreds of otherwise jobless farmers were clearing ditches, installing culverts and building bridges. Signs along the road announced that the work was financed by USAID. That program of public works, pitiful as the wages were, allowed those men to feed their families rather than pick up their rifles again. That sort of aid, grudging as it is, was withheld from Nicaraguans.

Bluntly and selfishly, aid programs to those countries would keep the people of Central America at home rather than seeking a new life here. American acceptance of refugees from Central America has always been distorted. Mexican wetbacks have been crossing the borders for all of this century, and it has been only in recent years that their numbers began to alarm not only nativists but social liberals as well as they threatened to swamp the abilities of the receiving communities to absorb them. As El Salvador political refugees made it to the United States and found refuge and sanctuary in American churches they wrote back to family members and friends who in turn came here. Federal policy hardened.

Few Salvadorans were considered genuine "political refugees" and immigration courts began sending them home, to fates that mostly have not yet been documented. The point is that those genuinely in fear of their lives encouraged others, perhaps not under immediate death threats, to come also. Separating the one from the other eventually became impossible. Must a Salvadoran show scars of torture before he or she can prove a threat to life? Is the refugee whose whole life has been an endurance of oppression, who has witnessed cousins or neighbors being killed for no provocation, is he or she a product of an unfortunate economic situation or legitimately in fear of death? And how do you prove either? Desperate people will take desperate chances.

Little recognized by those who resent or fear Mexican immigrants is the movement of refugees from the south *into* Mexico, particularly from the military regimes in Guatemala and El Salvador as well as the other countries of Central

America. Mexico, with a tradition of offering sanctuary to all persons fleeing political persecution, is hard pressed to care for these people, and their treatment by some Mexican relocation officials has been little better than they suffered at home. Local Mexicans often object to these newcomers, accusing them of working for even lower wages than the Mexicans themselves. This is the domino effect the United States should be watching with alarm.

All of this doesn't signify that Latin America's dilemmas, its poverty, social injustice, disease and general backwardness are entirely the fault of Uncle Sam. Latins are more than able to foul their own nests without any help from gringos. Individually, the people of Latin America are almost always more courteous to strangers, and to each other, than their counterparts in this country. But they are also inheritors of a Latin culture that goes back to arrogant "Iron Spain" on one side of the Latin American family tree, and on the other to the bloody indigenous regimes that ruled in what is now Mexico and Central America and South America. Those cultures were based on grim precepts, namely that might rules and right is seldom a factor.

As I wandered through Central America I pondered why Spanish America developed the way it did, why it turned so often to despotism while Anglo North America went in another direction which, in spite of our faults, still seems a paradise to so many of our southern neighbors. Was it because the English who first settled North America brought their wives and families to stay while Spanish younger sons came to Central and South America for loot to spend back home? Was it the difference between religions, relatively tolerant northern Protestantism versus authoritarian Catholicism in the south? Was it climate? Was it the ease with which the Spanish defeated the native Indians and enslaved them and interbred with them, while the English stole the lands of northern Indians and killed them when they resisted, but otherwise ignored them?

Were the Europeans better fighters, braver? Or was it their horses and gunpowder that made the difference? A partial answer, as modern historians re-examine the Conquest and all that came after it, is disease. The southern Indians fought as well as the Sioux, the Iroquois or the Blackfeet. But the Southerners, thanks to milder climates, were more numerous, and when the Spaniards brought small pox and other diseases with which the Indians' immune systems could not cope, the "disease boundaries" were more easily hurdled and they died by the hundreds of thousands. What Spanish blunderbusses couldn't do invisible germs did. To a lesser degree disease was also the ally of the English invaders in the north.

But all that does not answer the question: why has democracy failed to take root in most of Latin America? Until we and they can answer that question remedies are unlikely. I believe there is an answer. The clue lies in Cuban education. Fidel Castro brought learning to his countrymen and women, with Soviet money it is true, and he persecuted those who differed with him. But Cuba under Castro, as I have noted elsewhere, has far outdistanced all the other countries of Latin America in education and health care. Having missed our chance to tame Castro through common sense we could still make differences in those other countries by spending our weapons money on education there.

As a co-inhabitant of the hemisphere, Central America, indeed all of Latin America, was perceived in North America always as primarily an economic colony, a source of raw materials, and secondarily as a market. In the latter years of the 20th Century prospects of trade with the western side of the Pacific Rim dazzled American exporters who hadn't the foggiest idea of the geography of its eastern side with its four hundred million potential customers south of California and Texas. And even when Americans did seize on Latin markets their focus was pernicious. Arms sales, so often justified in the Middle East and other unruly areas of the world as tools for regional strategic balance, didn't have even that shallow justification in Latin America. The only stated purpose was the threat of an infiltrating Communism. Political instability, often the direct result of American policies, ie, arms sales, was an excuse for neglect when it wasn't used as justification for intervention.

Does the United States have a foreign policy? That question was being asked more frequently following the collapse of the communist governments of Eastern and Central Europe. Narrowed down to this hemisphere the question becomes: Is there a political policy, or an economic policy toward the countries of Central and South America and the Caribbean?

For the full span and more of the Reagan reign and well into the Bush Administration, our policy was singularly to root out communism in Central America without too much blood showing on our own hands. That was despite the knowledge of most of the professionals in the State Department and elsewhere in those administrations[85] that communist intervention in the region was, at its worst, Soviet needling. The Soviet purpose was to annoy by taking advantage of our paranoia rather than from any delusion that communism could take root. It posed no threat to the United States but it cost probably $10 billion of our money and the lives of several hundred thousand people. But since few Americans died, the administration's phobia went largely unchallenged at home, even by congressmen who also knew better.

But just because there were no body bags coming home doesn't mean the United States' low intensity warfare was and still is costing this nation only money. Immigration, legal and illegal, is a burden whose costs haven't yet been fully calculated. And probably never will be; they are real nevertheless, in social turmoil, in demands for housing, schools, added burdens on police agencies, welfare, health providers and more. Deep animosities over slights and insults, although incalculable in dollars, have added to our eventual burden. Immigration is bringing with it ethnic conflicts, which with racial differences, add to the decline in civil discourse in the country.

The United States hard right refuses to recognize that the wars it cheered on, in Southeast Asia as well as in Nica-

---

[85] Richard J. Barnet, The New Yorker, Jan. 1, 1990

ragua and El Salvador, have spawned the influx of illegal aliens it so dislikes and fears. No one, apparently, has done any serious thinking of the consequences of a Latin minority becoming a majority in California and the Southwest. Lamentations yes, thought, no. Not a few Mexicans dream of re-annexation. Were the governments of Latin America any more capable of formulating policy and carrying it forward than the United States is, one might suppose their purpose is to drive their surplus populations northward, to let *Tio Sam* take care of them. Policy or accident, Mexico, in collusion with multinational corporations, is exporting its population problem northward.

Policy questions take many guises. Should Panama have an army? I asked that question of a State Department person in Panama who didn't want to be identified, not even as a State Department person. It was two months after George Bush's "I'm no wimp" invasion.

"That's not up to us," the person said. "That's for the Panamanians to decide."

Well, they did. Panamanians decided they would not have an army, taking their cue from neighboring Costa Rica. But that's a temporary thing and don't count on it prevailing through the years. An opposing goal is harbored in the Pentagon; a United States force in Panama, like the Army and Air Force in Europe, enhances status and broadens career options. Panama is a comfortable United States outpost for the Indian wars of the late 20th Century and beyond.

The United States has an obligation to its inferiors in strength and wealth to establish a rational and just foreign policy or else keep out of their affairs altogether. Economic disparities and population pressures make the latter option impossible, but straight shooting with its own citizens makes a public, tangible foreign policy imperative. Policy is agreement on broad goals and methods between the executive and legislative branches, something the executive can then follow. We've never had that since the days of Manifest Destiny; perhaps it has never existed at any time, anywhere, in pure form, even among those brilliant statesmen who populate our history books. In spite of recent proclamations, history hasn't ended. It is very much alive; and still happening. Reagan Administration policy came from the gut of people heedless of long term consequences and following the imperatives of emotional politics. They were driven by delusions and we're all paying for their mistakes.

Is the public capable of assessing policy proposals and then deciding, with its votes for the candidate whose arguments it favors, which way policy will go? Or is the public too apathetic, too prone to diversion from serious policy issues by emotional tidbits thrown in its path and leading to dead ends? The answer is ambiguous. An rational policy for Central America would include clear positions on immigration, on trade, a foreign aid program metered by progress in human rights and reductions in or even elimination of the ridiculous armies of the region. The latter alone would require other policy initiatives, including whether to continue to provide the hardware for the world's small wars while maintaining a powerful military establishment. An enlightened policy would include educational incentives, scholarships to North American universities, even high schools, for promising Latin youths. If Latin American armies are indefensible, what can we say of the support, the lethal trinkets and money lavished on them by the United States? The billions of dollars this nation has poured into those countries and into their incompetent and corrupt militaries since before the first World War has accomplished nothing except to make even more miserable the lives of the people the aid was supposed to help. Anastasio Somoza, whose looting of his own country set new Latin American lows, was a graduate of the United States Military Academy at West Point, as was his older brother, Luis, the second in the Somoza dynasty. Thousands of Latin American officers have been entertained at United States military schools and there is no evidence they carried away anything worth knowing except new ideas for their versions of "crowd control."

Is Latin America capable of democracy? The example of Costa Rica would seem to say yes, but its experiment is still only little more than a generation old and it is fragile. Many influential Ticos are ashamed that theirs is the only real nation on earth with no army. More Costa Ricans, my travels there lead me to believe, are proud of that fact and their national example is a matter of envy to people of other nations not so fortunate. But wanting democracy and making it work, not to mention creating it in the first place, requires a toleration for differing views that most Latins have never been educated to accept. Thus I emphasize once again education.

One reason Costa Rica is politically tranquil is that its people are better educated than their neighbors. They know how to talk of the ideas of Jefferson and, as well, of how those ideas can be put into practice. No democracy will exist without a free exchange of ideas, an airing of differences in a civilized fashion and that can't happen without a press free to tell the truth. Multitudes of United States press failings notwithstanding, we have available to us, if we wish to know it, information about what is happening in our government. Powerful pressures attempt to shut up the press or to divert it with threats or glitz, but information does get out; the problem is that it is not always used.

The United States could help get a sturdy democracy on its way in a multitude of countries by abiding by its own ideals and if that is too difficult, by the rules by which we like to think civilized nations function. We expect the Germans to continue to show shame for atrocities under the Nazis, even unto the third generation. But we show no blushes when our outrages and hypocrisies are exposed. Trading weapons to our sworn enemies for hostages when we said we would never stoop to such dealings, aside from its collateral effect on our wars in Central America, seems not to have created a sense of shame among any sizable segment of the American public.

The Reagan Administration refused to recognize the trial in the World Court when Nicaraguans accused us of waging an illegal war against their country, including mining its harbors, and then brushed aside the 1986 verdict against us together with its call that we pay reparations. United States bullying, after the 1990 election in Nicaragua, forced that country to give up its award by the court of a paltry $12 million. By contrast, in 1990, when George Bush wanted a war over oil with Iraq he was quick to push the United Nations before him as a symbolic shield.

When Americans engaged illegally in foreign wars, in violation of the Neutrality Act, our government usually looked the other way. And when it did act, it was with obvious reluctance and, consistent with the press's attitude throughout the Central American wars, little public coverage. The defense in one of those Neutrality Act cases was far more candid than their prosecutor. A group supplying the Contra in the war against Nicaragua said they couldn't be guilty of defying the Act because "The U.S. government was in a *de facto* state of war against Nicaragua."

Mario Calero, brother of Contra kingpin Adolfo Calero, said in an interview that the charges against him and his companions were "ludicrous" because they were doing nothing more than the United States was doing, opposing the Sandinista government. "When you mine harbors and you run the show, then you really aren't de facto, you are at war," Calero said.[86] "Perhaps the U.S. hasn't been honest with itself that it was at war." That is as cogent a critique of Low Intensity Conflict as I have seen.

As I came to understand what politics meant in Central America and then later the influence of the United States on that politics, my views changed. Political freedom, I am convinced, can be maintained only when a populace has economic freedom. Deny a majority of people the goods available to the few and the majority will demand their share. Thus far in Latin America the poor have asked only for a small wedge of the abundance they know is available. The El Salvadoran campesino wants only to feed his family, to have available medical care for his children and for them to go to school. Eventually, given that little, he'll probably want more and that's what frightens the oligarchs. What

---

[86] Judith Gaines, The Boston Globe, April 20, 1982.

they don't recognize is that the campesino, forever denied, will eventually turn into the monster they fear.

The United States wrecked two countries, Nicaragua and El Salvador, in Reagan's holy war against communism. Guatemala, which has suffered more deaths than either of the other two, may eventually be in worse shape. Costa Rica, the ideal of what North Americans think a Latin country should be, has been compromised also and its democratic institutions are threatened although it will probably survive, at some internal cost. Honduras, rented by the United States as a base for the war against Nicaragua, was, relatively, in better social balance than the others, always with the exception of Costa Rica. Now it too is worse in every way than it was before we came bearing gifts of money and guns.

The natural world of Central America, its physical environment, has suffered over the latter two decades of the 20th Century as much as the social ambience, and for many of the same reasons: greed from abroad and among its willing collaborators at home, and the poverty that ripples out from that avarice. Blame for the destruction of rain forests can be laid at the feet of the multinational timber companies with stockholders and top level managers to satisfy. The other villain is the lonely campesino with a family to feed who cuts down the fragile forest to clear a plot for his corn and beans.

In my 1993 visit to Nicaragua the only reassuring sign was the growing recognition, by all levels of society, that the environment was in danger. That doesn't mean destruction was being reversed; on the contrary, most of the country's forests are gone and those remaining are under attack. But if lip service prevails now, deeper awareness should come next and action may, with luck and economic recovery, follow.

In the summer of 1992 the "developed" world met the south, the "emerging" world in Rio de Janiero to address common environmental problems. George Bush, president of the world's largest consumer of natural resources, refused not only to lead less well endowed countries, but balked at treaties whose goal was a rational balance between clean air, water and land and a decent life for the people who depend on them. The United States position seemed to be either, or: either we have thriving economies or we have clean water and air. We can't have both.

At home we make those compromises all the time, to the consternation of one side or another, sometimes of both. Germany is not only making its own environment livable through strongly enforced cleanups, but is preparing to do the same for the rest of the world, for a price. At Rio President Bush contented himself with lecturing the lesser world on our accomplishments, of which he was not a conspicuous author, while refusing to lend even the lip service that most such conferences degenerate into, to a cleaner world. It was not an inspiring moment nor a favorable augur of leadership in the times ahead as smokestacks grow in the Third World and the tendency to neglect earth, air and water needs only the excuse of example set by Big Brother.

It is probably simplistic to wonder why some issues, such as economic development, or more rightly economic freedom, must always be framed in such contrasts, such diametric opposites, leaving no middle way. Some Latin revolutionaries still insist, in defiance of the lessons of the Soviet Union's collapse, on a totally state run economy. The Sandinistas, in spite of the lies of the Reagan Administration, never intended a fully centrally controlled economy.

On the other hand, however, they allowed their own obsessives to chart a course too leftward for their revolution. That rigidity excused Yanqui intervention and nurtured seeds of rebellion against their own revolution. They not only tweaked Reagan's nose, they alienated many people who would have met them half way. Unschooled in democratic congress themselves and seeing all around them intolerance and heavy-handed, all-or-nothing examples, they fell into a trap of their own and Reagan's devising.

How many evils promoted by the United States could be avoided if the planning that goes into thwarting indigenous reforms were to be directed at solving Central America's problems? Or helping the locals solve them? What could our expertise in organization and our lead in materiel and equipment do if it were used to elevate all the peoples of Central America rather than the military and the oligarchs who rule through the armies' guns?

What miracles might we work, what miseries abate, what eventual wealth might we create, if we spent the money we waste on guns for those armies on educating the children of Latin America? Although most Americans are not aware of it, we do finance schools in foreign countries, out of taxpayer dollars. The State Department, when I asked for information about the American Schools it runs in many countries, was secretive as usual, even to the extent of refusing to tell me how many schools there are, how many students they educate and, most sensitive of all, their costs, which are hidden in State Department budgets.

The schools are maintained for the children of State Department officials posted to those countries. Other Americans working there may send their children also. A few locals may also attend, if they can pay, although I never learned just how many there were or how they were selected. They and the American families pay for the schooling, at least token amounts which seem to vary from country to country and apparently from family to family. A Honduran friend, a surgeon, works a second job to afford the $125 a month for each of his three children. "It is very difficult," he says, "but it's worth it." He is a graduate of the same school and it was the education he got there that made possible his later studies at the national university's medical school.

Another friend, in Guatemala, attended the school there and credits the education he received as well as the study habits he learned for his present substantial position in business. "It's the best education I could have received." Another friend, a Panamanian, has not fared as well in life although his command of the English language obtained at the American School assures him employment. The American School in Managua stands in a tranquilly beautiful campus and, a professor at the University of Nicaragua told me, it has the best library in the country. Its laboratories are the envy of faculty at local universities.

Most local public schools are abominable, teachers are generally poorly trained and underpaid. In some countries, Guatemala and El Salvador especially, teachers are almost automatically considered subversives and many have been specifically targeted for killing. Teaching, both in the common schools and in the universities, is mostly by rote and teachers brook no questions from their students, in the old Spanish pedagogic style. Nicaragua under the Sandinistas made a determined effort to improve lower level education and was succeeding until the Contra in Reagan's war killed or intimidated teachers and destroyed schools and books and other materials.

To some radical Latin Americans the American Schools are just other elements of United States imperialism, tools for misleading and manipulating the natives. I was savagely attacked in letters to the editor and to my face by liberal or leftist Americans when I wrote about them once, suggesting, as I do now again, that American taxpayer dollars could be better spent expanding the schools and creating a broad scholarship program for young Latin Americans. Some of my critics equated all that with the School of the Americas, an Army installation which the United States maintained in Panama for many years but which was moved to Fort Benning, Georgia, after Bush's invasion. That school is a genuine instrument of Yankee intervention.

"We need knowledge," I was told by Dr. Gustavo Parajon, the head of CEPAD, a Protestant church coalition whose goal is education for Nicaragua's poor. "We need capital to develop our country for the benefit of all. To accumulate capital you need more capital; with knowledge you accumulate capital.

"Graduates of high schools here can't go on to higher education, "Parajon said. "We are aware that we can't count on (our) government. We'd have to wait a long time. Do you still believe that your government stands for, of and by the people?"

The United States has a national, selfish reason for

spending money to expand education programs for young people from Latin America, as well as for other projects or ventures to help them improve their lot. As long as wide disparities exist between the cultures, of poverty in Central and South America and affluence in North America, pressures will continue on our southern borders. There is no way, short of drastic military action—gunning down migrants at the Rio Grande—that we can contain those hungry and oppressed people.

If we want to hold them back, to keep them out, the only solution is to help them make their homelands tolerable, to help them become educated, prosperous and healthy. Giving them a leg up to a level with our standard of living is self-interest of the most enlightened kind. Such a policy would require a leadership we have seldom seen. Even past well-intentioned overtures have always been short-lived either from indifference or inattention or, more usual, subverted by narrow commercial interests. Mass immigration has long since become a political reality. Whether it is met with demagoguery and possibly bullets or a moral and practical willingness to make available and spread our affluence will decide the course of our shared civilization.

Whatever happens in the days ahead *Tio Sam* has signaled that he is going to be a distant relative to his improvident nieces and nephews, quick to discipline at whatever cost but otherwise too busy to bother, especially if it does cost.

Index